# The Inexpressive Male

# The Inexpressive Male

Jack Balswick
Fuller Theological Seminary

**Lexington Books**
*D.C. Heath and Company/Lexington, Massachusetts/Toronto*

*Library of Congress Cataloging-in-Publication Data*

Balswick, Jack O.
  The Inexpressive male.

  1. Men—United States—Psychology.  2. Masculinity
(Psychology)  3. Expression.  4. Marriage—United
States—Psychological aspects.  I. Title.
HQ1090.3.B34  1988      305.3′ 1      87–45989
ISBN 0–669–17142–5 (alk. paper)

Published simultaneously in Canada
Printed in the United States of America
International Standard Book Number: 0–669–17142–5
Library of Congress Catalog Card Number 87–45989

The paper used in this publication meets the minimum requirements of
American National Standard for Information Sciences—Permanence of
Paper for Printed Library Materials, ANSI Z39.48–1984. ∞™

88  89  90  91  92  8  7  6  5  4  3  2  1

# Contents

# Figures, Tables, and Exhibits

## List of Figures

## List of Tables

## List of Exhibits

# Preface

I t was a Fall evening in 1964. My wife Judy had just returned, excited and enthusiastic, from a lecture given by Betty Friedan. I did not know anything about Betty Friedan except that I had just seen a notice on her recently published book, *The Feminine Mystique*. What began that evening as a questioning of the traditional female role, for both Judy and me, soon became a questioning of the traditional male role. For as Judy began to work through just what it meant to be a woman in contemporary marriage and society, I discovered that femininity and masculinity are as two sides to the same coin. Just as one cannot be defined without the other, one cannot be *redefined* without the other.

When I began to examine that which is called masculinity I realized that much of what I—and society as a whole—regarded as masculine was defined in negative terms. Being a "real man" was to a large extent "not acting like a woman." This can be translated as not crying, not showing any signs of weakness, and not expressing feelings like tenderness or love.

As a male who experienced boyhood during the 1940s and 1950s and grew into manhood by the 1960s, I was the epitome of what I have come to call the inexpressive male, more popularly known as the "strong and silent" or "John Wayne" type. This is not to say this type of male does not have any feelings; he certainly does. Neither does it imply that he does not express any feelings, for when it comes to expressing anger, hate, or rage—"real manly" feelings—this strong, silent type is not so silent. The inexpressive male has feelings of tenderness, warmth, or love but cannot verbally communicate them.

Having married in the early 1960s, to a therapist no less, I began to wonder if my society was engaged in a type of cultural discontinuity: socializing me one way, but expecting totally different behavior from me once I was married. For I learned, as did many men married in the 1960s and 1970s, that part of a wife's expectation for her husband is that he will be open and communicative to her about his feelings.

I have learned that much research in the behavioral sciences is conducted for very personal and not always "scientific" reasons. The reader can quickly detect that this is true also for me, for in my first article published on the inexpressive male I chose to include the subtitle, "A Tragedy of American Society." Although I have attempted to conduct my research according to the hallowed traditions of scientific method, I am somewhat less than dispassionate in wanting to see the findings applied to practical use.

My purposes in writing this book include both the "pure" and the "applied." In a scientific sense, it is my hope the research findings and theoretical constructs will add to the understanding of gender roles in general, and the male role specifically. I would emphasize that although the focus is on male inexpressiveness, most of the reported research includes information on female expressivity. In the applied sense it is my hope the ideas and information presented here can be used by individuals, couples, families, and communities to better understand why human feelings are not communicated and how they could be communicated better.

The material in this book represents research conducted by me, my colleagues, and students over the last fourteen years. While much of the material has been published piecemeal in journal articles and book chapters, no previous attempt has been made to publish the inexpressive male material as an organized whole. Where chapters contain material from joint research efforts, co-authorship credit for that chapter is given. My greatest assistance in studying the inexpressive male comes from being the recipient of the National Institute of Mental Health Grant # MH 221154-03, "The Inexpressive Male."

Chapter 1 is devoted to a discussion of the theoretical and practical importance of the concept of male inexpressiveness. An emphasis on this dual importance sets the tone for the entire book, in which the concern is for both the theoretical and practical implications of the findings. Chapter 2 contains a consideration of alternative theoretical explanations of male inexpressiveness, and chapter 3 attempts to give an integrated theory of male inexpressiveness. Chapter 4 represents my attempt to develop and describe what I believe are the major alternative types of inexpressive male roles. Presented in chapter 5 are the major scales and measuring instruments that have been developed to measure emotional expressiveness.

Each of the next three chapters reports on a major research attempt to identify the causes of male inexpressiveness. In chapter 6, coauthored with Christine Proctor Avertt, gender is established as a key factor on which people differ in emotional expressiveness. Chapter 7, coauthored by Katheleen Slevins, investigates the effect of parental expressiveness on children's expressiveness. Chapter 8, coauthored by David Dosser, considers the effect of situational factors on emotional expressiveness.

The relationship between emotional expressiveness and marriage is the topic of the next two chapters. Chapter 9 coauthored by Bernard Davidson, investigates the effect of emotional expressiveness on marital adjustment. Chapter 10, coauthored by Bernard Davidson and Donna Sollie, considers the relationship between emotional expressiveness and marriage, taking into account sex-role orientation and self-disclosure to friends.

Drawing upon the previous chapters, the concluding chapter presents some generalizations about the causes and consequences of male inexpressiveness, and after concluding that men express love too little, we address the question of how inexpressive males can become more expressive. It is argued that although many men are experiencing the clash between the traditional and modern male role as contradictory and inconsistent, the challenge can be viewed as an opportunity to change the social structures that hinder men from becoming more fully developed human beings.

# 1
# Why Study Male Inexpressiveness?

Another thing I learned—if *you* cry, the audience won't. A man can
cry for his horse, for his dog, for another man, but he cannot cry for
a woman. A strange thing. He can cry at the death of a friend or a
pet. But where he's supposed to be boss, with his children or wife,
something like that, he better hold'em back and let *them* cry.

—John Wayne

The traditional definition of manhood includes not only what "real"
men should do, but also what a real man should not do. Inexpressiveness is a male characteristic that traditionally has been defined in
negative terms. Simply put, an expressive male is one who has feelings and
verbally expresses them, while an inexpressive male is one who does not verbally express his feelings. While some inexpressive males do not believe they
have feelings to express, more typically, men are verbally inexpressive of their
feelings because they believe it is the way men should be. Given the current
redefinition of gender roles, an increasing number of men may want to express their feelings, but because of past restrictive socialization, are unable
to do so.

Men have traditionally been defined as independent, task-and-achieve-
ment oriented, objective, competitive, rational, unsentimental, and inexpressive, while women have been defined as dependent, interpersonally oriented,
sentimental, emotional, supportive, and expressive. Two factors have been
especially important in bringing about the redefinition of gender roles, the
rapid rate of social and cultural change, and the social and behavioral sciences' questioning of the "absolute role" that physiology plays in the formation of sexual temperament and behavior.

The modern definition of gender roles calls for greater flexibility and
interchangeability. For women this centers around the expansion of the female role beyond the acceptable definitions of wife and mother, to include
opportunity for participation in extra-familial positions of power and prestige traditionally reserved for men. For men, the male role has been redefined
to include the qualities that were once reserved for women, such as nurturance, tenderness, and expressiveness.

## The Practical Importance

The practical importance of understanding the causes, consequences, and possibilities for change in male inexpressiveness are many and varied. I contend that male inexpressiveness nearly always presents an obstacle to people attempting to develop intimate, meaningful relationships to the greatest extent possible. This is not to deny there may be some positive consequences that are a result of male inexpressiveness, given the existing societal and cultural normative patterns. However, in the best of all worlds I am committed to the position that both sexes benefit from the ability to freely and verbally express their feelings.

### Consequences

A number of personal and interpersonal problems have been attributed to inexpresssiveness and emotional distancing. Not the least of these are in familial relationships, where increased societal mobility and detachment have resulted in increased dependence on spouses or family members for affections, communication, and friendship. As Osherson (1986, 2) summarizes from his interviews of men who graduated from Harvard in the 1960s, "Many men showed confusion about the intimacy issues in their lives, particularly with wives, children, and their own parents." As a prime example of duality in cultural conditioning (Benedict 1938), society teaches the male that to be masculine is to be inexpressive, but at the same time teaches that the husband and father roles are defined in terms of sharing affection and companionship, which involve the ability to communicate and express feelings.

In a review of the literature on male socialization and the implications for marriage and family therapy, Phillips (1978) suggested that the traditional socialization of males in our culture inhibits the development of basic characteristics and skills that are important aspects of the ability to engage successfully in intimate and family relationships. He called the inability of many men to become intimate with another human being a "dysfunction in intimacy." Based on his review of research and clinical evidence, Phillips concluded that this dysfunction affects most men as they attempt to be friends, lovers, husbands, and fathers.

Jourard (1964) has described appropriate self-disclosure, the act of revealing personal information to others, as a necessary condition for a healthy personality. He was convinced that men, because of low self-disclosure, are beset with many psychosomatic disorders that do not affect women as frequently. He held that manliness seems to carry with it a chronic burden of stress that could be a factor related to man's shorter life span. Jourard (1964) concluded that the ability to suppress and express emotion selectively is the pattern of emotional control most compatible with psychological health. In a similar vein, Harrison (1978, 81) warned that the male sex role may endanger health and concluded, "a critical reading of presently available evidence confirms that male role socialization contributes to the higher mortality of men."

Male inexpressiveness can also be a hindrance to developing intimate relationships (Hunter and Touniss 1982; Prager 1986; Williams 1985). Tognoli (1980) points out the difficulty men often have in later life, when their support network of the "dependable woman" and the traditional male group disappears and they are unable to establish needed intimate relationships.

**Males Themselves.** Perhaps the greatest toll of emotional inexpressiveness is upon the inexpressive males themselves because they are robbed of potentially rich emotional experiences. The personal tragedy in emotional inexpressiveness was illustrated clearly to me one Saturday afternoon while my wife and I were attending a film version of Shakespeare's *Romeo and Juliet.* The roles of Romeo and Juliet were being played by sixteen-year-old youths; thus, the matinee performance was crowded with high school students. At the tragic and serious death scene, when my wife and I had lumps in our throats and tears in our eyes, we were surprised to hear the girls' sniffs accompanied by loud guffaws from the adolescent boys. Obviously, the emotional impact was being sidetracked and expressed in a reactional manner to cover up the sad and tender emotions that are not "cool" for adolescent males to express.

It can be physically and psychologically unhealthy for a person to not release and express emotions. Physically, the inability to cry and express emotions is thought to be related to the development of various physical symptoms. Psychologically, holding in emotions can result in a person's not being in touch with his feelings, which leads to not being in touch with himself. Articulating feelings helps us become aware of our emotions so that we can learn how to best deal with them. When we do not articulate what we feel, there is an uncertainty about the feelings. Just as talking over a problem with someone is a way to better understand it, so articulating emotions forces us to conceptualize what is being felt.

Other research has found self-disclosure to be related to various aspects of psychological health, and inversely, low self-disclosure related to psychological problems. Mayo (1968) found that normal people self-disclose more than neurotics or normal people with neurotic symptoms. Halverson and Shore (1969) found a relation between high self-disclosure and interpersonal openness and effectiveness. Thase and Page (1977) said high self-disclosure is related to positive mental health, self-awareness, and improved interpersonal functioning. Halpern (1977) said research has demonstrated that self-disclosure is positively related to personal adjustment and successful counseling outcome.

Research on androgyny suggests that increased emotional expressiveness will mean increased psychological health in males (Shichman and Cooper 1984; Downey 1984). Bem (1975) has reported findings that suggest androgynous individuals display more self-role adaptability across situations, and are able to engage in situationally effective behavior without regard to stereotypes. In finding that non-androgynous subjects display behavioral deficits of one sort or another, Bem concluded that the androgynous individual might someday come to define a new and more human standard of psychological health.

Recent research has supported Bem's suggestion, as Downey (1984) has found that middle-age men with traditional male sex-role orientation reported lower self-perceived levels of health than males considered to be androgynous. In their research on the relationship between sex-role orientation and life satisfaction, Shichman and Cooper (1984, 239) concluded that "androgynous people have a potentially wider range of sources for satisfaction and use their personality attributes more fully. They have therefore, less conflicts among various aspects of life, and a clearer picture of their way of life."

**Male Friends.** Men are less able than women to relate in an open, verbally expressive way to the same sex (Farrell 1986). There are two aspects of male inexpressiveness which may contribute to this: homophobia and competition (Lewis 1978; Hess 1981). Homophobia is the fear of being close to a person of the same sex. American males show many signs of fear of being branded homosexual or of having homosexual tendencies. Generally, the more secure a man is in his sexuality, the more open he can be in relating to a member of the same sex. The man who is secure in his own masculinity can put his arms around another man or verbally express his affection to him. Although most males would probably deny that they are "skin hungry," they often need to be physically stroked and held. James Kirkwood, in his play *P.S., Your Cat is Dead!*, captures the essence of this in an interchange between two male characters in his play:

"One evening about three months into our friendship, after we'd taken our dates home, we stopped by a bar for a nightcap. We ended by having three or four and when we left and were walking down the street, Pete suddenly slipped his arm around my shoulder. He surprised me; there was extreme warmth and intimacy about the gesture. When I looked over at him, he grinned and said, 'That bother you?' 'No . . . ' I shrugged in return. He then gave my shoulder a squeeze. 'Ever since I've known you, you got me pretending I don't have arms'" (Kirkwood 1973, 23 as quoted in Lewis 1978).

Compared to other cultures of the world, American males are undemonstrative and inhibited about showing love to someone of the same sex.

Competition can also be a barrier to the expression of love between male friends. From the time of birth, boys are indirectly taught to compete against other boys. If girls learn to compete for boys, boys learn to compete not only for girls, but also for status and respect. Although the more traditional status symbols are such things as achievement in sports, occupation, education, and salary, men can compete at almost anything, and will do so in order to gain status. In his book *Male Chauvinism: How It Works,* Korda (1973) relates how illicit sex becomes a status symbol in the corporate business world. In the seemingly sedate atmosphere of the university, men often compete fiercely for status with such things as the number and quality of professional publications or the number of lectureships one is invited to give. Some professors will not share important scientific information with their colleagues for fear someone else will publish the information first. Even in a prison, where all standards of status are stripped away, an inmate may establish status by being the best at playing cards or eating the most food. Homophobia and competition are concomitant factors of inexpressiveness which hinder the ability of males to establish close, intimate, sharing relationships.

In a recent literature review on friendship between men, Farrell (1986) stressed the need to look beyond social psychological factors to see the social structural hindrances to male friendship. Farrell (1986, 174–182) cites evidence that urbanization, social class, stages of the life and marital cycle, and organizational position all effect the potential intimacy level of male friends. A study comparing two work structures illustrates Farrell's point. Stensrud and Feldman (1982) found "that delivery men in a cookie company who held similar jobs, with low supervision and high security in a noncompetitive environment, developed intimate friendship ties and met frequently off the job. On the other hand, people working in a highly differentiated factory in a competitive environment developed only associative ties with infrequent outside contact" (Farrell 1986, 180–81).

**Marriage.** In light of the difficulties the inexpressive male has in relating as a single person to women, he may come to view marriage as an increasingly attractive alternative. As a husband, he can reduce the pressure to express such emotions by presenting the marriage itself as evidence of this affection. When expressions of verbal affection, tenderness, and gentleness toward a woman are necessary, it can be done with much less effort and awkwardness by the man when he is her husband rather than her date. Most couples, if together long enough, develop a set of shorthand symbols through which they express certain emotions and desires, such as a playful pat on the derriere, a certain look, or an arm around the shoulder. These symbols may connote the emotions the male is inept at expressing, and thus require reasonably little "gut-spilling" on his part. They clearly develop in nonmarital as well as marital relationships, but because marital relationships usually endure longer, there is ample opportunity for the development of a whole array of symbols that will facilitate the expression of "soft" and "feminine" emotions in the least painful way possible for the male.

While marriage may have useful consequences for the inexpressive male, the wife may not define the situation as a solution. Although the wife may resign herself to being married to a person who can communicate his feelings only through nonverbal symbols, she may still hold to the ideal of a verbally expressive husband. Such a marriage may not be too different from the highly incommunicative marriage that Cuber and Harroff (1965) describe as the *passive* marriage. The consequences of the husband's continued inexpressiveness toward his wife may then be dysfunctional to their marriage (Chelune, Waring, Vosk, and Sultan 1984; Davidson, Balswick, and Halverson 1983; Hendrick 1981; and Pascoe 1981).

The most serious and destructive effect of male inexpressiveness within marriages may be seen in accumulating evidence that links inability to express feelings to spouse abuse. Frin (1986) reports that men who held more traditional sex-role attitudes were more likely to endorse the use of physical force in the marital relationship. In their search for characteristics of abusive couples, Rosenbaum and O'Leary (1981) found that violent husbands were significantly less assertive than men in satisfactory, nonviolent relationships. In a study of men who had physically abused their wives, Coleman (1980) found that they believed that men must be strong, dominant, superior, and successful; but they themselves felt devastated and inadequate because they were none of these. "Their conflict about dependence explains why many of the men tended to distance themselves emotionally from their wives by complaining about their spouses' ineffectiveness as wives and mothers." Coleman (1980, 207) explained that violence and physical abuse followed because "the need to maintain an over-adequate facade causes many of the men to deny or repress feelings that indicate a vulnerability in their personalities."

Burgess and Locke (1955) made the initial suggestion that the present day American marriage is more oriented toward companionship, and thus carries a much heavier load than in the past. Blood and Wolfe (1960) concluded that "companionship has emerged as the most valued aspect of marriage today." Therefore, male inexpressiveness within modern companionship-oriented marriage relationships would decrease the chances of a marriage's survival by decreasing the wife's satisfaction with it, and thus giving her a smaller stake in its continuance.

Many males who are initially very inexpressive toward all women may learn to increase their level of expressiveness toward women with whom they become seriously involved because such relationships permit the development of symbols which make it less painful to express these emotions. Heiss (1962) investigated emotional expressiveness among casual daters, serious daters with no commitment to marriage, and daters committed to marriage. With increased involvement (that is, from casual to committed daters), males become more expressive; so that while females were clearly more emotionally expressive than males in the couples who were casual daters, among the serious daters committed to marriage, males were just as emotionally expressive as females. Leik (1963) conducted an intriguing experiment in which he looked at male-female differences when interacting with the spouse of a stranger and when interacting with their own mates. The male was clearly more task oriented and the female clearly more expressive with strangers, but these differences noticeably diminished when they were each other's mate.

Like the child who learns a rule and only begins to understand the exceptions to it through further experience, many American males may pick up the principle of inexpressiveness toward women, discovering exceptions as they become more experienced in the full range of man-woman relationships. Consequently, they may become more expressive toward their wives while remaining essentially inexpressive toward other women—they learn that the conjugal relationship is an exception to the cultural requirement of male inexpressiveness.

On the other hand, some inexpressive males may never "unlearn" their inexpressiveness, and many wives may, incongruently, come to value *and* expect an increased quality of nurturance and expression. Within these marriages, male inexpressiveness is certainly one of the contributing factors to the increased divorce rate, as "liberated" women are not as tolerant of the prospect of living the rest of their lives with a man who does not meet their need for emotional intimacy.

**Fathering.** Fatherhood may bring with it a whole new complexity of demands for the inexpressive male. To begin with, his wife, who is now a mother, may have increased needs for emotional support and expressiveness from him. While the mother is the primary source of gratification for the infant's rather taxing emotional requirements, the infant is not able to direct positive emotions toward her in return. It can be expected that she will turn to her husband for greater emotional input as a means of encouragement for continuing to meet the infant's emotional demands until she can replenish her own spent emotional resources. As a new mother, she probably will also be insecure in handling her new tasks of infant care, and will need reassurance from her husband in the form of emotional expressiveness. Having just gone through the physically altering state of pregnancy and finding that infant care leaves her much less time and energy to devote to personal beautification, she may strongly desire reassurances that she is still attractive and loved. The emotionally inexpressive male, whose main impact as a father during early infancy may be more determined by his interaction with the mother than the child (Bartemeier 1953, 277–280), may be unable to provide for her emotional needs (Pederson, Anderson, and Cain 1980; Lamb, Pleck, and Levine 1985).

Given the current redefinition of sex roles, greater expectations are being placed upon fathers to provide for the nurturant needs of their children starting from the time they are born (Lamb, Pleck, and Levine 1986). Benson (1968) suggests that "the modern father has more intensive nestling and comfort-giving relations with the infant than the peasant father in pre-industrial societies." As the infant grows, these expressive tasks expand to include activities such as providing bodily comfort to the child, exhibiting love and encouragement toward him or her, and playing with him or her.

If the inexpressive male has male children, these demands may be especially acute in the early years of his association with them. During their early years sons can be desirous of tenderness, gentleness, and verbal affection as daughters. Inexpressive fathers may be afraid their sons will not grow into "men" if they treat them tenderly and gently.

Fatherhood then requires a sudden increase in demands made upon the inexpressive male to produce emotions of tenderness, gentleness, and verbal affection. Although his emotional capacities may have been augmented through practice expressing such feelings toward his wife, they can still be limited. Marriage may serve as a lull between the turmoil of the single inexpressive male and the turbulence of fatherhood. If the inexpressive male continues at his same level of inexpressiveness or even slightly increases it, he will not be able to perform properly the role of father. Familial relationships may suffer as a consequence (Biller 1981).

**Society.** In discussing the consequences of male inexpressiveness thus far, I have concentrated on its effects upon interpersonal relationships. It may be helpful to consider the possible consequences of male inexpressiveness upon society as a whole. This is a difficult task to accomplish without falling into circular reasoning, for I have previously argued that the inexpressive male is a result of societal norms and social structures.

The fact that males are inexpressive allows for the continued justification that because they are that way, they are ill-suited for roles that call for a high degree of nurturant caring. Inversely, given the fact that success in the business world often demands that one act rationally and repudiate affection toward other people as a basis for making decisions, it can be argued that men rather than women are best suited to continue in such roles. The same argument might be used to justify political leadership by men rather than women (Lengermann and Wallace 1985).

I believe, however, that there will be no women's liberation without men's liberation. While the feminine role will be liberated when it is expanded to include opportunities for achievement, the masculine role will be liberated when it is expanded to include emotional expressiveness as acceptable behavior. If men are insecure in their own masculinity and position in society, they probably will be intolerant of increased freedom for women. As women begin to assume new roles, uncertainty and insecurity likely will occur among males who feel threatened by such new role behavior. As Brenton (1966, 188) wrote over twenty years ago:

> If a man is real—if he is fundamentally secure in his manhood—women do not threaten him; nor does he need to confirm his masculinity at their expense. . . . If he's secure, he can live his egalitarian life in an egalitarian marriage without fear of having his sexual identity shattered because roles merge or overlap. The secure man is warm, expressive, tender, and creative, yet quite capable of showing a sufficient amount of assertiveness when assertiveness is called for. The secure man can wash a dish, diaper a baby, and throw the dirty clothes into the washing machine—or do anything else women used to do exclusively—without thinking twice about it. . . . It's only when a man depends on arbitrary mechanisms outside himself to determine whether he's appropriately masculine, when he uses the stereotypes as strict guidelines to his identity, that he comes to feel somewhat beleaguered by changes taking place in the roles of men and women.

### Summary: Implications of Increased Male Expressiveness

Men need to be liberated from the emotional hangups that prevent them from becoming intimate in human relationships (Osherson 1986). Central to a traditional definition of masculinity has been "the stigma of all stereotyped feminine characteristics and qualities, including openness and vulnerability" (Guttman 1965, 229–240). Although increased emotional expressiveness is not a panacea for the difficulty men now experience in trying to work through a redefinition of masculinity and sex roles, expressive change can have vast implications for them, the people they know, and society in general.

The benefits of increased expressiveness for males themselves are both physical and psychological. Physically, release from an inability to cry and express emotions can result in reduction of various medical conditions caused by unreleased stress and pent-up emotions. Psychologically, the ability to recognize feelings will enhance self-awareness and in so doing provide a release from denial and repression. Articulating feelings is one way to get a better understanding of the problem, thus allowing one to go beyond it to do something active and constructive, rather than merely trying to deal with a vague feeling of depression or anxiety.

A second implication of increased male expressiveness has to do with the quality of love relationships. The strong need for nurturance, characteristic of newborn infants, is never outgrown. All of us need overt expressions of love from the time we are born until we die. As we mature from infancy to adulthood, we develop an increasing need for physical expressions of love. Increased male expressiveness will benefit the important people in a man's life—his wife, children, mother, father, and male and female friends.

The quality of relationships of males who have learned to express their feelings can be expected to vastly improve. A social relationship consists of a bond between two people who take each other into account. Intimate relationships are based upon *commitment* and maintained by *communication*. Although emotions are involved in love, more than anything else, love is a commitment. A commitment involves rights and responsibilities. From the recipient's point of view of a commitment, rights are involved. From the giver's point of view, responsibility is involved. True love relationships are always reciprocal and mutual—two-way, not one-way. Each person experiences the relationship as involving both rights and responsibilities.

In the same way that mutual commitment is the *basis* of a love relationship, so mutual communication is the *process* whereby a love relationship is maintained and enhanced. A love relationship does not grow when there is only one-way communication, i.e., when only one person attempts to express personal feelings to the other. At best, one-way communication may keep a love relationship alive; at worst, one-way communication is unable to sustain it.

The expressive person often makes valiant efforts to sustain the love relationship, while the inexpressive member of the relationship is either unwilling or unable to express his feelings. When an inexpressive person becomes expressive it can have dramatic effects in many areas of his or her life. Instead of the lack of responsiveness serving as a kind of negative reinforcement, the emergence of expressiveness can allow the relationship to grow and deepen. Instead of insecurity, resulting from not knowing where one stands in a relationship, the development of expressiveness can heighten security and reduce the need to resort to devious and often unproductive types of manipulative behavior designed to evoke some kind of positive response in others. The expression of love is the cement that maintains intimacy in close relationships.

## The Theoretical Importance

Male inexpressiveness as a concept began to be used in the early 1970s (Balswick and Peek 1970, 1971). Before 1970 only a limited number of researchers had carefully studied inexpressiveness by males. Komarovsky's (1962) study, based upon in-depth interviews of fifty-eight blue-collar married couples, is an early precursor of the proposed study. Komarovsky found that only one of every three marriages in her study measured up to the "prevailing

American ideal of psychological intimacy between married partners" (p. 149). When she looked for the reasons behind the lack of marital psychological intimacy, she found that one of the greatest barriers was the husband's inarticulateness—his "trained incapacity to share" (p. 156). Komarovsky states: "The ideal of masculinity into which they were socialized, inhibits expressiveness both directly, with its emphasis on reserve, and indirectly, by identifying personal interchange with the feminine role. Childhood and adolescence, spent in an environment in which feelings were not named, discussed or explained, strengthened these inhibitions. In adulthood they extended beyond culturally demanded reticence—the inhibitions are now experienced not only as 'I shouldn't' but as 'I cannot'" (p. 156). The blue-collar husband does not even share with his wife such feelings as worry or hurt, for it is a "strong man [who] bears his troubles in silence and does not 'dump his load on the family'" (p. 158). "Socialized to identify the expression of certain emotions with a lack of masculinity, the men inhibit self-disclosure" (p. 159).

Interestingly enough, Komarovsky found that even among a group of men as homogeneous as blue-collar workers, the less educated men were, the less revealing of themselves and the most withdrawn, and in general the least able to communicate intimately with their wives.

Two other early researchers, Rainwater (1965), doing research among poor families, and Hurvitz (1964), researching blue-collar families, have found results similar to Komarovsky's. Both found that one of the greatest contributions to marital strain is the wife's greater *desire* for emotional support and sharing and the husband's lower level of *providing* for such emotional support and sharing.

Alfred Auerback (1970), a psychiatrist relying largely upon case studies, has described the American male's inexpressiveness with women as part of the "cowboy syndrome." Auerback says that "the cowboy in moving pictures has conveyed the image of the rugged 'he-man,' strong, resilient, resourceful, capable of coping with overwhelming odds. His attitude toward women is courteous but reserved." Auerback goes on to explain that as the cowboy equally loved his girlfriend and his horse, so the present-day American male loves his car, or motorcycle, and his girlfriend. Although the cowboy does have tender feelings toward women, he does not express them, since, ironically, such expression would conflict with his image of what a male is.

The work of Blood and Wolfe as reported in their often-cited book, *Husbands and Wives* (1960), is probably the best evidence that the modern family is based upon the assumption that psychological intimacy between married couples is an American ideal. They conclude that in American marriages, "companionship has emerged as the most valued aspect of marriage today" (p. 172). Blood and Wolfe attempt to conjecture about the husband's ability to enter into the dynamics of a companionship-type marriage. However, since their sample did not include interviews with the men, I hesitate to cite evidence that reflects merely the wife's conception of the husband's marital role. There is a general lack of good research on the husband/father role in the family.

Inexpressiveness appears to negatively influence not only the marital relationship but also child development. For example, Hirschi (1969) has shown that the emotional bond between parents and children may have a direct influence on adolescent criminality. More recently, Conger (1976) has shown that parental behavior, either positive or negative treatment of male offspring, decreases or increases, respectively, the probability of delinquent behavior.

Male inexpressiveness has become a theoretically important concept then, precisely because contemporary institutions, especially the family, have come to expect greater expressiveness from males than they are apparently able to give. This incongruity is due in large part to the redefinition of sex roles. Although the greater stress has been put upon the redefinition of the female role, it is naive to believe that there can be a redefinition in only one gender.

A more social, psychologically oriented reason for the theoretical importance of male inexpressiveness is given by Brody (1985, 102,–103), who argues that emotions motivate and regulate adaptive behavior and are viewed by most personality theories "as either subsystems of, or as the primary determinants of other aspects of personality functioning." Brody goes on to point out that "abnormal personality functioning, or psychopathology, is often defined as the inability to cope with emotions . . . and/or as the expression or experience of inappropriately frequent or intense emotions." Brody (1985, 141) concludes his review article by arguing for "the study of gender differences in emotional development in the context of personality, familial, social and cultural variables."

## Summary

Although discussed separately, the practical and theoretical importance of male inexpressiveness are linked. The inability of men to express feelings has become identified as a practical problem and therefore, a theoretical concern. The present concern over the problem of family abuse can illustrate this point. It may be true that family abuse is no greater in today's family than in the past, but the awareness of abuse heightens theoretical efforts to identify factors associated with abuse. Accumulated evidence suggests that the inability of males to openly express their feelings is a major factor associated with physical abuse in the family (Edleson, Eisikovits, and Guttman 1985). Learning about the expressive capacities of males has taken on great practical *and* theoretical importance.

It has been said that there is nothing as practical as a good theory. In accepting this wisdom I have sought to balance practical and theoretical concerns in this book. An example of the dual concern can be seen in the following three chapters.

As a guide to what will be accomplished in the five databased chapters, the following summary generalization of the findings are offered. Regarding the causes of inexpressiveness we will learn that:

1. females are more expressive of their feelings than are males. Males are likely to be as expressive or more expressive of their feelings of anger as females. (chapters 6–10)

2. the greater the emotional expressiveness of parents, the greater the emotional expressiveness of children. (chapter 6–7)

3. in homes where fathers are expressive of their emotions, boys are as expressive as girls. (chapters 6–7)

4. whites are more expressive than blacks. (chapter 7)

5. among blacks, the expressiveness of the father is less related to children's expressiveness than the expressiveness of the mother. (chapter 7)

6. people are more expressive of their feelings to females than to males. (chapter 8 and 10)

7. people are more expressive of their positive feelings than of their negative feelings.(chapter 8)

8. people are more expressive of their feelings in an initiator role than in a respondent role. (chapter 8)

9. people are more expressive of their feelings in primary relationships than they are in secondary relationships. (chapters 8 and 10)

10. people are generally more expressive of their feelings to same-sex than to opposite-sex friends. Only in the expression of love is opposite-sex expressiveness greater than same-sex expressiveness. (chapter 8 and 10)

Regarding the consequences of inexpressiveness we will learn that:

1. the greater the expression of feelings between a couple, the greater the marital adjustment. (chapter 9)

2. the greater the inequality between spouses in their expression of feelings, the less their marital adjustment. (chapter 9)

3. where there is inequality between spouses in their expression of feelings, misperceiving such inequality as equality will result in greater marital adjustment. (chapter 9)

4. men who hold to the modern more than the traditional male role stereo-type are more expressive in their feelings. (chapter 10)

5. differences in expression of feelings are less between men and women who hold to the modern sex role stereotype than between men and women who hold to the traditional sex role stereotype. (chapter 10)

# 2
# Theoretical Explanations

T he first attempt to communicate my thinking on male inexpressiveness was based largely upon personal experience, culminating with a
description of male inexpressiveness as a tragedy of American society
(Balswick 1970a, 1974; Balswick and Peek 1970, 1971). Attempts to explain
this supposed male trait did not go beyond suggestions that the reasons for
male inexpressiveness can be found in the nature of the sex-role socialization.

In a critique of my earlier writing, Sattel (1976) suggested that male inexpressiveness might best be explained in terms of sexual politics. Sattel's paper
helped sharpen my explanation of male inexpressiveness theoretically in
terms of role theory. Thus followed a paper in which I compared and contrasted a role theory of male inexpressiveness with a sexual politics model
(Balswick 1979).

Given the limited attention paid to gender differences in expressiveness,
explanatory theories are still to be fully developed. The purpose of this chapter is to present a variety of theoretical orientations and approaches, some
merely brief statements which might make fruitful contributions to the theory
of male inexpressiveness to be developed in the following chapter.

## A Role Perspective

As a theoretical offspring of symbolic interactionism, role theory is more of
an organizing framework or theoretical orientation than a substantive theory
of behavior. Although the concept of "role" has been used in various sociological and social psychological approaches, the symbolic interactionist's use
of "role" places a more dynamic and evolving emphasis on the concept than
do other theories. Turner (1962), for example, suggested that the idea of
"role-taking" shifts emphasis from the simple process of enacting a prescribed
role to devising a performance on the basis of an imputed other role. Interpre-

tation, then, is a key variable and as Blumer (1969) pointed out, should not be regarded as a mere automatic application of established meanings but, rather, as a formative process in which meanings are used and revised as instruments for the guidance or formation of action.

Turner (1970, 185–186) has suggested three essential principles of role theory, which are freely paraphrased as follows: (a) that clusters of activities are assigned to a given role and once an individual assumes that role he should not dabble in the activities of another person's role; (b) that once a system of roles is developed, social interaction proceeds haltingly unless people play their respective roles; and (c) that people take the role of others in order to determine what role to play themselves and how to play it.

In our society, the male role has been imbued with activities that call for task achievement skills rather than emotional skills. As traditionally defined, the adult female role usually includes activities centered in the home and involves the emotional skills of caring for children; the adult male role carries an expectation to earn a living by working outside the home in occupations that require rational decision-making and non-emotional involvement with others (Zelditch 1955). The adult female's dominant role carries with it expressive expectations, while the adult male's role carries with it inexpressive expectations.

However, this is not to suggest that male inexpressiveness appears only when a male reaches adulthood. Children, from the time they are born, explicitly and implicitly are taught the male and female role. Male inexpressiveness is based upon a lifelong, institutionally based, socialization process that begins in infancy when girls are taught to act "feminine" and to desire "feminine" objects, and boys are taught how to be "manly." In learning to be a man, the boy in our society comes to value expressions of masculinity and devalue expressions of femininity. Masculinity is expressed largely through physical courage, toughness, competition, and aggression; femininity is, by contrast, expressed largely through gentleness, expressiveness, and responsiveness. The male child learns that expressing emotions is not a part of the male role.

When a boy begins to express his emotions by crying, his parents are quick to assert, "You're a big boy and big boys don't cry." Parents often use the term, "he's all boy," referring to his aggressiveness or mischievousness, but never use the term to denote behavior that expresses affection, tenderness, or emotion. What parents are really teaching their son is that a real man does not show his emotions.

(Hartley 1959, 458) and others (Brown 1957; Gray 1957; Hacker 1957), demonstrated nearly twenty years ago that families press these demands early in childhood and frequently enforce them harshly, so that by the time boys reach kindergarten, many feel "virtual panic at being caught doing anything traditionally defined as feminine, and in hostility toward anything even hinting at 'femininity,' including females themselves."

As the boy moves out from under the family umbrella and into the sphere of male peer groups, the taboo is reinforced against expressing feelings characteristic of females. Studies of the male subculture in schools (Coleman 1962; Hollingshead 1949) street-corner male groups (Hannerz 1969; Liebow 1967; Whyte 1943) and delinquent gangs (Keiser 1969; Miller 1958; Rosenberg and Silverstein 1969; Short and Strodtbeck 1965), show that affectionate, gentle, and compassionate behavior toward others is not to be "one of the boys." It is to misplay the male role.

The mass media seem to convey a similar message. From comics and cartoons to the more "adult" fare, the image of the male role does not usually include affectionate, gentle, tender, or soft-hearted behavior, except in a very small male child (for adults to appreciate, not as a model for other young male children) or an old, gray-haired grandfather.

In a similar vein, Phillips (1978) suggested that traditional male socialization is a process that demands males live up to an ideal concept of masculinity that emphasizes strength, control, and rationality, while denying expressions of feelings, vulnerability, gentleness, and sensitivity. Phillips believed that much male socialization focuses on what young men are not supposed to be like, and leads to denial and avoidance of feminine behaviors and attitudes.

Confronted with the image projected by this powerful triumvirate of the family, peer group, and mass media, most young males quickly learn that whatever masculine behavior is, it is not an expression of gentleness, tenderness, verbal affection, or similar emotions. Suppressing these types of emotions fits with other traits of the male role by helping the male avoid "sissy-like" displays of behavior, while correspondingly permitting open displays of anger, hostility, resentment, or rage—seen as distinctly "masculine." Such selective avoidance of emotional expressiveness is built into the early male role lessons, but is also reinforced throughout life.

This suggests that inexpressiveness is not merely the result of personality traits, but also of environment and instruction. A male is also influenced by his own view of himself in terms of his role and role performance. Male inexpressiveness is best understood in terms of a male's conception of himself, his perception of the role of the potential target person, and his perception of the potential target person's expectation of him.

## Social Learning Theory

Social learning theory includes most of the points of the general socialization explanations for male inexpressiveness. The gist is that males are not re-

warded, and are even punished, for expressions of emotion or any other behaviors that could be considered feminine. Notarius and Johnson (1982) describe the sex-role stereotype that females are more overtly expressive than
males:

> This sex difference is commonly reasoned to result from socialization proc-
> esses surrounding expressive displays. For example, expressive displays by
> boys are believed more likely to lead to negative consequences than the same
> displays by girls. This social learning history is thought to result in males
> who have learned to inhibit overt emotional reactions and females who have
> been encouraged in the expression of emotion. (p. 483).

Notarius and Johnson investigated the emotional expression and physiological reaction of husbands and wives as they discussed a salient interpersonal issue. In this study, wives were found to be more emotionally expressive
than husbands. In addition, an inverse relationship was found for husbands
between emotional expression and physiological reactivity. This finding was
seen by Notarius and Johnson as additional support for a suppression model
of emotion. They believed that a learning history of punishment for emotional displays might account for the attenuated show of emotion by husbands and their heightened physiological reactivity.

## Sexual Politics: A Functional-Conflict Perspective

Sattel (1976, 469) explained male inexpressiveness as resulting from sexual
politics—from the "instrumental requisites of the male power role." Sattel
reasoned that to wield power effectively, one must convince others that one's
decisions are based upon reason and not emotion. Within such a system, the
most powerful male is the one who can most soundly convince himself and
others that he has divested himself, or the role he plays, of any vestiges of
emotion.

Sattel (1976, 471–474) succinctly summarizes his explanation within
three propositions. First, *"Inexpressiveness* in a role is determined by the corresponding *power* (actual or potential) of that role." The more powerful the
role the more one will resort to an appearance of rationality and efficiency,
as opposed to emotionality, as an attempt to convince others that one's decisions are right. Thus, when an army general or a president of a large corpora-
tion announces an important decision, it will be done with an air of detachment. Boys are socialized to be inexpressive because, later, as men, they will
be expected to be decision-makers and wielders-of-power. The implication
contained within Sattel's first proposition is that "inexpressiveness is not just

learned as an end in itself; rather it is learned as a means to be implemented later in men assuming and maintaining positions of power."

Sattel's second position: "Male *expressiveness* in a sexist culture empirically emerges as an effort on the part of the male to *control* a situation (once again, on his terms) and to maintain his position." In this proposition, Sattel reacts to the suggestion that inexpressive males may learn to become expressive to their wives within the intimacy demands of marriage (Balswick and Peek 1971). Picking up on the suggestion that males might only be situationally inexpressive, rather than totally inexpressive, Sattel described situations of male expressiveness as attempts at controlling the situation. Male expressiveness may be "a way of 'coming on' with a woman—a relaxation of usual standards of inexpressiveness as a calculated move to establish a sexual relationship. Skill is dissembling in this situation may have less to do with handing a woman a 'line' than showing one's weaknesses and frailties as clues intended to be read by her as signs of authentic male interest" (Sattel 1976, 472). Thus, even those instances of male expressiveness that may appear on the surface to be authentic can actually be attempts by the male to control the situation.

Sattel's (1976, 469) third proposition: "Male *inexpressiveness* empirically emerges as an intentional manipulation of a situation when threats to the male position occur." Males are not inexpressive because they are unable to express their feelings, but because they *choose* to be inexpressive. The motivating force is to be secure and maintain power.

Perhaps Sattel perceived a need for a corrective to my explanations of male inexpressiveness, because he stressed: (a) the harm that male inexpressiveness does to the female rather than to the male; and (b) the intentional rather than the unintentional aspects of male expressive (Proposition B) and inexpressive (Proposition C) behavior.

## Complementarity Theory

In a reaction to my role theory approach, L'Abate (1980) has argued that male inexpressiveness can best be understood as a complementary reaction to women's overexpressiveness. In failing to find sex differences in research on conflict resolution methods, L'Abate concludes that males and females do not differ in emotional expressiveness. Besides, he argues, his clinical experience would suggest that in 20–30 percent of the couples is the male rather than the female who is more expressive. Very simply put, L'Abate believes an overexpressive female results in an inexpressive male; presumably when one partner is overexpressive, the other partner will be correspondingly less expressive. In reality, L'Abate's complementary theory suggests that expressiveness must be understood in the context of the dyadic relationship in which behavior occurs.

## Homophobia

The male role carries with it the belief that males should avoid any behavior that could be considered feminine, and especially any behavior that could be considered homosexual (Goldfried and Friedman 1982; Lewis 1978; Morin and Garfinkle 1978; Morin and Nungesser 1981; O'Neil 1982; Solomon and Levy 1982; Weinberg 1972). These beliefs have important implications for male expressiveness, and for male relationships with other males, and can be labeled fear of femininity and homophobia.

O'Neil (1982) believed that a man's fear of his femininity underlies much of current male gender-role strain and conflict, including both physical and psychological health problems. O'Neil described this fear as "a strong, negative emotion in self and others associated with feminine values, attitudes, and behaviors" (p. 18). He believed the fear is learned during early gender-role socialization and is related to the "masculine mystique and value system." According to O'Neil, when a man fears his feminine side, he is afraid that others will view him as stereotypically and negatively feminine rather than positively masculine. O'Neil wrote, "The fear of femininity produces six patterns of gender-role conflict and strain including (1) restrictive emotionality, (2) homophobia, (3) socialized control, power, and competition issues, (4) restricted sexual and affectionate behaviors, (5) obsession with achievement and success, (6) health care problems" (p. 23).

The fear of femininity and homophobia are related. According to O'Neil (1982), the fear of femininity is central to understanding homophobia because a male's stigma about his femininity is directly associated with his fears about homosexuality, femininity, and effeminate demeanor, so that if a man associates with gays, the conclusion is that he is feminine, effeminate, and homosexual (O'Neil 1982; Solomon 1982). Because of this, O'Neil believed that "femininity, labeled as homosexuality, breeds homophobia and threatens men and their masculine roles" (p. 27).

Homophobia has been defined in various ways, including the following: "the dread of being in close quarters with homosexuals" (Weinberg 1972, 4), "the fear of homosexual contact or of appearing to be homosexual to others" (Goldfried and Friedman 1982, 311); and "the fear of homosexuals or the fear of one's being or appearing to be homosexual" (Lewis 1978, 122). Although homophobia is found in both females and males, it appears to be more powerful and exaggerated in males (Morin and Garfinkle 1978; Weinberg 1972).

Homophobia can be thought of as the cause of male inexpressiveness in that it serves to restrict males to a very narrowly defined and rigid sex role that does not allow for emotional expression. In this sense, homophobia has been described by several authors as a powerful and central dynamic maintaining traditional male roles and keeping men within the confines of behavior culturally defined as sex-role appropriate (Morin and Garfinkle 1978; O'Neil 1982).

Homophobia is also important because of the effect it has on a male's relationship with another male. Homophobia is believed to prevent interpersonal and emotional intimacy between heterosexual men and to be a significant barrier to male self-disclosure, expressiveness, companionship, and touching (Goldfried and Friedman 1982; Lewis 1978; Mortin and Garfinkle 1978; O'Neil 1982; Solomon 1982).

The relation between homophobia and male inexpressiveness can be viewed as a reflection of the difficulty for many men in distinguishing between intimacy or affection and sexual behavior, even to the point of fearing that one will lead them to the other (Goldfried and Friedman 1982; Solomon 1982). This situation is clearly limiting to men because it makes emotional intimacy with another man difficult. When this point is coupled with the finding that men are more likely than women to perceive the world in sexual terms, to make sexual judgments, and to attribute sexual meaning and intent to a "friendly" situation (Abbey 1982), we then have a clearer understanding of the confusion between intimacy and sexual behavior. We also realize that this confusion has implications for male-female relationships as well because there is every reason to believe that males may confuse intimacy or affection with sexuality in relationships with females.

## The Reproduction of Mothering

In her book *The Reproduction of Mothering: Psychoanalysis and the Sociology of Gender* (1978), Nancy Chodorow manages to present a point of view from Freudian theoretical perspective that is, at the same time, consistent with feminist thinking. Although Chodorow does not directly present a theory of male inexpressiveness, such a theory is implied in her writing. Chodorow believes women rather than men do most of the parenting as a result of social, structurally induced, psychological mechanisms, rather than as an unmediated product of physiology. Women are more prepared for parenting because they more than men have received nurturant parenting from their parent of the same sex. This also results in a different process of maturation in boys than in girls. While both boys and girls begin their lives with an emotional attachment to their mother, boys must learn to identify with their father by denying attachment to their mother. On the other hand, girls can continue both their identity with and attachment to their mother.

The nature of a girl's relationship to her mother and the nature of a boy's relationship to his father are significantly different, however. While the girl is likely to be involved in a personal face-to-face relationship with her mother in the home, the fact that the father is likely to be absent from the home for periods of time means the boy must derive notions about masculinity from his mother and the culture at large in the absence of an ongoing personal relationship with his father. This results in girls' having more of an interactional orientation to the family, while boys receive more of an external orientation, away from the family.

The close ties girls have with their mothers will mean they most likely will desire to be nurturing mothers. Since boys are not closely tied to their fathers, and they deny their attachment to their mothers for the sake of their own masculinity, their resulting behavior as fathers will be characterized by emotional distance from their children.

Male inexpressiveness is further reinforced by the fact that mothers often turn to their children as potential sources for meeting unfulfilled emotional and erotic desires. Chodorow writes, "Sons may become substitutes for husbands, and must engage in defensive assertion of ego boundaries and repression of emotional needs." Chodorow also believes that "the very fact of being mothered by a woman generates in men conflicts over masculinity, a psychology of male dominance, and a need to be superior to women."

Although this brief attempt to "abstract" a theory of male inexpressiveness out of Chodorow's insightful writing does not do justice to the richness of her explanations, it does demonstrate how male inexpressiveness might be explained within a psychoanalytic perspective. However, it might be that if Freud were asked to explain male inexpressiveness he would give a little more credit to the influences of genetically acquired differences between the sexes than does Chodorow, although this suggestion is subject to debate.

## Inexpressiveness As a Different Voice

In her book *In A Different voice* (1982), Carol Gilligan builds upon Chodorow's work in reacting to what she believes is a male bias in Kohlberg's theory of moral development. Gilligan begins by pointing out that Kohlberg's theory is based upon responses to moral dilemmas from eighty male subjects, and that comparative research has found that women average one stage of moral development lower than men. In her own analysis of the reasons females and males gave for making a hypothetical moral decision, Gilligan came upon evidence that women's moral decisions were based upon the hearing of a "different voice."

While men base moral decision on a morality of rights and non-interference, women base their moral decisions on a morality of relationships and caring. Gilligan writes, "The moral imperative that emerges repeatedly in interviews with women is an injection to care, a responsibility to discern and alleviate the 'real and recognizable trouble' of this world. For men, the moral imperative appears rather as an injunction to respect the rights of others, and thus to protect from interference the rights to life and self-fulfillment" (p. 100).

The implications of Gilligan's ideas for an explanation of male inexpressiveness can best be seen when she contrasts the alternative visions of maturity for adult males and adult females. The mature female participates in acts of nurturance, care and intimacy with others as acts of strength. The mature male however, establishes an identity by individual achievement and separating himself from others. Levinson (1978) is cited as suggesting that men who seem distant in their relationships are seen as models of psychological health. Mature men may have a number of friends, but few close friends. Gilligan summarizes: "The view one gets from Levinson's research is that in maturity, relationships are subordinate to individuation and achievement. Men are described as "constricted in their emotional expression" (p. 335).

We have in Gilligan's thoughts not so much an explanation as to the origin of male inexpressiveness, but rather insight into psychological and socio-structural conditions that perpetuate it. Males are inexpressive because such behavior is functional to their own image and society's definition of what constitutes a mature male.


## Cultural-Ecological Theory

In her book *Female Power and Male Dominance* (1981), Peggy Sanday has proposed a theory explaining the origin of sexual inequality. The ideas contained in this work, however, might also be basis for a theory of male inexpressiveness. As Sanday sees it, dangerous or hostile environments create an outer-orientation in men, while safe, friendly environments create an inner-orientation. In hostile environments it is the practice of hunting large animals or killing other men that leads to an outer-orientation. The fishing or gathering economic activities featured in friendly environments leads to inner-orientation.

The behavioral patterns that correspond to an outer-orientation are segregation of work and child rearing, paternal distance from infants, and an emphasis on competition. An inner-orientation, on the other hand, is associated with a sharing of work and child rearing, paternal closeness to infants, and less emphasis on competition. When the environment is perceived as friendly the sexes tend to mingle in most activities, while the sexes tend to separate from each other when the environment is perceived as hostile. The nature of the physical environment determines the cultural selection of "appropriate" sex-role organization and expectations.

The sexual division of labor and emergence of sexual inequality also constitute a compelling explanation of the origins of expressive differences between the sexes. In going beyond Sanday it could be argued that one of the results of outer-orientation in men, along with distancing from infants and a competitive emphasis, is an inexpressiveness about communication of feelings. On the other hand, where men are inner-oriented they will more freely be able to verbally communicate their feelings, which can be expected among men who are close to their children and free of the excesses of competitiveness. This explanation attempts to identify a cause, or contributing factor, to male inexpressiveness which lies outside the socio-cultural arena.

## Sociobiology

Sociobiology explains existing differences between the sexes, not in terms of differential socialization, but rather in terms of genetic differences between the sexes. Sociobiology defines differences in social behavior between the sexes as based on differences in gene pools, emerging through a natural selection process over thousands of years. Thus in one version of sociobiology (Tiger 1969; Tiger and Fox 1971), men developed a bonding instinct and sense of adventure and protection toward their families because of the need for them to bond together, in hunting wild animals. Women developed nurturant abilities to bear and rear children. You may ask, what prevented women from going with the men on the hunt? Tiger's answer is that some women did, but in doing so diminished their chances of producing surviving offspring thus passing on their genes in the species gene pool. Women who spent their time caring for their children and safely giving birth were desired as marriage partners and were successful in having their genes passed on to further generations. The men who were desired as marriage partners were not those who stayed around the compound caring for children, but those who were successful on the hunt. Thus it was not the men with nurturant tendencies who were successful in contributing to the continuing species gene pool, but rather those with bonding tendencies. The result is that today men and women have different genetic packages, with women more capable of emotional bonding with small children and men more inclined to be adventurous, strong, and protective of their families.

Sociobiologists may agree that since we no longer live in a society dependent upon hunting dangerous animals, the gender differences between the sexes may no longer be functional. But they would argue that these genetically produced differences are real and cannot simply be dismissed.

A toned-down version of sociobiology is offered by Alice Rossi, who believes that "organisms are not passive objects acted upon by internal genetic forces, as some sociobiologists claim, nor are they passive objects acted upon by external environmental forces, as some social scientists claim" (Rossi 1984, 11). Rossi does believe there are innate temperament-producing genetic differences between the sexes, but that "genes, organisms, and environment interpenetrate and mutually determine each other" (Rossi 1984, 11).

From five areas of research, Rossi finds compelling evidence that biology is involved in gender differences. These are: (1) correlations between social behavior and physiological sex attributes; (2) gender differences in infants and young children prior to major socialization influences; (3) the emergence of gender differences with the onset of puberty when body morphology and hormonal secretion changes rapidly; (4) gender differences stable across cultures; and (5) similar gender differences across higher primate species.

Rossi cites evidence that suggests greater expressivity among females than males: females' higher sensitivity to touch, sound, and odor; earlier acquisition of language, verbal fluency, and memory retention; more sensitivity to context; greater skill in picking up peripheral information; quicker processing of information; more attraction to human faces; and greater responsiveness to the nuances of facial expression. These lead to the female's superior ability to express feelings. Rossi summarizes: "The female combination of sensitivity to sound and face, and rapid processing of peripheral information implies a quicker judgment of emotional nuance . . . (females have) an easier connection between feelings and their expression in words" (Rossi 1984, 13).

While Rossi would see females as having a "head start" in expressive abilities, she is careful not to accept a fatalistic genetic determinism as an indication of how the sexes must be different. She argues that co-parenting will produce the most creative and productive individuals because they "possess in equal measure the socially desirable traits of both sexes" (Rossi 1984, 14).

In a certain sense, cultural-environmental and sociobiology are identical theories in that they both view the physical environment within which a people must survive as the ultimate explanation of social behavior. The obvious difference lies in their temporal perspective: cultural-environmental theory emphasizes the immediate effect of the physical environment upon social behavior, while sociobiology views the physical environment as having an effect upon social behavior over long periods of time. The impact of the physical environment upon social behavior from the point of view of the cultural-environmental theorist is direct. Its impact to the sociobiologist is indirect, ultimately affecting social behavior through the impact it has on a gender's retention of genes within the species gene pool.

The socialization theories directly conflict with both cultural-environmental and sociobiology theories. It is possible, however, to attempt a synthesis. In such a synthesis the physical environment would be accepted as the ultimate cause of the social behavioral patterns found in a given culture. The social transmission of those cultural patterns of behavior would be the immediate cause of gender differences in expressiveness. Thus I see no ultimate contradiction between cultural-environmental theory and any of the varieties of socialization theories.

A synthesis between sociobiology and any one of the socialization theories is more problematic however. Those wishing to attempt such a task might best follow the example given by Alice Rossi. Any synthesis must begin by rejecting both as being in any sense determinative of gender differences. Having done this, one is then free to conceive of gender differences in genetic composition, and gender differences in cultural role expectation as interactive in their effect upon gender differences. Thus in some cultures the given genetically produced differences may be exaggerated, and in others they may be minimized and even reversed. If I have any argument with Rossi it is in her seemingly enthusiastic acceptance of the evidence from sociobiology. I, too, am convinced that we have had an overly socialized view of human behavior, but I remain skeptical of the ultimate interpretation placed on some of the evidence for genetic differences between the sexes. What genetically given differences that do exist between the sexes seem very pliable, especially given the rich differences in what is viewed as "acceptable" behavior from society to society.

Most societies take what nature gives in terms of differences between the sexes and accentuates those differences. In the next chapter we shall evaluate the social environmental theories presented in this chapter, and seek a unifying perspective to help us understand how our society accentuates expressive differences between the sexes.

## Summary

Eight theoretical explanations of male inexpressiveness have been presented; more could have been developed. The criterion I have used to select an explanatory model is the degree to which it seems to speak directly to the phenomena of male inexpressiveness. All but two attempt to explain male inexpressiveness in terms of social environmental factors. I will hold my evaluation of these theories until the next chapter, where they will be used as part of an integrated theoretical model of male inexpressiveness. I will argue that male inexpressiveness can best be understood as socialized behavior, but I do not negate the fact that nonsocial environmental theories, such as cultural-environmental and sociobiology, have contributions to make.

# 3
# Toward an Integrated Theory

In his important book *The Myth of Masculinity*, Pleck (1981) has given
revolutionary implications for understanding the male role. He believes
in and argues for a shift from the male sex role identity (MSRI) paradigm
to the sex role strain (SRS) paradigm. The MSRI paradigm, which since the
1930s has dominated the scientific and popular conceptions of sex roles
"holds that the fundamental problem of individual psychological development is establishing a sex role identity" (p. 3). Individuals are seen as being
"preprogrammed," as having an "innate psychological need" to develop a sex
role identity. The development of an adequate sex role identity can be a peril-
ous adventure, thwarted in the male by such factors as "paternal absence,
maternal overprotectiveness, the feminizing influence of the schools, and the
general blurring of male and female roles" (pp. 3–4).

A beginning understanding of the MSRI paradigm can perhaps best be
gained by perusing the eleven propositions Pleck (1981, 5–4) has identified
as constituting its core:

1. Sex role identity is operationally defined by measures of psychological
   sex typing, conceptualized in terms of psychological masculinity and/or
   femininity dimensions.

2. Sex role identity derives from identification-modeling, and, to a lesser
   extent, reinforcement and cognitive learning of sex-typed traits, especially among males.

3. The development of appropriate sex role identity is a risky, failure-prone
   process, especially for males.

4. Homosexuality reflects a disturbance of sex role identity.

5. Appropriate sex role identity is necessary for good psychological adjustment because of an inner psychological need for it.

6. Hypermasculinity in males (exaggerated masculinity, often with negative social consequences) indicates insecurity in their sex role identities.

7. Problems of sex role identity account for men's negative attitudes and behaviors toward women.

8. Problems of sex role identity account for boys' difficulties in school performance and adjustment.

9. Black males are particularly vulnerable to sex role identity problems.

10. Male adolescent initiation rites are a response to problems of sex role identity.

11. Historical changes in the character of work and the organization of the family have made it more difficult for men to develop and maintain their sex role identities.

Because of the accumulating anomalies inherent in the MSRI paradigm, Pleck believes we are now witnessing the development of the SRS paradigm, which views *social approval* and *situational adaptation,* rather than *innate psychological need,* as the central determinants of sex-typed traits. The current attempt to find the causes of sex role identity problems in men is analogous to using a finger to plug a widening hole in the dike. Rather than trying to fit men to an image of a traditional sex role, the SRS paradigm serves as a kind of cognitive release in which men can be viewed as subject to contradictory sex role expectations and as failing to live up to sex role expectations. Rather than operating from a static historical notion of a male sex role identity, SRS posits the current strain in the male sex role as due to social changes brought about by a clash between traditional and modern definitions of the male role.

Pleck summarizes the key elements in the SRS paradigm in the following ten propositions (p. 9, 135–153):

1. Sex roles are operationally defined by sex role stereotypes and norms.

2. Sex roles are contradictory and inconsistent.

3. The proportion of individuals who violate sex roles is high.

4. Violating sex roles leads to social condemnation.

5. Violating sex roles leads to negative psychological consequences.

6. Actual or imagined violation of sex roles leads individuals to overconform to them.

7. Violating sex roles has more severe consequences for males than females.

8. Certain characteristics prescribed by sex roles are psychologically dysfunctional.

9. Each sex experiences sex role strain in its paid work and family roles.

10. Historical change causes sex role strain.

Consistent with Thomas Kuhn's (1962) analysis of scientific paradigm clashes, it would be wrong to think of one of the above sex role paradigms as right and the other wrong. Rather, each must be evaluated in terms of its heuristic value, in its ability to consistently incorporate and explain all the accumulated evidence on sex roles, and its fruitfulness in generating further research. On the basis of Pleck's most detailed analysis I believe the SRS paradigm is more useful than the MSRI paradigm in understanding the male sex role characteristic of emotional inexpressiveness.

Six of the eight theories of male inexpressiveness discussed in the previous chapter can be classified as socialization theories. Some of these theories have in the past been used to support the MSRI paradigm, but I believe they can also be interpreted so as to consistently support the SRS model. Following a comparison and contrast of these seven theories in terms of their consistency with each other and the SRS model, I shall attempt to further develop a unified theory of male inexpressiveness according to the sex role strain paradigm.

## Theories: Comparison and Contrast

Of the theories presented in the previous chapter, role theory offers the most complete explanation of male inexpressiveness. As a theory it also allows for a range in the extent to which males are conceptualized as possessing an internalized psychological condition of inexpressiveness. At one extreme, role theory emphasizes that because society socializes males to be inexpressive, they are actually psychologically incapable of expressing their tender feelings. This view is consistent with SRS proposition number eight, which states that "certain characteristics prescribed by sex roles are psychologically dysfunctional." What may have started as an external expectation can result in a psychological dysfunction.

Role theory also allows for the possibility, however, that the learning of the male sex role may not actually result in an inability to be expressive, but rather only in his *thinking* he is not supposed to be expressive. Granted, according to the first explanation, the male cannot express himself precisely because he was taught that he was not supposed to be expressive, but in this second explanation, inexpressiveness is a result of present perceived expectations and not a psychological condition which resulted from past socialization. The male perceives cultural expectations as saying, "don't express yourself to women," and although the male may be capable of such expressiveness, he "fits" into cultural expectations. This explanation of male inexpressiveness is consistent with SRS proposition number four, which states that "violating sex roles leads to social condemnation." In the case of the married male, where familial norms do call for expressiveness to one's wife, it may be that the expectations for the expression of emotions to his wife are not communicated to him, or if they are, he does not perceive them.

There has been a trickle of evidence that would lend support to the first explanation, which stresses the male's incapacity to be expressive. Several studies (Balswick 1970; Hurvitz 1964; Komarovsky 1962; Rainwater 1965) have suggested that especially among the lower-educated, it is the wife playing the feminine role who is often disappointed in the lack of emotional concern shown by her husband. The husband, on the other hand, cannot understand the relatively greater concern and emotional expressiveness his wife desires, since he does not usually feel this need himself. As a result of her research, Komarovsky (1962, 156) has suggested that "the ideal of masculinity into which . . . (men are) . . . socialized inhibits expressiveness both directly, with its emphasis on reserve, and indirectly, by identifying personal interchange with the feminine role." My early research (1970) found that males are less capable than females of expressing or receiving companionship support from their spouses. This research also supports the view that inadequacy of expressiveness is greatest for the less-educated males. Although inexpressiveness may be found among males at all socioeconomic levels, it is especially among the lower-class male that expressiveness is seen as being inconsistent with his defined masculine role. SRS proposition number seven states that "violating sex roles has more severe consequences for males than females." I would suggest that this proposition holds true, more for low-income than for high-income people.

The seeming difference between a role perspective and a sexual politics perspective in explaining male inexpressiveness may be more apparent than real. It is not so much a question of which is right as it is of which theoretical explanation one prefers. While I have chosen to take a social psychological perspective in explaining male inexpressiveness, Sattel has chosen to take a functional-power or functional-conflict perspective. Rather than trying to refute Sattel's perspective, I would like to point out what that perspective perhaps overlooks.

First, we should consider that males "have considerable gains to make in loosening and changing their roles" (Pleck 1976), and that many, perhaps most males in our society, do truly want to become more expressive. One of the recurrent findings in my own research is the degree to which males are not satisfied with their inexpressive selves. Do males who hold power by means of inexpressive behavior really enjoy and find self-fulfillment by such tactics? Many men have come to realize they may have as much to gain as women by being liberated from their inexpressive hang-ups. Such gains can range from fewer ulcers and other physical and mental disturbances, to freer and more intimate interpersonal relationships with family members and friends.

Second, functional-conflict theory mistakenly classifies any situationally produced expression of affection by males as an attempt to control (proposition two). In my original article on inexpressiveness (Balswick and Peek 1971), I suggest two types of inexpressive males, the cowboy (feeling and nonverbal) and the playboy (nonfeeling and verbal). I would now stress that the cowboy and the playboy should not be thought of as personality types so much as inexpressive roles. As originally conceived, it is only the male assuming the playboy role who can be said to emit expressiveness as an effort to control a situation and maintain his position.

Men who have consistently related to women in the security of the cowboy role can learn to become genuinely expressive in a secure marital relationship. To explain such expressiveness as controlling behavior motivated to maintain a power position is unfair to those inexpressive males who are striving to become more genuine in their relationships.

Third, Sattel's second and third propositions involve inputing a radical degree of self-consciousness into the sexist behavior of men. Ascertaining the *motive* behind the behavior of any actor is an extremely delicate process. I would suggest that much, probably most, of the sexist behavior exhibited by males is not self-consciously intentional. It would seem the very emergence of the concept "male consciousness-raising" itself recognizes that most males have not been cognizant of the enormous amount of sexism built into their role behavior.. However, the question of how much of the male's sexist behavior is intentional may not only be impossible to assess, but also secondary to the real task at hand.

Males as a whole are inexpressive! One of the functions of this inexpressiveness is, as Sattel rightly points out, to keep males in positions of power is a sexist system. Males should change, but not only to put an end to the sexual politics that hold females in bondage to male domination, but also so that males can obtain more meaningful personal relationships with women, with children, with other men, and with people in general. As stated in SRS proposition number nine, "each sex experiences sex role strain in its paid work and family roles." A major source of role strain for males centers upon contradictory expectations about their expression of emotions at work and in the home.

Male inexpressiveness should not be understood solely in terms of a personality trait, although it is partly that, nor solely in terms of sexual power politics, although it is partly that also, but in terms of how men have internalized and constantly redefine their image of the role they play in society. Specifically, it would seem the sex role strain paradigm can beneficially serve as an integrating model capable of incorporating both the individual structure (the domain of psychology) and the social structure (the domain of sociology) in explaining male inexpressiveness. The limiting bias within the male sex role identity paradigm is to stress the psychological dimension at the neglect of the more external social structural determinants of gender role behavior.

Complementarity theory may be most popular among marriage and family therapists, who see powerful unconscious forces at work in the mate-selection process in the Western setting. There is undoubtedly some truth in complementarity theory as an explanation of who expressive or inexpressive people are likely to marry. It is, however, much too limited a theory to explain the vast evidence that across cultures, males tend to be less expressive than females.

Social learning is but a mere psychological or behavioristic version of what I have identified as socialization theory. *Both* seem to be intuitively true. Who can dispute the powerful evidence of the impact of cultural conditioning upon an individual's behavior? The strength of these three perspectives is that they manage to avoid either/or thinking as in trait psychology or strict environmental theories.

Homophobia is a useful concept that deserves further investigation, some of which will be reported later in this book. In reality it is a specialized version of socialization theory, and can be subsumed under it. As an explanation, homophobia refers to a specific fear of closeness with a member of the same sex, which males learn in the context of their social upbringing. Of the four theories evaluated to this point, it presents a viewpoint strongly rooted in the male sex role identity paradigm. Homophobia is usually seen as reflecting a disturbance of sex role identity, or as a reflection of problems in the identity-modeling process, which results in a male's insecurity with his own sexual identity.

The reproduction of mothering is a little more difficult to merely subsume within a socialization perspective. Contained within it is a subscription to the subtle subconscious and irrational dynamics that make Freudian theory so richly suggestive. Nevertheless, in its final analysis the reproduction of mothering does attribute male inexpressiveness to the way parents socialize their children. The solution to male inexpressiveness is clearly an alteration of parenting roles—bring father into more intimate relationships with both his sons and daughters.

An initial assessment of Chodorow's theory would probably result in a proclamation of its affinity to the male sex role identity paradigm, largely because both have developed out of the fertile grounds of Freudian theory. I believe, however, that many insights offered by Chodorow are true and can be integrated into the sex role strain paradigm. In his very brief discussion of Chodorow, Pleck (1981, 157) suggests that her analysis falls within proposition eight of the SRS paradigm. Proposition eight states that "certain characteristics prescribed by sex roles are psychologically dysfunctional."

In Gilligan's theory we have a continuation of the implications within Chodorow's theory. Male inexpressiveness is seen as a reflection of an orientation that stresses separation rather than attachment. Security for men is found not in the context of close relationships, but rather in aloneness—in achieving a position that puts distance between themselves and potential rivals. This tendency for men to seek security and maturity through distancing (Erickson 1968) is another example of a psychologically dysfunctional characteristic prescribed by the male sex role.

## A Sex Role Strain Perspective

The theories we've compared and contrasted are alternative but useful explanations of male inexpressiveness. Rather than seeing the different theories as conflictive and contradictory, I believe a far more fruitful strategy is to integrate the truths from each into a broader unifying perspective. The sex role strain perspective simply understands *male inexpressiveness as a reflection of sex role stereotypes and norms.*

Any social scientific understanding of sex roles stereotypes must begin with Parson's (1955) assertion that for men to assume instrumental roles and for women to assume expressiveness roles is functional to the maintenance of the family system. This amounts to a functional justification of traditional sex role stereotypes. Subsequent sex role stereotype research has found that, among other differences, *females are perceived to be less expressive than males* (Rosenkrantz et al. 1968; Broverman et al. 1972; Spence et al. 1974; Ruble 1983). It should be emphasized that the found difference in sex role stereotyping is in degree and not kind, "the typical male is not regarded as being unexpressive but as being less expressive than the typical female" (Spence, Deaux, and Helmreich 1985, 157).

It is also interesting to note that whereas males are stereotyped to be instrumental and females to be expressive, the most likeable males and females are those who are high in both characteristic, and the most unattractive are those who are perceived as low in both sets of qualities (Kulik and Harackiewicz 1979; Major, Carnevale, and Deaux 1981). This is an indication that although inexpressiveness is a stereotype of males, it is also a dysfunctional stereotype. There is some evidence that men in fact know that women desire greater expressiveness in men. Gilbert et al. (1978, 1981) asked men to indicate their beliefs about what women considered to be ideal in a man. They found that although men accurately described women's ideal man as being expressive, this ideal was more expressive than the ideal man held for themselves. It may be that men are bound by the cultural stereotype of inexpressiveness, a characteristic which proves to be dysfunctional in relating to women.

Inexpressiveness is anchored in males' self-concept. Numerous studies have shown that "as a group, males perceive themselves as being somewhat more instrumental than females and females perceive themselves as being somewhat more expressive than do males" (Spence, Deaux, and Helmreich 1985). The consistency of this finding is true across all ages from kindergarten children to mature adults (Bem 1974; O'Connor, Mann, and Bardwick 1978; Simms et al. 1978; Hall and Halberstadt 1980; Feldman, Biringen, and Nash 1981), across a wide range of ethnic and socioeconomic groups (Spence and Helmreich 1978; Romer and Cherry 1980), and with several cross-national studies (Block 1973; Spence and Helmreich 1978; Almeida 1980; Diaz-Loving et al. 1981; Runge, Frey, Gollwitzer, Helmreich, and Spence 1981).

Traditional sex role stereotypes are being challenged by a more modern definition of sex roles. This could lead us to expect that the traditional bifurcating model of sex roles will give way to a more androgynous model. However, it would be a mistake to assume that differences in sex role stereotypes are rapidly disappearing, for as Spence, Deaux, and Helmreich (1985, 156) have recently observed, "the resistance of trait stereotypes to change during a period in which sex role attitudes have become conspicuously more liberal is interesting to note." In a time when alternative sex role models are being offered, it can be expected that emotional inexpressiveness, as a characteristic of the traditional male sex role, will be both approved and disapproved, functional and dysfunctional. The concept of, and concern with male inexpressiveness, can best be explained in terms of contradictory, culturally prescribed, gender role expectations. Male inexpressiveness is an inherent part of the current sex role strain males are experiencing.

## Role Theory and the Sex Role Strain Paradigm

There is considerable overlap between the role theory perspective I have used in previous reports on the study of male inexpressiveness and Pleck's sex role strain paradigm. One may even suggest that the two perspectives may be identical, thus noting the acknowledgement both of us make to Ralph Turner's (1970) important writings on role theory. What I think Pleck has done is to "lift" role theory out of symbolic interaction as a perspective in understanding human behavior in general, and applied it to the understanding of a specific arena of human behavior, the male sex role. In this sense the SRS paradigm is more specific than role theory. But the SRS paradigm is also broader than role theory in the sense that it has taken into account historical change in explaining the current strain in sex roles.

Because of these two refinements, I find SRS the most useful "version" of role theory within which to study and understand male inexpressiveness.

I also believe the SRS perspective is general enough to include findings and insights generated from other theoretical perspectives.

At the risk of superficially forcing an exact fit, the following represents an attempt to couch the explanation of male inexpressiveness within each of Pleck's SRS propositions:

1. Inexpressiveness is a normative part of the traditional male sex role stereotype.
2. Because of the current clash between the traditional and modern male role, male inexpressiveness is contradictory and inconsistent.
3. Because of the changing nature of role commitments and the emergence of the modern male role, the proportion of men who violate the norm of inexpressiveness is high.
4. In a society that still values the traditional male role, male expressiveness leads to social condemnation.
5. Males who define themselves according to the traditional male role will experience negative psychological consequences if they are too expressive.
6. Actual or imagined violation of (not living up to) the traditional male role leads males to overconform to this role, as exemplified by extreme inexpressiveness.
7. Violating norms of inexpressivity has more severe consequences for males than females.
8. As a characteristic prescribed by the sex role, inexpressiveness is psychologically dysfunctional.
9. Inexpressiveness results in males' experiencing strain in their paid work and family roles.
10. Changing expectations of expressiveness has caused males to experience sex role strain.

## Summary: The Theory of Male Inexpressiveness

The sex role strain paradigm has been identified a useful for serving as an integrated theoretical model explaining male inexpressiveness. As a break from the MSRI paradigm, this paradigm provides a "release" from the burden of trying to explain male inexpressiveness in terms of some innate psychological need for sex-typed traits. The alternative theories of male inexpressiveness, as discussed in the previous chapter, were compared and contrasted in light of their consistency with each other and the SRS perspective. Although the truths and insights generated from each of the socialization theories might be incorporated within the SRS paradigm, the role theory perspective is an especially close fit.

Male inexpressiveness is a characteristic that reflects traditional societal definitions, stereotypes, and norms regarding the male sex role. Male inexpressiveness is not merely the result of personality traits, but of the interaction between a male's conception of himself and his definition of role-appropriate behavior in life situations. Because of the cultural discontinuity inherent in defining the male's role, inexpressiveness can be analyzed as both functional and dysfunctional at the same time. In short, male inexpressiveness is a part of the current sex role strain men can expect to experience.

There is some biological evidence suggesting that males may have a harder time than females in making a connection between feelings and their expression in words. If this evidence is true it may explain the origin, but not the magnitude, of average expressive differences between the sexes. Parents inadvertently accentuate tendencies that may already exist in their very young children. Such tendencies are *labeled* by parents, and when a child is thus labeled, it serves to draw forth the expected behavior from the child. In this sense, any inborn tendency toward inexpressiveness becomes part of a self-fulfilling prophecy. Biological evidence for expressive differences is still at the level of speculation, but if demonstrated to be a contributing factor, should not be thought of as a thread to the SRS explanation of male inexpressiveness.

Boys who are parented by mothers more than by fathers, and especially those who have cold and distant relationships with their fathers, can be expected to be inexpressive. This is not a result of serious sex role identity problems for the boys, but rather a result of observing an inexpressive adult role model. Such an adult male role model is likely to foster role overconformity in the son, whereby any real or imagined failure to live up to male sex role expectations results in the son's compensating by exaggerated forms of inexpressiveness. Expressive male behavior will be the result of having internalized expressive male sex role norms, or of being in situations in which the male role is defined in terms of expressive expectations. It can be expected that intimate and expressive relationships between fathers and sons will result in sons' incorporating norms of expressiveness into their male sex role. Social structural changes resulting from the industrial revolution, such as the removal of the father from the home for long periods of time during the day, has probably resulted in increased male inexpressiveness.

As traditionally defined, male inexpressiveness is gender-appropriate behavior. In the modern definition of the male role, inexpressiveness has come to be defined as a problem. The new male is expected to be able to express his feelings in marriage, with his children, with other men, and in social situations in general. Now, male inexpressiveness captures contradictory gender expectations. Once developed as normative components of the male sex role, inexpressiveness is difficult to undo. Not only is expressiveness a part of the male's self-concept, it is also incorporated into social structural constraints that foster its continuance. Any attempts to increase male expressiveness will have to focus on changing the systemic structures within which male inexpressiveness is considered normative behavior, as well as upon individual males themselves.

# 4
# Role Types

In the previous chapter the sex role strain paradigm was identified as a useful integrating perspective within which to consider male inexpressiveness. This chapter will attempt to illustrate several types of inexpressive male sex role strains. Each of these inexpressive male roles can be considered sex role strains because they constitute contradictory expectations for the male. They are also sex role strains because they involve behavior both functional and dysfunctional to males and the social relations of which they are a part.

Shakespeare said the whole world is a stage and that we each have our entrances and exits. Similar to a drama, inexpressive male behavior may be conceived in terms of role performance. The concept of *role,* as it is used within the sociological framework, especially of symbolic inteteraction, allows inexpressiveness to be viewed not only as a personality trait but also as behavior which results from interaction between the individual personality and others. The concept *role* serves to explain inexpressiveness as that which results from the ego's conception of himself, his perception of the alter's (potential target person's) role, and his perception of the alter's expectation of him.

However, unlike a staged drama, playing a role in the real world is often difficult and stressful because of contradictory cultural role expectations. This is especially true now. Thus the need to conceive of inexpressive male sex role *strain.*

A male's self-conception begins to form at the time he is born. There is perhaps no role stronger than the gender role in shaping one's self-concept and behavior. In learning to be a man, the boy in our society comes to value expressions of masculinity and to devalue expressions of femininity. Masculinity is expressed largely through physical courage, competitiveness, and aggressiveness. Gentleness, expressiveness, and responsiveness are often scorned as signs of femininity. The family, peer group, and mass media converge to help shape the male's view of masculinity—his self-concept. But the societal shapings of the male sex role are far from uniform, thus creating the distinct possibility that sex role strain may even exist within the males self-concept.

The ego's perception of the alter's role and his perception of the alter's expectation of him are important factors in understanding inexpressiveness because they widen the boundaries used to explain expressiveness from the ego (the individual level), to interaction with the alter (the social level). Turner (1962), for example, suggests that "role-taking" shifts emphasis from the simple process of acting out a prescribed role to devising a performance on the basis of an inputed other role. Interpretation of the social situation is a key variable in understanding inexpressiveness. In a contemporary society in which the normative expectations for a given social situation are often ambiguous at best and contradictory at worst, the attempt by males to appropriately express the right quantity and quality of emotions can only be described as sex role strain.

## Inexpressive Male Sex Role Strains

Male inexpressiveness can be categorized on the basis of at least three criteria: first, whether feelings are present in the male; second, whether there is an attempt to pretend to express feelings; and third, whether the potential object of expressiveness is female or male. As seen in figure 4–1, there are three groups of inexpressive male sex role strains, each of which contains two inexpressive roles.

|  |  | *FEELING* | *NON-FEELING* |
|---|---|---|---|
| *VERBAL* | Toward Females | EXPRESSIVE MALE (Parlor Room Boy) | PLAYBOY |
|  | Toward Males | EXPRESSIVE MALE (Locker-Room Boy) | CONBOY |
| *NON-VERBAL* | Toward Females | COWBOY | LOCKER-ROOM BOY (as seen by females) |
|  | Toward Males | GOOD OL' BOY | PARLOR-ROOM BOY (as seen by males) |

**Figure 4–1. Types of Inexpressive Males' Roles**

*Feeling, Verbal Roles: Expressive Male Roles*

A totally expressive male is one who has feelings and expresses those feelings to both females and males. However, it is not uncommon for males to express their feelings to one sex and not the other. While some males are expressive toward females and inexpressive toward males, others are inexpressive toward females and expressive toward males. A more thorough discussion of these two types of incomplete male roles will come later under the nonfeeling, nonverbal type of inexpressiveness.

*Feeling, Nonverbal Roles: Cowboys and Good Ol' Boys*

Some males are inexpressive because they have feelings but either cannot or will not verbally share those feelings with others. Feeling, nonverbal males play the role of cowboy toward females and the male role of a good ol' boy toward males.

**The Cowboy.** The feeling, nonverbal male learns to relate to females by assuming the strong, silent, rugged he-man role. Perhaps the best portrayal of the cowboy role can be seen in any one of the typecast roles played by the movie actor John Wayne. Around women, Wayne, in his films, appears to be uncomfortable and often unable to speak, especially if he really cares for the woman. He seems more comfortable around his horse than around "his woman." Any display of affection is likely to be disguised, rarely issued in a pronouncement of "I really love you." Such open verbal displays of affection would be out of character for the type of rugged frontiersman who supposedly won the West.

It would be a mistake to think of a cowboy as nonfeeling. Even the rugged cowboy portrayed by Wayne has emotional feelings—toward women, toward small children, and even toward other men, *but* they are never expressed directly. The cowboy type is feeling but is nonverbal in his expression of these feelings.

Upon entering marriage, the cowboy type may actually be relieved of expressive expectations. By presenting the marriage as evidence of his affection ("Would I have married you if I didn't love you?"), a husband can reduce the pressure to express such emotions.

His wife, too, can infer the existence of such emotions in the marriage ("He must love me or he never would have married me"), thus reducing the requirement for him to continually demonstrate affection and tenderness toward her. If together long enough, most couples develop shorthand symbols, such as an arm around the shoulder, a certain look, or a pat on the derriere, through which they express certain emotions and desires. These symbols come to represent the emotions the husband has, but is unable or unwilling to verbally express.

However, marriage can also represent added role strain for the cowboy, who is ill-prepared for a companionship-oriented marriage. Wives today are much more likely to expect their husbands to be expressive in the marital relationship than were wives in the past. Several researchers have commented on the male role strain that can result from contradictory demands and expectations males experience in their socialization and adult life (Hacker 1957; Bem 1975; Pleck 1976). American society "inconsistently teaches the male to be masculine is to be inexpressive, while at the same time, expectations in the marital role are defined in terms of sharing affection and companionship, which involves the ability to communicate and express feelings" (Balswick and Peek 1971, 366).

**The Good Ol' Boy.** The term *good ol' boy* is primarily a Southern expression coined by the flamboyant government of Louisiana's Huey Long. Good ol' boy relationships do not arise overnight; rather, they often begin during childhood and are nurtured through the trials and triumphs of growing up together. The good ol' boy is completely loyal to the other good ol' boys, who together form a strong ingroup or primary group. A good ol' boy will stick with you "through thick and thin."

Although good ol' boys spend much time talking together, they rarely communicate their personal feelings to each other. If asked why he did not talk about his feelings, the good ol' boy is likely to reply that it was not necessary. He may also say, "Man, if you have to say it, the feelings must not be there." He believes the expression of feelings is a "womanly" trait. The man who is expressive of his feelings is likely to be laughed at and joked about by the good ol' boys as one who is "too feminine" or lacks "manliness." Good ol' boys do have deep, enduring feelings for each other, demonstrated in the supportive *action* they will take on behalf of each other.

Good ol' boy roles are both fostered *by* and perpetuators *of* a male subculture. This subculture is a storehouse of folk philosophy, humor, wisdom, and stereotypes transmitted to males as they begin to learn the good ol' boy role. By the time adulthood is reached, each good ol' boy has a common storehouse of memories, stories, and wisdom that make lengthy conversation unnecessary. A brief statement or comment can conjure up a common memory in the good ol' boys group, drawing a collective laugh or response and then leading the group to another shared memory. It is difficult, if not impossible, for a woman to become a part of this subculture, as it would be for another male who does not share this heritage.

Role strain for the good ol' boy comes in two forms: First, when his level of expressiveness is not enough to sustain another member of the group in a crisis. While the hurting friend may need verbal affirmation of a feeling, the good ol' boy is capable of only joking about the hurt. Second, when the good ol' boy attempts to communicate to someone outside of the group. In many ways the good ol' boy does not communicate feelings to his buddies in non-verbal ways, but to outsiders who are not privy to these shared nonverbal codes, communication is difficult.

### Nonfeeling, Verbal Roles: Playboys and Conboys

Nonfeeling, verbal roles call for a display of feelings when in reality the male has no feelings within. The man who plays these roles must become skilled at pretending to have feelings. In relating to females, the non-feeling, verbal male assumes the playboy role, while in relating to males he plays the conboy role, as in "con man."

**The Playboy.** Although the playboy role can be considered a modern version of the cowboy role, it departs from the cowboy role in that it calls for the male to be verbal but also nonfeeling. A movie example of the playboy would be James Bond. Bond interacts with women with a cool air of detachment. Women fall passionately in love with Bond, but he remains aloof. It is interesting to note that in the one film where Bond does fall in love with the heroine, she dies—no doubt the tragic consequences of Bond's shedding his emotional detachment.

As reflected in the philosophy of his namesake, *Playboy* magazine, a playboy "is a skilled manipulator of women, knowing when to turn the lights down, what music to play on the stereo, which drinks to serve, and what topics of conversation to engage in" (Balswick and Peek 1971, 265). The playboy reduces sexuality to a packageable consumption item that he can handle because it demands no responsibility. A successful encounter with a woman is when the bed is shared, but the playboy emerges free of any emotional attachment or commitment. When playtime is over, the plaything can be discarded in a manner befitting our consumer, disposable-oriented society.

**The Conboy.** Webster's defines *con* as a swindler or as an attempt to direct the course of another. The conboy role includes the types of manipulative behavior we associate with the "con man," "con artist," or "wheeler-dealer" in our society. The conboy becomes a skilled manipulator of other males through his ability to convince them he really likes and cares for them.

Certain occupational roles, such as the traveling salesman, may place a man in the conboy role. To the extent that the techniques of selling involve flattering and ego-building of a would-be client, the salesman is playing the role of the conboy. In the competitive structure of much of the work-a-day world, males learn to be on guard against such manipulative behavior in other males.

The conboy's attempt at manipulation may even be ethically justified within certain male subcultures. The conboy learns to rationalize his manipulation of other men by believing that the "sucker" or naive "mark" deserves to be taken advantage of. The skilled conboy may even achieved status in such a subculture because of his reputation as a skilled manipulator. Conboys may well agree with W. C. Fields' famous line, "Never give a sucker an even break."

The ethics and philosophy of the conboy role are those of a modified type of rugged frontier individualist who makes it to the top on his own. Instead of succeeding purely by hard work, self-discipline and honesty, the conboy models his behavior after the equally hard-working folk hero who had to scheme, connive, and sometimes "claw" his way to the top. The fact that many men report they feel suspicious of other men and have a difficult time trusting them may be indicative of the extent to which the conboy role is used by males in our society.

### Nonfeeling, Nonverbal Roles: Locker-Room Boys and Parlor-Room Boys

To be both nonfeeling and nonverbal undoubtedly results in few meaningful interpersonal relationships. Not much can be said to describe the behavioral roles of such males, other than that they are inexpressive because they in fact have no feelings to express. As such, their behavior is more consistent with their emotional state, unlike the playboy or conboy. Many males, however, may learn to express their feelings toward members of one sex but not the other. Males who are nonfeeling and nonverbal toward females but expressive of their feelings toward males will be viewed by females as locker-room boys. Males who are nonfeeling and nonverbal toward males but expressive of their feelings toward females will be viewed by other males as parlor-room boys.

**The Locker-Room Boy.** This role calls for the expression of feelings to men but not to women. There is a certain extent to which all inexpressive male roles allow the male to feel more comfortable around men than women; that is in the security of a male subculture. The locker-room boy is dependent upon such "masculine" subcultures as men's athletic clubs, sports teams, bars, and gaming rooms. In such environments, where masculine identity is secure, the locker-room boy is better able to express his more gentle feelings and even physical affections.

Examples of locker-room boy behavior transcend the boundaries of social stratification. After a few beers at the neighborhood tavern, men who have spent the day working in a factory will begin to share their feelings and concerns with each other. Such emotional sharing does not take place between them and their wives (Balswick 1970; Hurvitz 1964; Komarovsky 1962; Rainwater 1965).

Football players will enthusiastically hug each other after a touchdown. In the locker room, they will openly weep after defeat or express affection or love for each other after a victory or defeat. After one of the 1976 World Series baseball games, the New York Yankees' fiery manager, Billy Martin, announced to the media that he *loved* his ball players. Since the athlete's masculinity has been established through his physical prowess, he is free to *be* expressive of his feelings without having his masculinity questioned. The locker-room boy is more comfortable and also more able to share his feelings with certain other men in sufficiently "masculine" environments.

**The Parlor-Room Boy.** This role calls for a greater expression of feelings toward females than toward males. There is much within the male subculture that encourages a male to take on the parlor-room boy role—competitiveness, power-grabbing, aggressiveness, and one-upmanship. To be comfortable in such a male subculture, one must be sufficiently competitive and aggressive not to feel threatened or overwhelmed. The male who has an insufficient quantity of these "masculine" traits may find herself more comfortable around females than males.

There is some evidence to suggest that a male's greater ability to relate to females may originate in the home. Several studies have found that fathers are more expressive toward their daughters than their sons (Bronfenbrenner 1961; Johnson 1963; Slevins and Balswick 1980). Johnson (1963) noted that while mothers have an expressive attitude toward male and female children indiscriminately, fathers are expressive with their daughters and instrumental with their sons. Because of the role model provided by their father and the greater expressiveness shown to them by their mother, male children may become freer in expressing their feelings to females than to males.

Much of the literature on male relationships suggests that males often fear and distrust other males. Sattel (1976) suggested that males are inexpressive as a conscious effort to maintain power in a relationship, implying that a male will become vulnerable when he expresses his feelings to another male. The fear exists that another male cannot be trusted to use such revelations in a nonexploitive way. Given these fears, and the reality that many males are capable of assuming the conboy role, it is understandable that a male response to sex role strain would be to restrict expressiveness to females.

## Conclusions

The ideas presented in this chapter are based upon a major value assumption and a major theoretical assumption, neither of which can be completely discussed apart from the other. The implied value assumption is that behavioral maturity involves expressing feelings to another person when such feelings are present. This value is derived from the modern definition of the male sex role. The careful reader will have visualized by now that the inclusion of the word *boy* in the title of the six types of inexpressive male roles is intentional. However, it is easy to misinterpret this value assumption as meaning that inexpressiveness is simply the result of an inadequate sex role identity within certain males.

Males inexpressiveness is problematic, not because of inadequate male sex role identity, but because it represents behavior which is both functional and dysfunctional within the cultural discontinuity of contemporary society. (Male inexpressiveness can best be understood within the interactive social process, rather than merely as a sex role identity problem existing within the individual. Although individuals behave inexpressively, they do so within socially perceived, and socially prescribed, situations). In this sense male inexpressiveness is functional. At the same time, however, on the basis of the modern definition of the male sex role, inexpressiveness is dysfunctional. (Conceptualized within a developmental perspective [Erickson 1968; Levinson 1978] *resorting to the type behavior called for within any of the inexpressive role is to operate on an immature behavioral level.* This statement accepts the developmental implication that inexpressive behavior is immature, while at the same time understanding that this behavior may be called forth by roles that exist within the social structure of our society.) The contradictory definitions of the male sex role means that men are likely to experience sex role strain when they behave as they think a man should.

# 5
# Measuring Expressiveness

**M**y first attempt at constructing emotion and expression of emotion instruments consisted of assembling a number of statements about a variety of affective, or emotionally, situations. Pretesting soon revealed these statements to be so indirect it was not at all clear whether emotional feelings and their expression were actually being measured. Attempting to construct items capable of measuring emotionality and the expression of emotions can be summarized as having begun with the fairly indirect types of measurements and gradually changing to more direct types. The final scales developed and described in this chapter are based upon the conviction that the best way (within survey research) to measure something as abstract as emotionality and the expression of emotions is by directly asking people how they feel certain emotions and how they express these emotions to others. Blalock (1960, 10) has argued that "operations and theoretical definitions should be associated on a one-to-one basis." If this is the ideal, then the direct way the scales attempt to measure emotionality and the expression of emotions should give us confidence in their face validity. The early phases of scale construction were aided very much by the National Institute of Mental Health funded research project on "The Inexpressive Male," Grant #22156–01, University of Georgia, Jack Balswick, principal investigator.

## The Emotion Scale and Expression of Emotion Scale

The constructed *Emotion Scale* is contained in exhibit 5–1 and the constructured *Expression of Emotion Scale* is contained in exhibit 5–2 (see pages 63–64). Each of the Lickert-type scales consists of sixteen statements to which subjects are asked to respond in one of the four forced categories of "Never,"

"Seldom," "Often," or "Very often." Each of the sixteen statements in the *Emotion Scale* seeks to measure the degree to which each of sixteen types of emotions are present in the subject. Thus, the presence of "anger" is based upon the subject responding to the statement, "I feel anger," in terms of either "never," "seldom," "often," or "very often." Each of sixteen statements in the *Expression of Emotion Scale* seeks to measure the degree to which each of the same sixteen types of emotions is expressed by the subject. Thus, the expression of "anger" is based upon the subject responding to the statement, "When I *do* feel angry toward people I tell them," in terms of "never," "seldom," "often," or "very often."

Each of the sixteen-item scales were constructed so as to include four subscales of four items each. Within the *Emotion Scale,* the items measuring love, tenderness, warmth, and affection constitute the *Love Scale;* the happiness, delight, joy, and elation items constitute the *Happiness Scale;* the sorrow, grief, sadness, and blues items constitute the *Sadness Scale;* and the anger, hate, resentment, and rage items constitute the *Hate Scale.* The *Expression of Emotion Scale* contains the same groups of emotions in each subscale.

By giving weights of one to a "never" response, two to a "seldom" response, three to an "often" response, and four to a "very often" response, the potential scale scores for the *Emotion Scale* and the *Expression of Emotion Scale* are from a low of sixteen to a high of sixty-four. The potential scale scores for all of the subscales are from a low of four to a high of sixteen.

## Factor Analysis of the Scales

To determine the nature of the scale items, an analysis procedure was carried out to determine more accurately the factor structure of the scales. Four factors were expected to emerge in each of the scales—Love, Hate, Happiness, and Sadness factors. The factor analysis of the *Emotion Scale* is presented in table 5–1 and the factor analysis of the *Expression of Emotion Scale* is presented in table 5–2.

**Emotion Scale.** As can be seen in table 5–1, the four items measuring Love clearly load on Factor One; the four items measuring Sorrow load on Factor Two; the four items measuring Hate load on Factor Three; and the four items measuring Happiness load on Factor Four. On Factor One the Love Scale items load extremely high, .713, .690, .812, and .707 respectively, with the next highest loading at only .341. On Factor Two the Sadness Scale items load high at .795, .729, .573, and .485 respectively, with all other items loading at .287 or less. On Factor Three the Hate Scale items load high at −.713, −.707, −.548, and −.753 respectively, with all other items loading at −.322 or below. On Factor Four the Four Happiness items load high at

# Table 5-1
## Rotated Factor Loadings for Emotion Scale Items*

| | | | Total Sample | | |
|---|---|---|---|---|---|
| Criteria — Item | Factor 1 | Factor 2 | Factor 3 | Factor 4 | Communality** |
| (1) I feel anger | .042 | .094 | −.713 | −.074 | .524 |
| (2) I feel love | .713 | −.017 | .082 | .168 | .543 |
| (3) I feel sorrow | .027 | .795 | −.040 | .000 | .635 |
| (4) I feel happy | .294 | −.088 | .148 | .698 | .603 |
| (5) I feel tenderness | .690 | .102 | .083 | .274 | .569 |
| (6) I feel grief | −.126 | .729 | −.108 | .184 | .593 |
| (7) I feel delight | .292 | .023 | .034 | .702 | .580 |
| (8) I feel hate | −.142 | .117 | −.707 | −.028 | .535 |
| (9) I feel affection | .812 | −.040 | −.012 | .134 | .679 |
| (10) I feel resentment | −.004 | .287 | −.548 | −.079 | .389 |
| (11) I feel sad | .138 | .573 | −.322 | −.353 | .576 |
| (12) I feel joy | .341 | −.042 | .001 | .674 | .572 |
| (13) I feel rage | −.080 | −.028 | −.753 | .069 | .579 |
| (14) I feel warmth | .707 | −.004 | .056 | .302 | .594 |
| (15) I feel blue | .164 | .485 | −.317 | −.404 | .526 |
| (16) I feel elation | .316 | .127 | −.203 | .402 | .319 |
| Eigenvalue (Sum of Squares) | 2.622 | 1.872 | 2.174 | 2.148 | 8.816 |
| Percentage of Variance | 16.4 | 11.7 | 13.6 | 13.4 | |
| Cumulative Variance | 16.4 | 38.1 | 51.7 | 65.1 | |

*The factor loadings were derived from the varimax rotation, the procedure being the Principal Factor Analysis with iterations.

**The *communality* ($h_i^2$) indicates the amount of the variance of a variable that is shared by at least one other variable in the set. The complement of communality ($1-h_i^2$) indicates the proportion of the variance of a variable that is not accounted for by the common factors or by any variable in the set.

Table 5–2
Rotated Factor Loadings for Expression of Emotion Scale Items*

| Criteria | Item | Total Sample | | | | |
|---|---|---|---|---|---|---|
| | | Factor 1 | Factor 2 | Factor 3 | Factor 4 | Communality** |
| | (1) I tell anger | .200 | .636 | .029 | .132 | .462 |
| | (2) I tell love | .839 | .077 | .047 | .066 | .716 |
| | (3) I tell sorrow | .176 | .046 | .041 | .754 | .603 |
| | (4) I tell happy | .231 | -.070 | .728 | .194 | .626 |
| | (5) I tell tenderness | .791 | .044 | .228 | .142 | .699 |
| | (6) I tell grief | .139 | .241 | .139 | .659 | .531 |
| | (7) I tell delight | .253 | .017 | .754 | .204 | .674 |
| | (8) I tell hate | .027 | .780 | -.059 | .062 | .617 |
| | (9) I tell affection | .814 | .106 | .237 | .028 | .730 |
| | (10) I tell resentment | .141 | .667 | .035 | .149 | .489 |
| | (11) I tell sad | .060 | .103 | .220 | .705 | .560 |
| | (12) I tell joy | .259 | .037 | .774 | .195 | .706 |
| | (13) I tell rage | -.096 | .670 | .190 | .160 | .521 |
| | (14) I tell warmth | .706 | .100 | .324 | .128 | .630 |
| | (15) I tell blue | -.053 | .200 | .241 | .576 | .433 |
| | (16) I tell elation | .068 | .180 | .644 | .082 | .459 |
| Eigenvalue (Sum of Squares) | | 2.805 | 2.087 | 2.497 | 2.067 | 9.455 |
| Percentage of Variance | | 17.5 | 13.0 | 16.2 | 12.9 | |
| Cumulative Variance | | 17.5 | 30.5 | 46.7 | 59.6 | |

*The factor loadings were derived from the varimax rotation, the procedure being the Principal Factor Analysis with iterations.

**The *communality* ($h_i^2$) indicates the amount of the variance of a variable that is shared by at least one other variable in the set. The complement of communality ($1-h_i^2$) indicates the proportion of the variance of a variable that is not accounted for by the common factors or by any variable in the set.

.698, .702, .674, and .402 respectively, with all other items loading at .302 or below. Factor One, Love, explains 16.4 percent of the variance; the Sorrow Factor explains 11.7 percent of the variance; the Hate Factor explains 13.6 percent of the variance; the Happiness Factor explains 13.4 percent of the variance; and all four together explain 65.1 percent of the variance in the scale.

**Expression of Emotion Scale.** As can be seen in table 5–2, factor analysis of the *Expression of Emotion Scale* strongly supports the theoretical soundness of the four dimensions of emotions that make up its subscales. Factor One items all load high at .839, .791, .814, and .706 respectively, while all other items load at .253 or below. Factor Two items all load high at .636, .780, .667, and .670 respectively, while the next hightest loading item is .241. Factor Three items all load high at .728, .754, .774, and .644 respectively, while all other items load at .324 or lower. Factor Four items all load high at .754, .659, .705, and .576 respectively, while all other items load at .204 or less. For the *Expression of Emotion Scale,* the Love Factor accounts for 17 percent of the variance; the Hate Factor accounts for thirteen percent of the variance; the Happiness Factor accounts for 16.2 percent of the variance; the Sadness Factor accounts for 12.9 percent of the variance; and all four together account for 59.6 percent of the variance in the scale. Test-retest reliability coefficients for the *Expression of Emotion Scale* were .83 at one week for adults (N = 34) and .72 at six weeks for college students (N = 33) (Davidson and Dosser 1982).

Needless to say, the almost "textbook" results of the factor analyzing supports the notion that the four items that make up each of the dimensions of emotionality are actually measuring a variety of the same type of emotion.

## Conclusion

The construction of the *Emotion Scale* and the *Expression of Emotion Scale* attempts to establish some quantitative measurements of emotions. I have elected to conceive of emotions along the polar dimensions of Love–Hate and Happiness–Sadness. There are undoubtedly other dimensions of emotions which can and should be included.

Further work can also be done in specifying the conditions under which certain types of emotion are felt and expressed. We not only need to know how expressive a person is of emotions in general, but to *whom* one is expressive of various kinds of emotions. It would be a mistake to conceive of emotions and the expression of emotions as merely being a function of individual personality traits. The feeling and expression of emotions, like all psychological phenomena, are also a function of the role or roles an individual may perform at any one time. The following two scales are elaborations of the

*Expression of Emotion Scale,* both measuring a dimension of situational expressiveness.

## Expression of Emotions Scale, Varied by Target Person

This scale is a variation of the *Expression of Emotion Scale* and requires subjects to report how often they expressed each of sixteen emotions to each of six targets (father, mother, female friend, male friend, female stranger, and male stranger). The same emotions and response categories as in the *Expression of Emotion Scale* are used and it is scored in the same manner. The *Expression of Emotions Scale, Varied by Target Person* is contained in exhibit 5–3 (see pages 65–66).

## Expression of Emotions Scale, Varied by Size of Group

This scale requires subjects to report how often they express each of the sixteen feelings given in the *Expression of Emotion Scale* to someone in three different conditions: alone with the person, in a small group, and in a large group. This scale uses the same response categories as the expressiveness scale and is scored in the same manner. The *Expression of Emotions Scale, Varied by Size of Group* is presented in exhibit 5–4 (see page 67). Results of both are reported in chapter 9, "Situational Factor."

## The Expression of Emotion Scale for Couples

This scale, as shown in exhibit 5–5, is a direct extension of the *Expression of Emotion Scale* (see page 68). Individuals were asked to respond to four-point Likert scales that measure the "outputs" or degrees to which each of sixteen different emotions are disclosed to one's spouse. Thus, the husband's disclosing of resentment is based upon his response to the statement, "When I *do* feel resentment toward my wife I tell her," in terms of "never," "seldom," "often," or "very often," which are assigned values of one to four, respectively. The wife was asked similar questions about the husband. As with the *Expression of Emotion Scale,* these sixteen emotions may be combined into four subscales each consisting of four items. The subscales yield scores measuring the affective self-disclosure of love, happiness, sadness, and anger, and are summed to produce a total score.

*Perception of Expression of Emotion Scale*

Another similar series of four-point Likert scales was included to measure individuals' perceptions of how much their spouses disclose to them on these same sixteen emotions (see exhibit 5–6 on page 69). As with the prior measure, four subscales of four items each measured individuals' perceptions of how much their spouses disclose love, happiness, sadness, and anger to them. As in the first measure, these subscales are summed to yield a perception of total emotional expressiveness.

The *Expression of Emotion Scale for Couples* and the *Perception of Expression of Emotion Scale for Couples* are two of the major instruments used to assess the relationship between emotional expressiveness and marital adjustment discussed in chapters 10 and 11. These measures allow for the computation of one's expressiveness to spouse, the difference between partners' levels of expressiveness to each other, one's perception of expressiveness received from spouse, and the difference between one's stated expressiveness to spouse and one's perception of expressiveness received from spouse.

*Factor Analysis*

The *Expression of Emotion Scale for Couples* and the *Perception of Expression of Emotion Scale for Couples* separate principal components analyses with oblique rotation (Kim 1975). As shown in tables 5–3 and 5–4, four factors were obtained for each and represent the subscales of love, happiness, anger, and sadness expression. The rationale for performing an oblique rotation rests on the assumption that emotional expressiveness should be measured by propensity for expression in specific emotional areas as well as a general willingness to reveal. Translated into a methodological context, it was presumed that separate factors comprising the expression of different emotions would emerge and are presumed to be somewhat correlated.

An examination of the factor structures reveals that those items presumed to measure *Love* output and input (love, tenderness, affection, and warmth) do, in fact, load highly on the same factor. Those items presumed to measure *Happiness* output and input (happiness, delight, joy, and elation) load on the same factor. In addition, those items presumed to measure *Anger* output and input (anger, hate, resentment, and rage) and those items presumed to measure *Sadness* output and input (sadness, sorrow, grief, and blue) also load on their respective factors.

The four factors of the *Expression of Emotion Scale for Couples* account for 71.1 percent of the total variance associated with these variables. The four factors of the *Perception of Expression of Emotion Scale for Couples* account for 75.1 percent of the total variance associated with the variables comprising that scale. The results of these factor analyses support the notion

Table 5–3

**Factor Pattern Matrix of the Affective Self-disclosure Scale Items Following Oblique Rotation**

| | Loadings on Factors | | | |
|---|---|---|---|---|
| *Expression Item* | *Factor 1* | *Factor 2* | *Factor 3* | *Factor 4* |
| love | −.007 | .005 | .849 | .083 |
| happy | .648 | .005 | .050 | −.108 |
| angry | −.210 | .470 | .150 | −.284 |
| sorrow | −.046 | .035 | .054 | −.740 |
| tenderness | .065 | −.019 | .777 | −.032 |
| delight | .761 | .037 | .070 | .069 |
| hate | .017 | .843 | −.046 | .098 |
| grief | .088 | .145 | .061 | −.630 |
| warmth | .446 | .040 | .343 | −0.53 |
| joy | .863 | −.002 | −.040 | −.056 |
| resentment | .079 | .690 | −.005 | −.037 |
| sad | .089 | .002 | −.015 | −.845 |
| affection | .076 | −.036 | .734 | −.093 |
| elation | .610 | .071 | .110 | −.103 |
| rage | .093 | .507 | .001 | −.169 |
| blue | .071 | −.032 | −.037 | −.789 |

that the four items in the four dimensions of emotion expressiveness actually measure a variety of the same type of emotion.

To test the stability of the derived factors, congruency coefficients were computed between the *Expression of Emotion Scale for Couples* factors and the original factor structure as resulting from a factor analysis of the original *Expression of Emotion Scale*. Basically this procedure (Ryder 1967) correlates the loadings between the unrotated principal factors, from the two separate factor analyses, and allows for an interpretation of the stability of each factor. As shown in table 5–5, these coefficients show a high stability for the whole factor structure. Essentially, the structure obtained in the original factor analysis replicated almost identically five years later. This marked resiliency, as well as the test-retest correlations of the *Expression of Emotion Scale* which range from .71 and .83 (Davidson and Dosser 1982), suggests a more than adequate attainment of reliability for the use of this instrument.

Validation for this scale comes from the content nature of the self-report items that do appear to measure the emotional expressiveness of the four proposed emotions as evidenced by the factor structure of the scale. It can also be noted that with all the scales, greater female emotional expressiveness

Table 5–4
Factor Pattern Matrix of the Perception of Receiving Affective Self-disclosure from Spouse Scale Items Following Oblique Rotation

| Expression Received from Spouse | Loadings on Factors | | | |
|---|---|---|---|---|
| | Factor 1 | Factor 2 | Factor 3 | Factor 4 |
| love | .141 | .013 | .687 | .064 |
| happy | .750 | −.053 | .090 | −.076 |
| angry | −.061 | .574 | .155 | −.151 |
| sorrow | .076 | .162 | .045 | −.646 |
| tenderness | .001 | .031 | .840 | −.111 |
| delight | .888 | .039 | −.046 | −.011 |
| hate | .067 | .674 | −.138 | .039 |
| grief | .163 | .146 | −.142 | −.677 |
| warmth | .332 | −.050 | .519 | −.116 |
| joy | .740 | .038 | .099 | −.042 |
| resentment | .080 | .763 | −.030 | −.028 |
| sad | −.007 | −.110 | −.016 | −.953 |
| affection | .114 | .017 | .768 | .017 |
| elation | .712 | .017 | .137 | −.015 |
| rage | −.110 | .724 | .226 | −.088 |
| blue | −.027 | .081 | .119 | −.756 |

Table 5–5
Correlations among Unrotated Principal Factors between Balswick's Expression of Emotion Scale and Affective Self-disclosure Scale for Couples

| Self-Disclosure Scale For Couples | Balswick's Expression of Emotion Scale | | | |
|---|---|---|---|---|
| | Factor 1 | Factor 2 | Factor 3 | Factor 4 |
| Factor 1 | .73 | | | |
| Factor 2 | | .97 | | |
| Factor 3 | | | .93 | |
| Factor 4 | | | | .84 |

Note: All correlations significant $p < .001$.

in the areas of love, happiness, and sadness is consistent with the wider literature on sex roles.

## Pretend Expression of Emotion Scale

It is possible for a person to not have a certain feeling, but deem it advantageous to pretend to have that feeling. This is especially true of a male in the
playboy role (see chapter 4) seeking to manipulate a woman toward his own
sexual ends. Although the playboy may say, "I love you," in reality these are
empty words uttered with the intent of gaining sexual favors. The *Pretend
Expression of Emotion Scale* is intended to measure the extent to which a
person pretends to express feelings that in fact are not there.

As can be seen in exhibit 5–7, this scale represents a simplification rather
than an elaboration of the *Expression of Emotion Scale* (see page 70). The
pretend scale has the disadvantage of relying upon only one scale item to
collectively represent four related, but possibly distinct emotions. It does,
however, collect data in very little precious questionnaire space.

## Self-Report Performance Test

The *Self-Report Performance Test* is a revised version of a test developed by
Highlen and Voight (1978) and is used in other studies (Highlen and Gillis
1978; Highlen and Johnston 1979). It consists of sixteen situations that required an equal number of responses to situations requiring the expression
of love, happiness, sadness, and anger. In addition, subjects made responses
both as initiators and respondents. Therefore, type-of-subject role (initiator,
respondent) and type-of-feeling response (love, happiness, sadness, anger),
were crossed factors with each situation presented twice (one for a male best
friend and once for a female best friend) for each of the eight combinations.
This was done to allow for direct comparison between responses to male and
female best friends.

The emotionally expressive situations are open-ended, with adequate
space for subjects to write in their responses to the sixteen situations. All
situations are presented in the same fashion and followed one after the other.
Exhibit 5–8 is a copy of the *Self-Report Performance Test* (see pages 70–74).

Two raters were trained to score subjects' written responses to the self-
report performance test. This training included practice on simulated performance tests. Inter-rater reliability coefficients were calculated during rater
training on ten simulated performance tests; training continued until reliability was satisfactory. Inter-rater reliability coefficients were also calculated on
thirty-five jointly rated self-report performance tests taken from three points

in time on control for rater drift. Reliability coefficients at the end of rater training ranged from .90 to .96 for the situational factors subscores, with a coefficient of .93 for the total expressiveness scores across all situational factors. During the actual rating of the self-report performance tests the reliability coefficients from the three reliability checks ranged from .75 to 1.00 for the situational factor subscores and from .94 to .98 for the total expressiveness scores. Final scores for the jointly rated performance tests were determined by alternating the raters' scores when discrepancies occurred.

Each response was rated using this six-point scale adapted for Highlen and Gillis (1978): Five—clear, self-referenced feeling with clear reason for the feeling given; four—clear self-referenced feeling with no or unclear reason for the feeling given; three—unclear feeling or a response to feeling in an indirect, unclear or confusing way; two—response to content, cognitive statement, or affect that is other referenced; one—irrelevant response or response with inappropriate feelings; zero—no response to the situation (see exhibit 5–9 for the coding manual on pages 74–76). Responses received a score ranging from zero to five. For example, the statement "I feel angry" in response to a negative stimulus situation would receive a score of four. Mean scores for each level of the situational factors were calculated, which maintained the scores for all levels within the zero-to-five range. An additional measure of expressiveness, number of words, was also computed by the raters. Raters were kept naive as to the sex of the subject and to the subject's scores on any other measure.

## Behavioral Performance Test

The behavioral performance test is identical to the self-report performance test just described, except that the subjects are asked to respond verbally to role-playing situations instead of writing responses. This procedure requires the use of videotape and is best conducted in an experimental room with a two-way mirror. For ethical reasons, the subject is advised of the videotaping, but the equipment should be as inconspicuous as possible. Also, help subjects feel comfortable and relaxed. One additional advantage with this assessment procedure is that, since the same sixteen situations are used in the self-report and the behavioral sections of the assessment, it is possible to compare self-report and behavioral data directly.

The following instructions were presented verbally and in writing to each subject to the start of the session:

*In this study, you will be asked to respond to typical situations which arise in people's lives. It is important that you try to imagine that you are actually in the situations, and are interacting with your best male or best female friend. It is also important that you try to express your true feelings that you would experience if you were in that particular situation with your best friend. Take a few seconds now to think of the name of your best female friend and your best male friend to help you keep in mind the people you are imagining you are with in these situations. Try throughout this experience to imagine the actor as your best male friend and the actress as your best female friend. In order to better imagine the situations that will be described, you could think about what it would feel like to be in the situation, where it would occur, and what you would see, hear, and smell. Then, when you are certain that you understand the situation and can imagine it, you may proceed to respond to the actor or actress. Try to respond just as you would to your best friend. Remember, express your feelings as well as you can. After each situation, I will explain the next situation and you will have time to get ready. In some of the situations, you will respond first, and, in others, you will respond after the actor or actress speaks to you.*

When the subject understands the instructions, the situation is presented on a card and given to the subject. After the subject has a chance to understand and imagine the situation, an actor or actress enters the room and the subject responds. The situations are presented to the subjects in random order to control for any order response bias and proceed from one situation to another until all sixteen situations have been presented and responses have been obtained. Although subjects' responses are not limited by time, each response ends with their first response, and does not include any further interaction with the actor or actress.

Two practices are held to ensure that subjects understand the instructions, to acquaint each subject with the task, and to further relax them. These situations are very similar to the experimental situation, and can be videotaped for later use in rater training. If subjects have difficulty following the instructions, try this method:

Videotaping begins at the end of the introduction of the situation and when the first words are spoken by either the actor/actress or the subject. At the end of the subject's response to each situation, the actor/actress states the number of the situation for the videotape and audiotape, for identification purposes.

After each response to the situation, turn off the video equipment and ask each subject to rate the anxiety he or she would actually feel if he or she had made that response to his or her best male or female friend. A one-to-seven Likert scale, ranging from "very calm and relaxed" to "extremely nervous," is used to report anxiety for each situation (Highlen and Gillis 1978). The entire behavioral portion of this procedure takes twenty to thirty minutes per subject to administer. The rating, although requiring raters and video equipment, is reliable and straightforward.

Two trained raters score the performance audiotape as described with the self-report performance test and exhibit 5–9, and also for length of response (number of words). Two additional raters are trained to rate nonverbal expression of emotion by observing the videotapes. Reliability measures should be calculated for these raters.

Each of the sixteen videotaped responses for each participant is rated using methods similar to those used to assess nonverbal components of assertive behavior. Eisler et al. (1973) and Eisler et al. (1975) suggested eight nonverbal units of behavior that are useful for this study: duration of looking, smiles, duration of reply, latency of response, loudness of speech, fluency of speech, affect, and overall assertiveness. The scale suggested for use in this assessment procedure has been adapted from Eisler et al (1973), and consists of these eight behaviors: loudness of speech, effective voice tone, fluency of speech, animation of body, latency of response, facial expression, distracting behavior, and overall assertiveness. Each category is on a scale from one to eleven (see exhibit 5–10 for all scales and definitions on pages 77–79).

For all behavioral measures the participant's score is obtained by taking the mean value averaged over the eight situations. It should be noted that the adapted measurement and scoring procedure has been used for a sample of thirty-five correctional officers with acceptable reliability (reliabilities for the three raters corrected by the Spearman-Brown Prophecy Formula ranged from .69 to .88) and demonstrated ability for scores to differentiate between high and low assertive subjects. With only brief training of raters in the above mentioned pilot study, the scale proved useful and reliable. Other nonverbal rating methods exist (Izard 1971, 1972; Mehrabian 1972), but they are more complex and less straightforward.

Research results support the contention that rating videotape, rather than live behavior, will not affect the reliability of the ratings. For example, Eisler et al. (1973) concluded that videotaped observation of nonverbal interaction for the behaviors they studied (looking and smiling) is highly reliable and equal to reliabilities obtained by observing the interactions live. They also suggested a distinct advantage to the use of videotapes, in that they can be viewed more than once to facilitate precision in defining and measuring behaviors.

## Conclusion

In this chapter a number of instruments of varying length, complexity, and nature have been discussed and presented for the help they might be measuring in emotional expressiveness. Most measuring techniques can be classified as either self-report methods of behavioral methods. It is not my intent here to describe the long-term, expansive, and continuing debate over the relative merits of each of these approaches to assessment. Only a few points will be made to this issue; the reader is referred to other sources for a more thorough review of this issue (Mischel 1968; Sackett 1978; Ciminero, Calhoun, and Adam 1977; Walsh 1967, 1968). It is important to note that most authors in the assessment area make the distinction between self-report and behavioral methods of assessment and present examples of each approach (Hall 1978; Heimberg et al 1977; Hersen and Bellack 1977; Jackubowski and Lacks 1975; Lange and Jackubowski 1976; Rich and Schroeder 1976).

Behavioral self-report and observer subjective report are two other methods of assessment that have been suggested by Olsen (1977). These two, he claimed, help bridge the gap between self-report and behavioral methods. In distinguishing between these four methods of research and assessment, Olsen divided them on two dimensions: (a) reporter's frame of reference (Insider versus Outsider) and (b) type of data (subjective versus objective). Olsen defined each method as follows: (a) self-report is subjective data from an insider's perspective; (b) behavioral is objective data from an outsider's perspective; (c) observer subjective report is subjective data from an outsider's perspective; and (d) behavioral self-report is objective data from an insider's perspective. Cromwell et al. (1976) made the same distinctions when discussing diagnosis and assessment in marital and family therapy, giving primary attention to the self-report and behavioral methods, since these methods are more frequently used. Because of that, this discussion will consider only these two primary methods.

## Self-Report Methods

In areas related to expressiveness (assertiveness, social skills, and self-disclosure), many self-report methods of assessment exist. Hall (1978) believed that the issues surrounding the validity of self-report data have been widely discussed, but that many questions relating to reliability, social desirability, and the usefulness of self-report methods as measures of social skills remain unclear. Despite these unanswered questions, self-report is a major approach to the assessment of assertiveness because of the economy and quantifiability of self-ratings and self-report inventories. The difficulties of self-reported assessment, including its susceptibility to subject-induced distortion, have also been noted by Hollandsworth and Wall (1977), who argued that more direct and objective measures of behavior are needed at some point. They agreed with Mischel (1968) that self-reports have the advantage of being as good a predictor of future behavior as any other nonbehavioral measure, while being easily and inexpensively administered. Although self-report methods of assessment are important, necessary, and useful, Jackubowski and Lacks (1975) have cautioned therapists to be aware of the contradictory findings about how self-reports correlate with overt measures of assertion when attempting to evaluate the effectiveness of assertion training.

## Behavioral Methods

Several authors have been less charitable toward self-report measures. For example, Warren and Gilner (1978) have cited research that compared behavioral and self-report measures and concluded that assessment of behavior is more predictive of future events and more sensitive to changes resulting from treatment in assertive training than are self-report measures. Their findings also support the common finding that self-report measures do not correlate highly with behavioral data. A number of researchers have attempted to avoid difficulties usually associated with self-report methods through the use of behavioral tasks and role-playing tests of assertiveness that attempt to bring assessment samples as close to real-life situations as possible. While admitting the desirability of assessing behavior directly, it has been pointed out that the major limitation presently of role-playing assessment is that no validation studies have been reported. Hollandsworth and Wall (1975) and Hall (1978) have discussed the limits of behavioral assessments, in that the influence of varying response types and situational contexts must be considered. However, this could be an overwhelming and expensive task unless the wide range of situations can be narrowed to those that exhibit a potential for productive investigation.

## Advantage of Both Methods

Several authors have argued for the importance of both in combination for research and assessment. The importance of approaching assessment from a subjective—self-report—insider frame of reference as well as from an objective—behavioral—outsider frame of reference to gain a comprehensive picture of interpersonal relationships has been stressed by Olson (1977), who argued that each offers a different and valuable perspective, and that their combination has benefits too often ignored by researchers. Cromwell et al. (1976) has argued that different methods provide different kinds of information and that from both a research and a therapeutic perspective, data from each can provide a more comprehensive understanding. They believe that, since these methods tap different perspectives (insider's and outsider's) and generate different types of data (subjective and objective), one should not expect agreement across methods. Conflicting data may be considered additional sources of clinical information that the therapist might effectively apply during the treatment. Self-report, overt behavioral, and psyiological response measures have had consistently low relationships with one another in the assessment of social skills and there appears to be no indication that any one approach is sufficient to adequately represent the social skills complex. This view is supported by Olsen (1977), who believes the insider's and outsider's perspectives are mutually exclusive frames of reference with neither sufficient alone.

# Exhibits

**Exhibit 5–1.  Emotion Scale**

---

*Instructions:*  *Please respond to the next items by circling the number that best describes how often the following occur:*

|  | 1 = NEVER | 2 = SELDOM | 3 = OFTEN | 4 = VERY OFTEN |
|---|---|---|---|---|

| | 1 | 2 | 3 | 4 |
|---|---|---|---|---|
| 1. I feel anger | 1 | 2 | 3 | 4 |
| 2. I feel love | 1 | 2 | 3 | 4 |
| 3. I feel sorrow | 1 | 2 | 3 | 4 |
| 4. I feel happiness | 1 | 2 | 3 | 4 |
| 5. I feel tenderness | 1 | 2 | 3 | 4 |
| 6. I feel grief | 1 | 2 | 3 | 4 |
| 7. I feel delight | 1 | 2 | 3 | 4 |
| 8. I feel hate | 1 | 2 | 3 | 4 |
| 9. I feel affection | 1 | 2 | 3 | 4 |
| 10. I feel resentment | 1 | 2 | 3 | 4 |
| 11. I feel sadness | 1 | 2 | 3 | 4 |
| 12. I feel joy | 1 | 2 | 3 | 4 |
| 13. I feel rage | 1 | 2 | 3 | 4 |
| 14. I feel warmth | 1 | 2 | 3 | 4 |
| 15. I feel blue | 1 | 2 | 3 | 4 |
| 16. I feel elation | 1 | 2 | 3 | 4 |

## Exhibit 5–2.  Expression of Emotion Scale

*Instructions:*  *Please respond to the next items by circling the number that best describes how often the following occur:*

| | 1 = NEVER | 2 = SELDOM | 3 = OFTEN | 4 = VERY OFTEN |
|---|---|---|---|---|
| 1. When I do feel angry toward people I tell them. | 1 | 2 | 3 | 4 |
| 2. When I do feel love toward people I tell them. | 1 | 2 | 3 | 4 |
| 3. When I do feel sorrow I tell people. | 1 | 2 | 3 | 4 |
| 4. When I do feel happy I tell people. | 1 | 2 | 3 | 4 |
| 5. When I do feel tenderness toward people I tell them. | 1 | 2 | 3 | 4 |
| 6. When I do feel grief I tell people. | 1 | 2 | 3 | 4 |
| 7. When I do feel delight I tell people. | 1 | 2 | 3 | 4 |
| 8. When I do feel hate toward people I tell them. | 1 | 2 | 3 | 4 |
| 9. When I do feel affection toward people I tell them. | 1 | 2 | 3 | 4 |
| 10. When I do feel resentment toward people I tell them. | 1 | 2 | 3 | 4 |
| 11. When I do feel sad I tell people. | 1 | 2 | 3 | 4 |
| 12. When I do feel joy I tell people. | 1 | 2 | 3 | 4 |
| 13. When I do feel rage I tell people. | 1 | 2 | 3 | 4 |
| 14. When I do feel warmth I tell people. | 1 | 2 | 3 | 4 |
| 15. When I do feel blue I tell people. | 1 | 2 | 3 | 4 |
| 16. When I do feel elation I tell people. | 1 | 2 | 3 | 4 |

**Exhibit 5–3. Expression of Emotion Scale, Varied by Target Person**

*Following is a list of sixteen feelings you might feel toward another person. Simply indicate how often you tend to tell each type of person each of the following types of feelings.*

1 = NEVER    2 = SELDOM    3 = OFTEN    4 = VERY OFTEN

| | Father | Mother | Female Friend | Male Friend | Female Stranger | Male Stranger |
|---|---|---|---|---|---|---|
| 1. When I *do* feel *angry* toward this person I tell him/her: | 1 2 3 4 | 1 2 3 4 | 1 2 3 4 | 1 2 3 4 | 1 2 3 4 | 1 2 3 4 |
| 2. When I *do* feel *love* toward this person I tell him/her: | 1 2 3 4 | 1 2 3 4 | 1 2 3 4 | 1 2 3 4 | 1 2 3 4 | 1 2 3 4 |
| 3. When I *do* feel *sorrow* toward this person I tell him/her: | 1 2 3 4 | 1 2 3 4 | 1 2 3 4 | 1 2 3 4 | 1 2 3 4 | 1 2 3 4 |
| 4. When I *do* feel *happy* toward this person I tell him/her: | 1 2 3 4 | 1 2 3 4 | 1 2 3 4 | 1 2 3 4 | 1 2 3 4 | 1 2 3 4 |
| 5. When I *do* feel tenderness toward this person I tell him/her | 1 2 3 4 | 1 2 3 4 | 1 2 3 4 | 1 2 3 4 | 1 2 3 4 | 1 2 3 4 |
| 6. When I *do* feel *grief* toward this person I tell him/her: | 1 2 3 4 | 1 2 3 4 | 1 2 3 4 | 1 2 3 4 | 1 2 3 4 | 1 2 3 4 |
| 7. When I *do* feel *delight* toward this person I tell him/her: | 1 2 3 4 | 1 2 3 4 | 1 2 3 4 | 1 2 3 4 | 1 2 3 4 | 1 2 3 4 |

(cont.)

**Exhibit 5-3. (Continued)**

1 = NEVER    2 = SELDOM    3 = OFTEN    4 = VERY OFTEN

| | Father | Mother | Female Friend | Male Friend | Female Stranger | Male Stranger |
|---|---|---|---|---|---|---|
| 8. When I *do* feel *hate* toward this person I tell him/her: | 1 2 3 4 | 1 2 3 4 | 1 2 3 4 | 1 2 3 4 | 1 2 3 4 | 1 2 3 4 |
| 9. When I *do* feel *affection* toward this person I tell him/her: | 1 2 3 4 | 1 2 3 4 | 1 2 3 4 | 1 2 3 4 | 1 2 3 4 | 1 2 3 4 |
| 10. When I *do* feel *resentment* toward this person I tell him/her: | 1 2 3 4 | 1 2 3 4 | 1 2 3 4 | 1 2 3 4 | 1 2 3 4 | 1 2 3 4 |
| 11. When I *do* feel *sad* toward this person I tell him/her: | 1 2 3 4 | 1 2 3 4 | 1 2 3 4 | 1 2 3 4 | 1 2 3 4 | 1 2 3 4 |
| 12. When I *do* feel *joy* toward this person I tell him/her: | 1 2 3 4 | 1 2 3 4 | 1 2 3 4 | 1 2 3 4 | 1 2 3 4 | 1 2 3 4 |
| 13. When I *do* feel *rage* toward this person I tell him/her: | 1 2 3 4 | 1 2 3 4 | 1 2 3 4 | 1 2 3 4 | 1 2 3 4 | 1 2 3 4 |
| 14. When I *do* feel *warmth* toward this person I tell him/her: | 1 2 3 4 | 1 2 3 4 | 1 2 3 4 | 1 2 3 4 | 1 2 3 4 | 1 2 3 4 |
| 15. When I *do* feel *blue* toward this person I tell him/her: | 1 2 3 4 | 1 2 3 4 | 1 2 3 4 | 1 2 3 4 | 1 2 3 4 | 1 2 3 4 |
| 16. When I *do* feel *elation* toward this person I tell him/her: | 1 2 3 4 | 1 2 3 4 | 1 2 3 4 | 1 2 3 4 | 1 2 3 4 | 1 2 3 4 |

## Exhibit 5-4. Expression of Emotion Scale, Varied by Size of Group

*Following are a number of situations in which you might feel more or less free to express your feelings about another person. Simply indicate how often you are likely to express your feelings to others in the various types of situations.*

1 = NEVER   2 = SELDOM   3 = OFTEN   4 = VERY OFTEN

| | Alone with the Person | In a Small Group | In a Large Group |
|---|---|---|---|
| 1. When I *do* feel *angry* toward this person I tell them: | 1 2 3 4 | 1 2 3 4 | 1 2 3 4 |
| 2. When I *do* feel *love* toward people I tell them: | 1 2 3 4 | 1 2 3 4 | 1 2 3 4 |
| 3. When I *do* feel *sorrow* toward people I tell them: | 1 2 3 4 | 1 2 3 4 | 1 2 3 4 |
| 4. When I *do* feel *happy* toward people I tell them: | 1 2 3 4 | 1 2 3 4 | 1 2 3 4 |
| 5. When I *do* feel *tenderness* toward people I tell them: | 1 2 3 4 | 1 2 3 4 | 1 2 3 4 |
| 6. When I *do* feel *grief* toward people I tell them: | 1 2 3 4 | 1 2 3 4 | 1 2 3 4 |
| 7. When I *do* feel *delight* toward people I tell them: | 1 2 3 4 | 1 2 3 4 | 1 2 3 4 |
| 8. When I *do* feel *hate* toward people I tell them: | 1 2 3 4 | 1 2 3 4 | 1 2 3 4 |
| 9. When I *do* feel *affection* toward people I tell them: | 1 2 3 4 | 1 2 3 4 | 1 2 3 4 |
| 10. When I *do* feel *resentment* toward people I tell them: | 1 2 3 4 | 1 2 3 4 | 1 2 3 4 |
| 11. When I *do* feel *sad* toward people I tell them: | 1 2 3 4 | 1 2 3 4 | 1 2 3 4 |
| 12. When I *do* feel *joy* toward people I tell them: | 1 2 3 4 | 1 2 3 4 | 1 2 3 4 |
| 13. When I *do* feel *rage* toward people I tell them: | 1 2 3 4 | 1 2 3 4 | 1 2 3 4 |
| 14. When I *do* feel *warmth* toward people I tell them: | 1 2 3 4 | 1 2 3 4 | 1 2 3 4 |
| 15. When I *do* feel *blue* toward people I tell them: | 1 2 3 4 | 1 2 3 4 | 1 2 3 4 |
| 16. When I *do* feel *elation* toward people I tell them: | 1 2 3 4 | 1 2 3 4 | 1 2 3 4 |

## Exhibit 5–5. Expression of Emotion Scale for Couples

(Husband's form)

*Please respond to the next thirty-two items by circling the number that best describes how often the following occur.*

1 = NEVER        2 = SELDOM        3 = OFTEN        4 = VERY OFTEN

| | |
|---|---|
| When I do feel love toward my wife I tell her. | 1 2 3 4 |
| When I do feel happy I tell my wife. | 1 2 3 4 |
| When I do feel angry toward my wife I tell her. | 1 2 3 4 |
| When I do feel sorrow I tell my wife. | 1 2 3 4 |
| When I do feel tenderness toward my wife I tell her. | 1 2 3 4 |
| When I do feel delight I tell my wife. | 1 2 3 4 |
| When I do feel hate toward my wife I tell her. | 1 2 3 4 |
| When I do feel grief I tell my wife. | 1 2 3 4 |
| When I do feel warmth I tell my wife. | 1 2 3 4 |
| When I do feel joy I tell my wife. | 1 2 3 4 |
| When I do feel resentment toward my wife I tell her. | 1 2 3 4 |
| When I do feel sad I tell my wife. | 1 2 3 4 |
| When I do feel affection toward my wife I tell her. | 1 2 3 4 |
| When I do feel elation I tell my wife. | 1 2 3 4 |
| When I do feel rage I tell my wife. | 1 2 3 4 |
| When I do feel blue I tell my wife. | 1 2 3 4 |

(Wife's form)

*Please respond to the next thirty-two items by circling the number that best describes how often the following occur.*

1 = NEVER        2 = SELDOM        3 = OFTEN        4 = VERY OFTEN

| | |
|---|---|
| When I do feel love toward my husband I tell him. | 1 2 3 4 |
| When I do feel happy toward my husband I tell him. | 1 2 3 4 |
| When I do feel angry toward my husband I tell him. | 1 2 3 4 |
| When I do feel sorrow toward my husband I tell him. | 1 2 3 4 |
| When I do feel tenderness toward my husband I tell him. | 1 2 3 4 |
| When I do feel delight toward my husband I tell him. | 1 2 3 4 |
| When I do feel hate toward my husband I tell him. | 1 2 3 4 |
| When I do feel grief toward my husband I tell him. | 1 2 3 4 |
| When I do feel warmth toward my husband I tell him. | 1 2 3 4 |
| When I do feel joy toward my husband I tell him. | 1 2 3 4 |
| When I do feel resentment toward my husband I tell him. | 1 2 3 4 |
| When I do feel sad toward my husband I tell him. | 1 2 3 4 |
| When I do feel affection toward my husband I tell him. | 1 2 3 4 |
| When I do feel elation toward my husband I tell him. | 1 2 3 4 |
| When I do feel rage toward my husband I tell him. | 1 2 3 4 |
| When I do feel blue toward my husband I tell him. | 1 2 3 4 |

## Exhibit 5–6.   Perception of Expression of Emotion Scale for Couples

(Husband's form)

*Please respond to the next thirty-two items by circling the number that best describes how often the following occur.*

1 = NEVER          2 = SELDOM          3 = OFTEN          4 = VERY OFTEN

| | |
|---|---|
| When my wife does feel love toward me she tells me. | 1  2  3  4 |
| When my wife does feel happy she tells me. | 1  2  3  4 |
| When my wife does feel anger toward me she tells me. | 1  2  3  4 |
| When my wife does feel sorrow she tells me. | 1  2  3  4 |
| When my wife does feel tenderness toward me she tells me. | 1  2  3  4 |
| When my wife does feel delight she tells me. | 1  2  3  4 |
| When my wife does feel hate toward me she tells me. | 1  2  3  4 |
| When my wife does feel grief she tells me. | 1  2  3  4 |
| When my wife does feel warmth she tells me. | 1  2  3  4 |
| When my wife does feel joy she tells me. | 1  2  3  4 |
| When my wife does feel resentment toward me she tells me. | 1  2  3  4 |
| When my wife does feel sadness she tells me. | 1  2  3  4 |
| When my wife does feel affection toward me she tells me. | 1  2  3  4 |
| When my wife does feel elation she tells me. | 1  2  3  4 |
| When my wife does feel rage she tells me. | 1  2  3  4 |
| When my wife does feel blue she tells me. | 1  2  3  4 |

(Wife's form)

*Please respond to the next thirty-two items by circling the number that best describes how often the following occur.*

1 = NEVER          2 = SELDOM          3 = OFTEN          4 = VERY OFTEN

| | |
|---|---|
| When my husband does feel love toward me he tells me. | 1  2  3  4 |
| When my husband does feel happy he tells me. | 1  2  3  4 |
| When my husband does feel anger toward me he tells me. | 1  2  3  4 |
| When my husband does feel sorrow he tells me. | 1  2  3  4 |
| When my husband does feel tenderness toward me he tells me. | 1  2  3  4 |
| When my husband does feel delight he tells me. | 1  2  3  4 |
| When my husband does feel hate toward me he tells me. | 1  2  3  4 |
| When my husband does feel grief he tells me. | 1  2  3  4 |
| When my husband does feel warmth he tells me. | 1  2  3  4 |
| When my husband does feel joy he tells me. | 1  2  3  4 |
| When my husband does feel resentment toward me he tells me. | 1  2  3  4 |
| When my husband does feel sadness he tells me. | 1  2  3  4 |
| When my husband does feel affection toward me he tells me. | 1  2  3  4 |
| When my husband does feel elation he tells me. | 1  2  3  4 |
| When my husband does feel rage he tells me. | 1  2  3  4 |
| When my husband does feel blue he tells me. | 1  2  3  4 |

## Exhibit 5–7. Pretend Expression of Emotion Scale

*Please respond to the following statements by circling the number that best describes how often this occurs:*

1 = NEVER    2 = SELDOM    3 = OFTEN    4 = VERY OFTEN

1. I pretend to feel *anger, hate, rage* or *resentment*.    1  2  3  4
2. I pretend to feel *love, tenderness, affection* or *warmth*.    1  2  3  4
3. I pretend to feel *sadness, sorrow, grief,* or *blue*.    1  2  3  4
4. I pretend to feel *happiness, delight, elation* or *joy*.    1  2  3  4

## Exhibit 5–8. Self-Report Performance Test

*On this section of this questionnaire, you will write your responses to typical situations which arise in people's lives. It is important that you try to imagine that you are actually in the situations and talking to your best male or best female friend. It is also important that you try to express your true feelings that you would experience if you were in that particular situation with your best friend. Take a few seconds now and write down the name of your best female friend and your best male friend to help you keep in mind the people you are to be imagining in the situations. In order to better imagine the situations you could think about what it would feel like to be in that situation, where it would be, and what you would see, hear, and smell. Then, after carefully reading each situation, write down exactly what you would say in the space provided. Try to write it just as you would say it. Remember, express your feelings as well as you can.*

*Situation 1:* It's the worst day of your life. You overslept and missed an important class and then got back a test on which you had done poorly. Then on the way to an important afternoon meeting your car broke down. Finally, your plans for the evening, which you had been very excited about, fall through, and you are left with nothing to do except think of the terrible day. Your best

*male* friend comes by and says: "How's it going?" and you say _____

_____

_____

*Situation 2:* Your grandfather has been very sick for a long time, and you have just returned from visiting him at the hospital. He looked very bad, didn't even recognize you, and had clearly deteriorated. This has upset you so much that

you need someone to talk to. You go to your best *male* friend and say _____

_____

_____

*Situation 3:* You have worked very hard preparing an exotic and delicious dinner for your best *female* friend and had looked forward to enjoying it with *her.* You had arranged for her to arrive at 7:30 P.M. At 9:30 P.M., after the dinner has been ruined, *she* arrives and says: "Gee, I'm really sorry I'm late, I got busy with my studies and forgot about our plans." You respond to *her* by saying

_____

_____

_____

_____

*Situation 4:* You're giving a party, and the behavior of one of your best *female* friends has become increasingly objectionable and obnoxious over the course of the evening. You're upset with *her* behavior, so you go over to *her*

and say _____

_____

_____

_____

*Situation 5:* A *female* friend is taking a carpentry course and has really struggled with it. Secretly, you think it's kind of a crazy thing for *her* to do, but for your birthday *she* brings you a really nice coffee table that *she* made. After *she*

gives you the gift, you say _____

_____

_____

_____

_____

*Situation 6:* Your best *male* friend has finally convinced you to go to a play with *him.* Much to your surprise as the play ends, you find that you've enjoyed it and *his* company immensely. This evening has reminded you how much *his*

friendship means to you. You turn to *him* and say _____

_____

_____

_____

_____

(*cont.*)

**Exhibit 5–8. (*Continued*)**

---

*Situation 7:* Your best *female* friend's parents have just filed for divorce. Your friend is really upset and feels torn between them. You and *she* talk several hours, and you assure *her* that *she* can still love both of them. *She's* visibly relieved and says, "Thank you so much. I really needed to talk to someone,

and you've helped a lot." You reply _____

_____

_____

_____

*Situation 8:* You're camping with your best *male* friend. It's night, and you're sitting together by the fire watching the stars. *He* turns to you and says, "Hey! Isn't this fantastic?! Thanks for asking me to come. Listen, I think you're a really

special person—I care for you a lot." You respond by saying _____

_____

_____

_____

*Situation 9:* It's the worst day of your life. You overslept and missed an important class and then got back a test on which you had done poorly. Then on the way to an important afternoon meeting your car broke down. Finally, your plans for the evening, which you had been very excited about, fall through, and you are left with nothing to do except think of the terrible day. Your best

*female* friend comes by and says: "How's it going?" and you say _____

_____

_____

_____

*Situation 10:* Your grandfather has been very sick for a long time, and you have just returned from visiting him at the hospital. He looked very bad, didn't even recognize you, and had clearly deteriorated. This has upset you so much that you need someone to talk to. You go to your best *female* friend and say

_____

_____

_____

*Situation 11:* You have worked very hard preparing an exotic and delicious dinner for your best *male* friend and had looked forward to enjoying it with *him*. You had arranged for *him* to arrive at 7:30 P.M. At 9:30 P.M., after the dinner has been ruined, *he* arrives and says: "Gee, I'm really sorry I'm late, I got busy with my studies and forgot about our plans." You respond to *him* by saying _____

_____

_____

*Situation 12:* You're giving a party, and the behavior of one of your best *male* friends has become increasingly objectionable and obnoxious over the course of the evening. You're upset with *his* behavior, so you go over to *him* and say

_____

_____

_____

*Situation 13:* A *male* friend is taking a carpentry course and has really struggled with it. Secretly, you think it's kind of a crazy thing for *him* to do, but for your birthday *he* brings you a really nice coffee table that *he* made. After *he* gives you the gift, you say _____

_____

_____

_____

*Situation 14:* Your best *female* friend has finally convinced you to go to a play with *her*. Much to your surprise as the play ends, you find that you've enjoyed it and *her* company immensely. This evening has reminded you how much *her* friendship means to you. You turn to *her* and say _____

_____

_____

_____

*Situation 15:* Your best *male* friend's parents have just filed for divorce. Your friend is really upset and feels torn between them. You and *he* talk several hours, and you assure *him* that he can still love both of them. *He's* visibly relieved and says, "Thank you so much. I really needed to talk to someone, and you've helped a lot." You reply _____

_____

_____

_____

(*cont.*)

## Exhibit 5–8. (*Continued*)

*Situation 16:* You're camping with your best *female* friend. It's night and you're sitting together by the fire watching the stars. *She* turns to you and says, "Hey! Isn't this fantastic?! Thanks for asking me to come. Listen, I think you're a really special person—I care for you a lot." You respond by saying

_____

_____

_____

## Exhibit 5–9. Coding Manual for Rating Emotional Expressiveness on the Self-Report Performance Test

*Each response should be considered in its entirety; i.e. the response, no matter how many sentences long, is rated as one unit. The highest score for any one sentence within the response is the score for that response, unless a sentence within a response causes the rest of the response to be unclear. In that case, the rating should be lowered.*

### SCORE of 1: Irrelevant Response

The first determination to be made is whether the response is relevant or irrelevant. This determination should be made by considering the context of the stimulus situation including the circumstances, the setting, the sex of the target person, the type of feeling appropriate, and the role of the subject. Just because a statement fails to respond to feeling does not make it irrelevant; the fact that is responds to an inappropriate feeling or to a totally unrelated context does make it irrelevant.

> *Example:* In response to the presentation of a coffee table by best friend:
> "I'm really angry that you made this table"—irrelevant due to inappropriate feeling.
> "I really enjoy weekends"—irrelevant due to unrelated context.

> *Example:* In response to camping scene and positive statement of caring from best friend:
> "It really upsets me when you talk like that"—inappropriate feeling.
> "Which tent are you sleeping in?"—unrelated context.

## SCORE of 2: Response to Content, Cognitive Response, or Affect that is Other-Referenced

Once the relevance of the response has been determined, the next determination is whether there is affect present in the response. In order for a response to be classified as containing affect, the following criteria must be met:

a. an affect word contained in either of the two lists of feeling words must be present and the affect word must be used as a verb, adverb, or an adjective, or

b. the words "I feel" followed by "like" or "as", and some descriptive words, e.g. "I feel like everything is going wrong at once," or "I feel as if my life has taken a turn for the better."

If the response is relevant and there is no response to feeling as per the above criteria, the response is to content or a cognitive statement. This type of response includes those that reiterate the content of the stimulus situation, those that evaluate or judge, and those that order or give instructions, etc. In addition, responses that respond to feelings that clearly belong to someone else are given a score of 2. Also, opinions and desires; e.g., I wish, I want, I need, etc.

*Examples:* In response to the camping scene and positive statement of caring from best friend:

"I agree with you"—no affect stated, just agreement.

"I can tell you're really excited about this trip"—feeling responded to is the other person's.

*Examples:* In response to presentation of coffee table by best friend:

"The carpentry work here is nearly perfect, you must have learned a lot"—no affect, just evaluative comment.

"I think that table looks good"—good is a feeling word, but "feel" is used here in a cognitive statement.

"You must be really proud of your work"—feeling responded to is the other person's.

## SCORE of 3: Unclear Feeling, Response to Feeling in an Indirect Way

This category includes all responses to feeling that use metaphor or simile to express feelings.

*Examples:* "I feel that tomorrow will be a better day."

"I feel like I did the best I could."

"I feel it was a nice thing for you to do."

(*cont.*)

**Exhibit 5–9.** (*Continued*)

---

A score of 3 is also given to a response that may contain a statement with a higher rating, but which becomes unclear due to the other portions of the response that are irrelevant or unclear.

*Example:* "I feel good being here with you tonight; would you like to have sex?"

Another example of an indirect feeling would be a statement to feeling that is not referenced.

*Examples:* "Super" or "Great" or "Wonderful"

Statements that indirectly give reference for the feeling or give reference to the situation are scored as a 3. For example, "that was great" could be interpreted as "I feel great about that," but the reference to that and the structure of the statement make it unclear and indirect.

Statements of courtesy are scored a 3 since they might be true expressions of feeling or trite, nonthinking responses and are thus unclear.

*Example:* "I appreciate it—thank you very much."

## SCORE of 4: Clear, Self-Referenced Feeling with Absent or Unclear Reason for that Feeling

A score of 4 is given to a response when a clear feeling is stated in a self-referenced fashion, with either no reason given or an unclear or implied reason given for that feeling.

*Examples:* "That makes me fel good"—a 4 as there is an unclear reason for the feeling.
"I feel really sad because that happened"—is unclear and implied reason for the feeling.

## SCORE of 5: Clear, Self-Referenced Feeling with Clear Reason for the Feeling

When the feeling is clearly stated in a self-referenced fashion with a clear and precise reason for the feeling given, the response received a score of 5.

*Examples:* "I feel happy when I am with you and I care for you very much."
"I am very sad because my grandfather is so sick and will probably die."

---

## Exhibit 5–10. Nonverbal Expressiveness Rating Scales

**A.** *Loudness of Speech*

Loudness of speech is an important characteristic of assertive behavior. For purposes of this experiment, loudness of speech will be determined in comparison to the confederate.

11 very loud
10
9
8
7
6 equal to confederate
5
4
3
2
1 very low, not able to hear

**B.** *Affective Voice Tone*

This scale considers the communication of emotion through the voice tone or the paralinguistic qualities of the voice.

11 full, lively, sincere, appropriate voice tone
10
9
8
7
6 not monotone, but not lively voice tone
5
4
3
2
1 very flat, unemotional, monotone, insincere voice tone

**C.** *Fluency of Speech*

This scale considers how easily the speech flows. Fluent speech avoids fillers or interruptions such as "you know", "ah", "er", etc. and inappropriate pauses.

11 very fluent, easily flowing speech with no fillers
10
9
8
7
6 somewhat fluent with some fillers but without frequent interruptions
5
4
3
2
1 not fluent at all with speech frequently interrupted with fillers

*(cont.)*

## Exhibit 5–10. (*Continued*)

D. *Animation of Body*

This scale considers the communication of body language. It includes the consideration of gestures, body posture, and body movement.

11 very animated with use of gestures and posture appropriate to the situation
10
 9
 8
 7
 6 some use of gestures with some animation
 5
 4
 3
 2
 1 no animation of body, remains still and stiff, inappropriate to the situation

E. *Latency of Response*

This scale considers how quickly the response follows the stimulus or the initiation of the situation.

11 no hesitation, immediate response
10
 9
 8
 7
 6 some hesitation, but response follows within a reasonable amount of time
 5
 4
 3
 2
 1 too much hesitation; extremely slow to respond; inappropriate delay

F. *Facial Expression*

This scale considers communication through facial expression and changes in facial expressions. It considers specifically three important facial regions: the brow, eyes and eyelids, and the mouth and lower face.

11 very expressive face with eyes, brow, mouth all appropriate for the situation; active and congruent
10
 9
 8
 7
 6 some expression facially, but not clear or congruent
 5

4
3
2
1 totally inexpressive, blank face inappropriate to situation

G. *Distracting Behavior*

This scale considers behaviors that limit the communication by distracting the speaker or the listener, or both. These behaviors include: nervous gestures, tics, inappropriate smiles; inappropriate body posture; playing with pencil; scratching; rattling change, etc.

11 no distracting behavior; nonverbal behavior appropriate
10
9
8
7
6 some appropriate; some distracting nonverbal behavior
5
4
3
2
1 very much distracting behavior; nonverbal behavior totally inappropriate

H. *Overall Expressiveness*

This scale considers the global rating of expressiveness, integrating voice tone, facial features and body movements to generate an overall impression of expressiveness.

11 very expressive
10
9
8
7
6 moderately expressive
5
4
3
2
1 not expressive

# 6
# Gender Differences

The expression of certain emotions is often mentioned as a characteristic that distinguishes males from females. Boys are reprimanded for expressing sentimental or affectionate feelings, but girls are allowed and, in fact, encouraged to do so. Certain emotions as are even described as feminine—tenderness, compassion, sentimentality, gentleness, soft-heartedness—while aggressive feelings, such as anger and hostility, are described as masculine.

As we have seen in chapter 1, the literature on sex roles assumes and demonstrates that expressiveness is a part of the feminine stereotype and that a lack of expressiveness is part of the masculine stereotype. Little research has been done, however, to determine if there are *actual* sex differences along these lines. This chapter presents findings that can help determine whether and why differences in expressiveness exists.

## Rationale and Hypothesis

Prevalent stereotypes reflect sex differences along any expressive-inexpressive continuum. Some studies have found that females are perceived or stereotyped to be more expressive than males (Bardwick and Douvan 1971; Chafetz 1974; Lunneborg 1970; Ruble 1983; Romer and Cherry 1980; Ward and Balswick 1978). Similar differences, although less extreme, have also been found in studies in which males and females were asked to give expressive characteristics about themselves (Abrahams, Feldman, and Nash 1978; Spence and Helmreich 1979; Feldman, Biringen, and Nash 1981; Hall and Halbertstadt 1980; Almeida 1980; Diaz-Loving et al 1981; Runge, Frey,

Some of the findings reported in this chapter appeared in A. C. Proctor, 1975. *Sex Differences In Expressiveness,* unpublished masters thesis, University of Georgia.

Gollwitzer, Helmreich, and Spence 1981; Lunneborg 1970; Rosenkrantz et al 1968; Biller 1971; and Broverman, Vogel, and Broverman 1972).

Whether discussing sex-role stereotypes or self-reported sex differences, much of the literature would lead one to predict that females are more emotionally expressive than males. Although the reasons for this are not clear, two trends do seem to be relevant in both the child development and sex-role literature.

First, parents seem to interact with children differentially according to gender. They expect, as well as reward, "masculine" behavior in boys and "feminine" behavior in girls (Biller 1981; Johnson 1963; Lynn 1969; Lamb 1977, 1981; Lamb, Owen, and Chase-Landsdale 1979; Lamb, Pleck, and Levine 1985; Lewis 1972).

Second, some of the sex-role literature points to a greater need for affiliation or interpersonal orientation for females than males (Oetzel 1966; Hoffman 1972; Gilligan 1982; Lamb et al. 1986; Rossi 1984). The etiology of this difference is not apparent but may be related to both the different expectations placed upon children according to gender and objective criteria for self-esteem of males. In addition, three attempts to summarize research on the psychology of women conclude that females are more interpersonally oriented than males (Bardwick 1971; Sherman 1971; Gilligan 1982).

However, not all the literature finds that parents interact with their children differentially according to gender, nor that females are more interpersonally oriented than males. The most extensive review of the literature on sex differences concludes that there is little evidence that parents practice differential socialization toward daughters and sons (Maccoby and Jacklin 1974, 303–348), and that females are not more interpersonally oriented than males (Maccoby and Jacklin 1974, 191–226).

Because the literature is mixed, it would seem important to examine the relationships between each of the variables—gender, parental differentiation in socialization, and interpersonal orientation—and expressiveness. Our strategy in this study is to examine these relationships and then to relate two of the variables—interpersonal orientation and perceived parental expressiveness—to the supposed sex difference in expressive behavior. As noted before, females are expected to be more expressive than males. However, it is proposed that because female expressiveness is largely a result of *interpersonal orientation* and *parental expressiveness,* controlling for these factors will substantially reduce the difference in expressiveness between the sexes. Since it would be nearly impossible, given the nature of this study, to ascertain actual parental expectations or behavior, the focus will be on the recall of parental expressiveness. Moreover, neither can the causes of sex differences in interpersonal orientation be studied within the context of this work. Rather, it will be assumed that this interpersonal orientation is learned (as opposed to innate) and that it acts as an intervening variable between gender and emotional expressiveness. From this rationale, the following hypotheses can be derived:

1. Females will be more expressive of love, happiness, and sadness than males.

2. Males will be more expressive of anger than females.

3. Females will be more interpersonally oriented than males.

4. Females will have had parents who were expressive of love, happiness, and sadness more often than males.

5. People who are more interpersonally oriented will be more expressive of love, happiness, and sadness.

6. People whose parents were expressive to them will be more expressive.

7. Controlling for interpersonal orientation and expressiveness of parents toward self, there will be no significant difference between females' and males' expressiveness of love, happiness, and sadness.

## Methodology

### Sample

The data on which this study is based consist of written responses to questionnaires given by a sample of 523 undergraduate students in social studies classes at three Southeastern universities. All questionnaires were considered confidential and were filled out and collected during a class period. Although there were no refusals, two respondents were omitted from the study because of obvious dishonesty in responses. Although a probability sample of all adults would be desirable, resources available at the time did not allow for such a sample. Our logic must be that if the relationships investigated hold true for all adults, then certainly they must hold true for these adults. Since the results presented here are based upon a nonprobability sample, care must be taken in generalizing the findings.

This sample, composed of 50.3 percent (163) males and 49.7 percent (160) females, adequately represents the gender ration of a population of all adults. However, on other demographic characteristics the sample is more homogenous than the larger population. The mean age was twenty for both males and females. The sample was predominantly white, with only 4 percent black and 1 percent others; 95 percent of both males and females were white. This sample consisted of mostly middle-class and upper-middle-class subjects. Using Hollingshead's Two Factor Index, which ranks subjects into five classes, 95 percent of the sample fell into the top three classes, while only 5 percent were in class four and none in class five. The mean social class, by this measure, was class two (2.032), or upper middle class, for both males and females. Moreover, only 7 percent of both male and female subjects had fathers whose income was less than ten thousand dollars, and 17 percent had fathers whose incomes were greater than fifty thousand dollars. Thus, social class is essentially controlled for by means of the sample selection.

Since this is a homogenous sample, one might expect that any variance found will be a conservative estimate of the true variation: differences arising within a college sample might be considerably less than those found in a random sample of all adults.

### Instituting Concepts

*Gender* was determined by answers to the question "Which sex are you?" *Interpersonal orientation* was determined from a question in which respondents were asked to rank the following items from one to eight as to their importance in the respondent's life: having close friends; being successful in school; getting married; financial security; being a good parent; self-fulfillment of intellectual development; being with the one I love; having a successful career. A score of one was given to each of the top four ranked items and a score of zero to the last four, with an individual's interpersonal orientation score computed by summing the scores of the interpersonal items.

*Perceived parental expressiveness* was determined from responses to an eight-item Lickert-type scale, in which subjects responded "never," "seldom," "often," or "very often," to the question(s), "When your mother (father) felt anger, hate, resentment, or rage (love, warmth, tenderness, or affection; sadness, sorrow, grief, or blue; and happiness, delight, joy, or elation) how often did she (he) tell you?" Perceived parental expressiveness was divided into most equal thirds based on frequencies, making a respondent's score of low, medium, or high (relative to that of the other respondents). Throughout this chapter, it should be remembered that the parental expressiveness being discussed is *perceived* parental expressiveness.

*Expressiveness* was determined from responses to the sixteen-item *Expression of Emotion Scale* (see chapter 5 for a detailed discussion of the scale).

### Statistical Tests

Nonparametric statistical techniques were used to test the hypotheses, as the measurement levels of all of the variables are nominal and ordinal. *Chi-square* was used to test for the relationship in Hypotheses One through Three. Goodman and Kruskall's *Gamma* was used as a measure of association. Partial *gammas* were used in testing Hypothesis Four. A relationship was considered significant when it reached the .05 level of probability, based upon a one-tailed test of significance.

## Findings

The literature reviewed in chapter 1 suggests that sex differences exist in expressiveness, sex-role stereotypes, self-concepts, and self-disclosure. Females are said to be more emotional and more willing to express these emotions with others than males. Feelings of hostility (being more aggressive) seem to be more acceptable for males to express than females. The first and second hypotheses of this study reflect this literature:

Hypothesis One:  Females will be more expressive of love, happiness, and sadness than males.

Hypothesis Two:  Males will be more expressive of anger than females.

As can be seen in table 6–1, females in this sample are significantly more expressive of feelings of love, happiness, and sadness than males. Further, this relationship is quite strong: the gammas are .43, .44, and .51 for love, happiness, and sadness, respectively.

On the other hand, the second hypothesis predicts males to be more expressive of anger than females. Although the findings were in the predicted direction, males were not found to express anger more often than females (see table 6–1); there were no significant differences between the two. It is interesting, though, that there is no difference given the substantial differences between males and females in expressing the other feelings. Anger seems to be the only type of emotion studied here that females do not express more often than males.

Hypothesis Three states: Females will be more interpersonally oriented than males. Although it was expected that relationships with loved ones and family would be more important to females than males, these data do not support such a conclusion; there were no significant differences between males and females on this variable (see table 6–2). A rank ordering of the items by means (see table 6–3) reveals that "Being with the one I love" was ranked highest by both males and females. In fact, over half of the males (57.3 percent) and the females (60.7 percent) ranked this item first or second. The only major discrepancy between males and females occurred on the financial security item which was ranked higher by males than females. Interestingly enough, although being with a loved one was consistently ranked high in importance, getting married was consistently ranked low: 76.5 percent of the males and 67.4 percent of the females ranked getting married in the bottom four.

**Table 6–1**
**Expressiveness by Sex**

| Subjects' Expressiveness | | Male | Female | Total |
|---|---|---|---|---|
| Love:[1] | | | | |
| | Low | 41.5 | 19.6 | 30.7 |
| | Medium | 39.6 | 42.0 | 40.8 |
| | High | 18.8 | 38.4 | 28.5 |
| | Totals | 100.0 | 100.0 | 100.0 |
| | N | 260 | 255 | 515 |
| Happiness:[2] | | | | |
| | Low | 44.4 | 21.5 | 32.9 |
| | Medium | 37.4 | 39.1 | 38.2 |
| | High | 18.3 | 39.5 | 28.8 |
| | Totals | 100.0 | 100.0 | 100.0 |
| | N | 257 | 256 | 513 |
| Sadness:[3] | | | | |
| | Low | 40.2 | 16.7 | 28.6 |
| | Medium | 34.9 | 28.0 | 31.5 |
| | High | 24.9 | 55.3 | 40.0 |
| | Totals | 100.0 | 100.0 | 100.0 |
| | N | 261 | 257 | 518 |
| Anger:[4] | | | | |
| | Low | 35.4 | 35.9 | 35.7 |
| | Medium | 34.2 | 39.1 | 36.6 |
| | High | 30.4 | 25.0 | 27.7 |
| | Totals | 100.0 | 100.0 | 100.0 |
| | N | 257 | 256 | 513 |

[1] $x^2 = 37.655$, df $= 2$, p $< .001$; gamma $= 0.43$
[2] $x^2 = 40.380$, df $= 2$, p $< .001$; gamma $= 0.44$
[3] $x^2 = 56.802$, df $= 2$, p $< .001$; gamma $= 0.51$
[4] $x^2 = 2.149$, n.s.; gamma $= 0.06$

Females were expected to be more expressive of love, happiness, and sadness and were also expected to more often have had parents who were expressive of these same emotions. Hypothesis Four states: Females will have had parents who were expressive of love, happiness, and sadness more often than males. Table 6–4 shows that there were significant sex differences in

Table 6–2
Interpersonal Orientation by Sex

|  |  | *Male* | *Female* | *Total* |
|---|---|---|---|---|
|  | Low | 22.9 | 19.7 | 21.3 |
| Interpersonal | Medium | 50.2 | 44.7 | 47.4 |
| Orientation | High | 26.8 | 35.7 | 31.4 |
|  | Total | 100.0 | 100.0 | 100.0 |
|  | N | 231 | 244 | 475 |

$x^2 = 7.307$, n.s.; gamma $= 0.15$

parental expressiveness of only love and happiness. There were no differences between males and females in parental expressiveness of sadness, so this hypothesis must be rejected for that emotion. Sex differences in parental expressiveness of anger were not hypothesized and, in fact, there were no differences. Although a relationship between sex and parental expressiveness does exist, it appears that this relationship is not as strong as the one between the subject's expressiveness and sex; gammas for parental expressiveness and subject's expressiveness of love and happiness were 0.14 and 0.23, respectively. Moreover, the gamma (0.14) for love is not statistically significant; therefore, while there is a relationship between sex and parental expressiveness of love, it is not necessarily monotonic.

A person to whom relationships with "significant others" are important is expected here to be more expressive of love, happiness, and sadness. Hy-

Table 6–3
Ranking of Interpersonal Orientation Items by Sex[1]

|  | *Male* | | *Female* | |
|---|---|---|---|---|
|  | *Rank* | *Mean* | *Rank* | *Mean* |
| Being with the one I love | 1 | 6.26 | 1 | 6.32 |
| Having close friends | 2 | 5.09 | 3 | 5.36 |
| Self-fulfillment | 3 | 5.05 | 2 | 5.79 |
| Having a successful career | 4 | 4.68 | 4 | 4.15 |
| Financial security | 5 | 4.52 | 8 | 3.43 |
| Being a good parent | 6 | 3.70 | 6 | 3.68 |
| Being successful in school | 7 | 3.69 | 5 | 3.77 |
| Getting married | 8 | 3.11 | 7 | 3.56 |

[1]Scores were reversed; i.e., a rank of 1 received a score of 8; therefore, the higher the mean the higher the average rank.

**Table 6–4**
**Parental Expressiveness by Sex**

|  |  | Male | Female | Total |
|---|---|---|---|---|
| Parental Expressiveness of Love[1] | Low | 44.4 | 41.5 | 42.9 |
|  | Medium | 35.6 | 26.5 | 31.0 |
|  | High | 20.0 | 32.0 | 26.0 |
|  | Totals | 100.0 | 100.0 | 100.0 |
|  | N | 250 | 253 | 503 |
| of Happiness[2] | Low | 38.8 | 29.1 | 33.9 |
|  | Medium | 38.8 | 35.8 | 37.3 |
|  | High | 22.4 | 35.0 | 28.8 |
|  | Totals | 100.0 | 100.0 | 100.0 |
|  | N | 250 | 254 | 504 |
| of Sadness[3] | Low | 20.9 | 17.3 | 19.1 |
|  | Medium | 35.3 | 32.7 | 34.0 |
|  | High | 43.8 | 50.0 | 46.9 |
|  | Totals | 100.0 | 100.0 | 100.0 |
|  | N | 249 | 284 | 500 |
| of Anger[4] | Low | 36.3 | 27.4 | 31.8 |
|  | Medium | 47.0 | 51.6 | 49.3 |
|  | High | 16.7 | 21.0 | 18.9 |
|  | Totals | 100.0 | 100.0 | 100.0 |
|  | N | 251 | 252 | 503 |

[1]$x^2 = 10.587$, df = 2, p < .01; gamma = 0.14, n.s.
[2]$x^2 = 10.764$, df = 2, p < .01; gamma = 0.23
[3]$x^2 = 2.136$, n.s.; gamma = 0.11
[4]$x^2 = 4.877$, n.s.; gamma = 0.16

pothesis Five thus states: Persons who are more interpersonally oriented will be more expressive of love, happiness, and sadness. These data lead us to accept this hypothesis (see table 6–5): the more interpersonally oriented a person is, by this measure, the more often he or she is likely to express these emotions. Again, this relationship is not quite as strong as the one between expressiveness and sex (see gammas, table 6–5). The same test applied to anger reveals that there are no significant differences due to interpersonal orientation.

Given the relationships between sex and expressiveness and between in-

## Table 6–5
## Expressiveness by Interpersonal Orientation

| Subjects' Expressiveness | | Low | Medium | High | Total |
|---|---|---|---|---|---|
| Love:[1] | Low | 42.7 | 31.2 | 22.3 | 30.9 |
| | Medium | 41.7 | 36.7 | 48.0 | 41.3 |
| | High | 15.5 | 32.3 | 29.7 | 27.8 |
| | Totals | 100 | 100 | 100 | 100 |
| | N | 103 | 221 | 148 | 472 |
| Happiness:[2] | Low | 52.5 | 31.5 | 18.8 | 32.0 |
| | Medium | 29.7 | 39.2 | 44.3 | 38.8 |
| | High | 17.8 | 29.3 | 36.9 | 29.2 |
| | Totals | 100 | 100 | 100 | 100 |
| | N | 101 | 222 | 149 | 472 |
| Sadness:[3] | Low | 42.2 | 26.7 | 20.3 | 28.0 |
| | Medium | 25.5 | 32.4 | 35.8 | 32.0 |
| | High | 32.4 | 40.9 | 43.9 | 40.0 |
| | Totals | 100 | 100 | 100 | 100 |
| | N | 102 | 225 | 148 | 475 |

[1] $x^2 = 18.227$, df $= 4$, $p < .01$; gamma $= 0.21$
[2] $x^2 = 32.205$, df $= 4$, $p < .001$; gamma $= 0.32$
[3] $x^2 = 14.742$, df $= 4$, $p < .01$; gamma $= 0.19$

terpersonal orientation and expressiveness, and the lack of such a relationship between sex and interpersonal orientation, the possibility of a relationship between interpersonal orientation and expressiveness within each sex was then examined (see tables 6–6 and 6–7). As can be seen, only for happiness does the relationship between interpersonal orientation and expressiveness hold true among males and females. Among males, interpersonal orientation (IPO) does not seem to relate to the expression of sadness, while among females such a relationship does exist. There seems to be no relationship between IPO and the expression of love for males and females. An examination of the percentages reveals that among females, IPO seems to have no effect in the expression of sadness and a small but inconsistent effect upon the expression of love. Among males, however, the relationship between the expression of love and IPO, while not statistically significant, is consistently in the correct direction. It seems, then, that interpersonal orientation does

## Table 6–6
### Expressiveness by Interpersonal Orientation among Males

| Males' Expressiveness | | Low | Medium | High | Total |
|---|---|---|---|---|---|
| Love:[1] | Low | 52.8 | 43.0 | 32.3 | 42.4 |
| | Medium | 39.6 | 35.1 | 45.2 | 38.9 |
| | High | 7.5 | 21.9 | 22.6 | 18.8 |
| | Totals | 100 | 100 | 100 | 100 |
| | N | 53 | 114 | 62 | 229 |
| Happiness:[2] | Low | 63.5 | 43.0 | 24.2 | 42.5 |
| | Medium | 28.8 | 39.5 | 48.4 | 39.5 |
| | High | 7.7 | 17.5 | 27.4 | 18.0 |
| | Totals | 100 | 100 | 100 | 100 |
| | N | 52 | 114 | 62 | 228 |
| Sadness:[3] | Low | 60.4 | 38.8 | 27.9 | 40.9 |
| | Medium | 24.5 | 35.3 | 44.3 | 35.2 |
| | High | 15.1 | 25.9 | 27.9 | 23.9 |
| | Totals | 100 | 100 | 100 | 100 |
| | N | 53 | 116 | 61 | 230 |

[1]$x^2 = 8.575$, n.s.; gamma $= 0.23$
[2]$x^2 = 19.141$, df $= 4$, $p < .001$; gamma $= 0.41$
[3]$x^2 = 13.024$, df $= 4$, $p < .05$; gamma $= 0.29$

have an effect among the inexpressive group, males, while females remain expressive regardless of interpersonal orientation.

Hypothesis Six states: Persons whose parents were expressive to them will be more expressive than those whose parents were not as expressive. This hypothesis is accepted for all emotions (see table 6–8). A subject's expressiveness of love, happiness, sadness, and anger were all found to be related to his or her parents' expressiveness of those same feelings. Moreover, this relationship is quite strong except in the case of anger (note gammas, table 6–8).

Using a role model approach, it could further be expected that a subject's same-sex parent will be a better predictor of expressiveness than the opposite-sex parent. The data gathered here are inconsistent and inconclusive. The same-sex parent's expressiveness is not consistently more strongly related to the subject's expressiveness than the opposite-sex parent's expressiveness (see table 6–9 for males and table 6–10 for females). Moreover, a test of signifi-

Table 6–7
Expressiveness by Interpersonal Orientation among Females

| Females' Expressiveness | | Low | Medium | High | Total |
|---|---|---|---|---|---|
| Love:[1] | Low | 31.3 | 19.0 | 15.1 | 20.1 |
| | Medium | 43.8 | 38.1 | 50.0 | 43.5 |
| | High | 25.0 | 42.9 | 34.9 | 36.4 |
| | Totals | 100 | 100 | 100 | 100 |
| | N | 48 | 105 | 86 | 239 |
| Happiness:[2] | Low | 38.3 | 19.8 | 14.9 | 21.7 |
| | Medium | 31.9 | 38.7 | 41.4 | 38.3 |
| | High | 29.8 | 41.5 | 43.7 | 40.0 |
| | Totals | 100 | 100 | 100 | 100 |
| | N | 47 | 106 | 87 | 240 |
| Sadness:[3] | Low | 21.3 | 14.0 | 14.9 | 15.8 |
| | Medium | 25.5 | 29.0 | 29.9 | 28.6 |
| | High | 53.2 | 57.0 | 55.2 | 55.6 |
| | Totals | 100 | 100 | 100 | 100 |
| | N | 47 | 107 | 87 | 241 |

[1] $x^2 = 8.604$, n.s.; gamma = 0.13
[2] $x^2 = 10.283$, df = 4, $p < .05$; gamma = 0.21
[3] $x^2 = 1.45$, n.s.; gamma = 0.03

cance between the gammas measuring the relationships between the mother's and subject's expressiveness and the father's and subject's expressiveness reveals no significant differences between the two. Some of these findings were in the predicted direction—namely, the expression of love among males and the expression of love and sadness among females—while the rest were not. These results indicate that while parental expressiveness is important as a general determinant of expressiveness, neither parent in particular is more important in predicting expressiveness.

Given the finding of general male inexpressiveness (see table 6–1), it was thought that the relationship between a father's expressiveness of love and his son's expressiveness in general should be further investigated. Table 6–11 reveals that only when the father expresses love very often are the significant differences between the sexes reduced substantially. Accordingly, then, only when a father is *very* expressive is the amount of male expressiveness brought up to the level of that of females. This does not occur when mother's expres-

**Table 6–8**
**Expressiveness by Parental Expressiveness**

| Subjects' Expressiveness | | Low | Medium | High | Total |
|---|---|---|---|---|---|
| Love:[1] | Low | 43.6 | 24.1 | 16.7 | 30.3 |
| | Medium | 38.4 | 47.5 | 35.6 | 40.5 |
| | High | 18.0 | 28.5 | 47.7 | 29.1 |
| | Totals | 100 | 100 | 100 | 100 |
| | N | 211 | 158 | 132 | 501 |
| Happiness:[2] | Low | 49.7 | 31.2 | 14.6 | 32.7 |
| | Medium | 33.3 | 45.7 | 32.6 | 37.7 |
| | High | 17.0 | 23.1 | 52.8 | 29.5 |
| | Totals | 100 | 100 | 100 | 100 |
| | N | 171 | 186 | 144 | 501 |
| Sadness:[3] | Low | 44.2 | 29.5 | 19.9 | 27.8 |
| | Medium | 32.6 | 35.8 | 29.7 | 32.3 |
| | High | 23.2 | 34.7 | 50.4 | 39.9 |
| | Totals | 100 | 100 | 100 | 100 |
| | N | 95 | 173 | 236 | 504 |
| Anger:[4] | Low | 44.6 | 32.0 | 31.6 | 35.9 |
| | Medium | 33.8 | 42.5 | 27.4 | 36.9 |
| | High | 21.7 | 25.5 | 41.1 | 27.3 |
| | Totals | 100 | 100 | 100 | 100 |
| | N | 157 | 247 | 95 | 499 |

[1] $x^2 = 49.974$, df $= 4$, p $< .001$; gamma $= 0.40$
[2] $x^2 = 72.757$, df $= 4$, p $< .001$; gamma $= 0.46$
[3] $x^2 = 30.260$, df $= 4$, p $< .001$; gamma $= 0.33$
[4] $x^2 = 18.440$, df $= 4$, p $< .01$; gamma $= 0.20$

siveness of love is controlled. Similar findings occur with the expression of happiness and sadness; only when the father is perceived to have expressed happiness often or very often and sadness very often are the differences between the sexes for these same emotions not significant.

Expressiveness, therefore, has been demonstrated to be affected independently by one's sex, interpersonal orientation, and perceived parental expressiveness. It was thought that the two intervening variables, IPO and parental expressiveness, would account for most of the sex differences. Hypothesis Seven states: Controlling for interpersonal orientation and expressiveness of

## Table 6–9
## Expressiveness by Mother's and Father's Expressiveness among Males

| | Parental Expressiveness | | | | | | | |
|---|---|---|---|---|---|---|---|---|
| | Mother | | | | Father | | | |
| | N & S | Often | Very Often | Total | N & S | Often | Very Often | Total |
| **Male's Expressiveness** | | | | | | | | |
| **Love:[1]** | | | | | | | | |
| Low | 49.0 | 47.2 | 26.8 | 40.9 | 48.9 | 33.3 | 20.0 | 40.7 |
| Medium | 34.7 | 38.2 | 45.1 | 39.8 | 38.2 | 43.1 | 26.7 | 39.5 |
| High | 16.3 | 14.6 | 28.0 | 19.3 | 13.0 | 23.5 | 53.3 | 19.8 |
| Totals | 100.0 | 100.0 | 100.0 | 100.0 | 100.0 | 100.0 | 100.0 | 100.0 |
| N | 49 | 123 | 82 | 254 | 131 | 102 | 15 | 248 |
| **Happiness:[2]** | | | | | | | | |
| Low | 77.3 | 43.9 | 21.2 | 43.8 | 63.0 | 30.0 | 26.9 | 43.1 |
| Medium | 22.7 | 38.8 | 43.9 | 37.3 | 26.0 | 49.2 | 30.8 | 37.8 |
| High | 00.0 | 17.3 | 34.8 | 18.9 | 11.0 | 20.8 | 42.3 | 19.1 |
| Totals | 100.0 | 100.0 | 100.0 | 100.0 | 100.0 | 100.0 | 100.0 | 100.0 |
| N | 44 | 139 | 66 | 249 | 100 | 120 | 26 | 246 |
| **Sadness:[3]** | | | | | | | | |
| Low | 46.9 | 31.5 | 31.3 | 39.4 | 40.8 | 32.5 | 42.9 | 39.5 |
| Medium | 36.9 | 34.3 | 37.5 | 35.8 | 39.3 | 25.0 | 14.3 | 36.3 |
| High | 16.2 | 34.3 | 31.3 | 24.8 | 19.9 | 42.5 | 42.9 | 24.2 |
| Totals | 100.0 | 100.0 | 100.0 | 100.0 | 100.0 | 100.0 | 100.0 | 100.0 |
| N | 130 | 108 | 16 | 254 | 201 | 40 | 7 | 248 |
| **Anger:[4]** | | | | | | | | |
| Low | 38.2 | 36.6 | 28.2 | 36.0 | 40.5 | 35.4 | 25.0 | 36.4 |
| Medium | 39.1 | 24.7 | 17.9 | 34.0 | 34.5 | 35.4 | 25.0 | 33.6 |
| High | 22.7 | 28.7 | 53.8 | 30.0 | 25.0 | 29.3 | 50.0 | 20.0 |
| Totals | 100.0 | 100.0 | 100.0 | 100.0 | 100.0 | 100.0 | 100.0 | 100.0 |
| N | 110 | 101 | 39 | 250 | 116 | 99 | 32 | 247 |

[1]Mothers: $X^2 = 11.771$, df = 4, $p < .05$; gamma = 0.27
Fathers: $X^2 = 18.443$, df = 4, $p < .01$; gamma = 0.35
[2]Mothers: $X^2 = 39.741$, df = 4, $p < .001$; gamma = 0.57
Fathers: $X^2 = 34.624$, df = 4, $p < .001$; gamma = 0.48
[3]Mothers: $X^2 = 12.071$, df = 4, $p < .05$; gamma = 0.30
Fathers: $X^2 = 11.522$, df = 4, $p < .05$; gamma = 0.27
[4]Mothers: $X^2 = 14.009$, df = 4, $p < .01$; gamma = 0.20
Fathers: $X^2 = 7.789$, df = 4, $p < .05$; gamma = 0.19

## Table 6–10
## Expressiveness by Mother's and Father's Expressiveness among Females

| | Parental Expressiveness | | | | | | | |
|---|---|---|---|---|---|---|---|---|
| | Mother | | | | Father | | | |
| | N & S | Often | Very Often | Total | N & S | Often | Very Often | Total |
| Female's Expressiveness | | | | | | | | |
| Love:[1] | | | | | | | | |
| Low | 34.9 | 17.9 | 11.6 | 19.8 | 25.5 | 15.0 | 17.0 | 19.7 |
| Medium | 38.1 | 56.8 | 28.4 | 41.5 | 42.2 | 29.0 | 25.5 | 41.8 |
| High | 27.0 | 25.3 | 60.0 | 38.7 | 32.4 | 26.0 | 57.4 | 38.6 |
| Totals | 100.0 | 100.0 | 100.0 | 100.0 | 100.0 | 100.0 | 100.0 | 100.0 |
| N | 63 | 95 | 95 | 253 | 102 | 100 | 47 | 249 |
| Happiness:[2] | | | | | | | | |
| Low | 29.3 | 24.0 | 15.1 | 21.6 | 27.8 | 22.3 | 13.3 | 21.9 |
| Medium | 26.6 | 47.1 | 29.0 | 28.8 | 44.3 | 45.5 | 16.7 | 38.2 |
| High | 34.1 | 28.9 | 55.9 | 39.6 | 27.8 | 32.1 | 70.0 | 39.8 |
| Totals | 100.0 | 100.0 | 100.0 | 100.0 | 100.0 | 100.0 | 100.0 | 100.0 |
| N | 41 | 121 | 93 | 255 | 79 | 112 | 60 | 251 |
| Sadness:[3] | | | | | | | | |
| Low | 21.6 | 11.5 | 14.3 | 16.5 | 16.6 | 8.9 | 35.7 | 16.3 |
| Medium | 32.8 | 27.9 | 14.3 | 28.2 | 30.1 | 24.4 | 14.3 | 28.2 |
| High | 45.7 | 60.6 | 71.4 | 55.3 | 53.4 | 66.7 | 50.0 | 55.6 |
| Totals | 100.0 | 100.0 | 100.0 | 100.0 | 100.0 | 100.0 | 100.0 | 100.0 |
| N | 116 | 104 | 35 | 255 | 193 | 45 | 14 | 252 |
| Anger:[4] | | | | | | | | |
| Low | 45.7 | 30.1 | 32.9 | 35.8 | 44.3 | 25.3 | 24.9 | 35.7 |
| Medium | 32.1 | 46.6 | 35.7 | 39.0 | 36.5 | 46.2 | 32.6 | 39.4 |
| High | 22.2 | 23.3 | 31.4 | 25.2 | 19.1 | 28.6 | 32.6 | 24.9 |
| Totals | 100.0 | 100.0 | 100.0 | 100.0 | 100.0 | 100.0 | 100.0 | 100.0 |
| N | 81 | 103 | 70 | 254 | 115 | 91 | 43 | 249 |

[1]Mothers: $X^2 = 37.978$, df=4, p<.001; gamma=0.43
Fathers: $X^2 = 12.792$, df=4, p<.05; gamma=0.23
[2]Mothers: $X^2 = 17.806$, df=4, p<.01; gamma=0.30
Fathers: $X^2 = 31.129$, df=4, p<.001; gamma=0.37
[3]Mothers: $X^2 = 10.821$, df=4, p<.05; gamma=0.29
Fathers: $X^2 = 7.437$, n.s.; gamma=0.12
[4]Mothers: $X^2 = 7.532$, n.s.; gamma=0.15
Fathers: $X^2 = 10.032$, df=4, p<.05; gamma=0.22

Table 6–11
Expressiveness of Love by Sex, Controlling for Father's Expressiveness

| | | Father's Expressiveness of Love | | | | | |
|---|---|---|---|---|---|---|---|
| | | Never & Seldom | | Often | | Very Often | |
| | | Male | Female | Male | Female | Male | Female |
| Expression | Low | 48.9 | 25.5 | 33.3 | 15.0 | 20.0 | 17.0 |
| of | Medium | 38.2 | 42.2 | 43.1 | 49.0 | 26.7 | 25.5 |
| Love | High | 13.0 | 32.4 | 23.5 | 36.0 | 53.3 | 57.4 |
| | Totals | 100.0 | 100.0 | 100.0 | 100.0 | 100.0 | 100.0 |
| | N | 131 | 102 | 102 | 100 | 15 | 47 |

$X^2 = 18.366$, $p < .001$; gamma $= 0.45$        $X^2 = 10.017$, $p < .01$; gamma $= 0.34$        $X^2 = 0.097$, n.s.

parents toward self, there will be no significant difference between females' and males' expressiveness of love, happiness, and sadness. This, however, was not the case. As can be seen in table 6–12, the relationship between sex and expressiveness is still quite strong when interpersonal orientation and parental expressiveness are controlled; partial gammas are .45, .38, and .57 for love, happiness and sadness respectively. These do not represent a substantial reduction in the strength of the original sex-expressiveness relationship (see table 6–1). As neither interpersonal orientation nor parental expressiveness substantially reduces the relationship between sex and expressiveness, they must be ruled out as intervening variables (see Rosenberg 1968).

Since interpersonal orientation and parental expressiveness do not act as intervening variables between sex and expressiveness, and since all three variables are related to expressiveness, the interpersonal orientation-expressiveness relationship and the parental expressiveness-expressiveness relationship were examined when the two other factors were controlled. Table 6–13 reveals that the relatively small interpersonal orientation-expressiveness relationship does not hold when the other two factors are controlled. On the other hand, the parental expressiveness-expressiveness relationship is still quite strong when both interpersonal orientation and sex are taken into account.

From this analysis, then, it seems that sex and parental expressiveness are two important factors in explaining expressiveness, while the orientation-expressiveness relationship is apparently spurious. Both the relationship between sex and expressiveness and the relationship between parental expressiveness and expressiveness still hold when the other factor is controlled: par-

**Table 6–12**
**Expressiveness by Sex, Controlling for Interpersonal Orientation and Parental Expressiveness**

| | | Interpersonal Orientation | | | | | | | |
| | | Low | | | | High | | | |
| | | Parental Expressiveness | | | | | | | |
| | | Low | | High | | Low | | High | |
| | | M | F | M | F | M | F | M | F |
|---|---|---|---|---|---|---|---|---|---|
| Love[1] | Low | 63.2 | 33.3 | 32.6 | 15.2 | 38.5 | 30.8 | 27.8 | 6.9 |
| | Med | 26.5 | 42.0 | 43.5 | 36.7 | 38.5 | 53.8 | 50.0 | 48.3 |
| | High | 10.3 | 24.6 | 23.9 | 48.1 | 23.1 | 15.4 | 22.2 | 44.8 |
| | N | 68 | 69 | 92 | 79 | 26 | 26 | 36 | 58 |
| Happiness[2] | Low | 69.4 | 26.0 | 35.1 | 26.0 | 45.0 | 26.3 | 14.3 | 12.1 |
| | Medium | 24.2 | 42.0 | 44.3 | 33.0 | 35.0 | 52.6 | 54.8 | 36.4 |
| | High | 6.5 | 32.0 | 20.6 | 41.0 | 20.0 | 21.1 | 31.0 | 51.5 |
| | N | 62 | 50 | 97 | 100 | 20 | 19 | 42 | 66 |
| Sadness[3] | Low | 51.1 | 18.9 | 36.8 | 13.2 | 44.8 | 19.1 | 12.9 | 7.9 |
| | Medium | 31.9 | 31.1 | 35.3 | 25.0 | 41.4 | 34.0 | 45.2 | 26.3 |
| | High | 17.0 | 50.0 | 27.9 | 61.8 | 13.8 | 46.8 | 41.9 | 65.8 |
| | N | 94 | 74 | 68 | 76 | 29 | 47 | 31 | 38 |

[1] X² = 36.559 with 8 d.f., p < .002; gamma = 0.45
[2] X² = 39.052 with 8 d.f., p < .002; gamma = 0.38
[3] X² = 58.367 with 8 d.f., p < .002; gamma = 0.57

Table 6–13

**Second-Order Partial Gammas between the Expressiveness Dimensions and, Respectively, (a) Sex, (b) Parental Expressiveness, and (c) Interpersonal Orientation, with the Other Two Controlled.**

|  | *Sex* | *Parental Expressiveness* | *Interpersonal Orientation* |
|---|---|---|---|
| Love | .45 (.43) | .46 (.40) | .08 (.21) |
| Happiness | .38 (.44) | .38 (.46) | .28 (.32) |
| Sadness | .57 (.51) | .28 (.33) | .10 (.19) |

*Note:* The corresponding zero-order gammas are given in parentheses.

tial gammas for the sex-expressiveness relationship, controlling for parental expressiveness, are .41, .28, and .49 for love, happiness, and sadness respectively; controlling for sex are .41, .45, and .32 for love, happiness and sadness respectively.

## Discussion

### Gender

In this study, females have been found to be more expressive of love, happiness, and sadness than males. This finding is consistent with what one would expect on the basis of the sex role stereotype literature. The inability or unwillingness of males to express love, affection, warmth, or tenderness may pose a problem, because these are characteristics prescribed by the male sex roles and yet are psychologically dysfunctional. This observation expresses the *socialized dysfunctional characteristic theory* of sex role strain (Pleck 1981, 147). The dilemma for these inexpressive males is that "even if they successfully live up to the male role, they suffer adverse consequences" (Pleck 1981, 147).

As discussed in Chafetz (1974), people enter into relationships with expectations of each others' behavior. Chafetz further states that while females need affection, the masculine stereotype discourages the open display of affection ( 1974, 171). Balswick (1970a) has found that wives are disappointed at their husbands' inability to show companionship support. The present study has found that not only is inexpressiveness a part of the masculine stereotype, but also that males report that they express these feelings less often than females. Therefore, Chafetz may be correct in her analysis of incompatible expectations in romantic relationships, a further adverse consequence of male inexpressiveness.

Moreover, in today's world of changing sex-role definitions, males are expected to play a more expressive role, especially within the family, while females pursue self-fulfillment outside the home. These expectations further contribute to male sex role strain. The fact that males have not been allowed to be emotional has been pointed out by Lewis (1972), Balswick and Peek (1970), and Bardwick (1973). But of equal significance is Spence, Deaux, and Helmreich's recent conclusion that expressive differences between the sexes have remained resistant to change, even as "sex role attitudes have become conspicuously more liberal" (1985, 156). When discussing inequalities by sex, Bardwick (1973, 16) notes, "These are devastating sex-related inequities—women kept from achieving and men from feeling." It has been a part of the feminine stereotype that females are both more dependent upon, and involved in, interpersonal relationships (Bardwick and Douvan 1971; Chafetz 1974; Spence, Deaux, and Helmreich 1985). In fact, the occupations in which females are traditionally found in are those which require competence in interpersonal relationships, such as teaching, social work, and nursing. It seems obvious, therefore, that those who are most involved with significant others will have more of the skills useful in maintaining such relationships, and our results show it is the female more than the male who has these qualities. Moreover, in keeping with an inherently sociological interest in social interaction, it is interesting to note that the finding of females to be better equipped than males in affective interaction may demonstrate that inexpressiveness among males is a psychological dysfunction that adversely affects their attempts to build personal relationships.

*Perceived Parental Expressiveness*

While differential parental expressiveness does not explain the gender-expressiveness relationship, it does have an independent effect upon expressiveness in general. In a general learning context, it seems obvious that those who are around expressive people will learn to be expressive. Maccoby and Jacklin (1974) conclude that a modeling theory approach is inadequate to account for sex differences in personality traits. However, a more general application of modeling theory would expect parents (both mother and father) to be important models of expressiveness for their children (both sons and daughters). Parents are the key socializers of their children; it can be expected that their personalities will be reflected in their children (Lamb, Pleck, and Levine 1986). Our evidence suggests that expressive children come from expressive parents, or at the very least, from parents who are perceived as expressive.

*Interpersonal Orientation*

It was thought that people to whom relationships with significant others are important would report that they express love, happiness, and sadness more often—this was the case. However, the relationship is not as strong as that between gender and expressiveness, and when the other factors, gender and parental expressiveness, are controlled, the relationship between interpersonal orientation and expressiveness disappears. Perhaps another measure that reveals interaction patterns rather than interpersonal values would be a better predictor of expressiveness.

Parenthetically, it should be mentioned that in the wider study, of which the data reported in this paper are a part, males and females were found *not* to differ in interpersonal orientation. Although much of the literature on sex roles and sex role stereotypes would lead one to expect significant differences, with females being more interpersonally oriented than males (Bardwick 1971; Hoffman 1972; Gilligan 1982; Sherman 1971; Chafetz 1974), Maccoby and Jacklin (1974, 191–226) conclude that there are few sex differences in various components of interpersonal behavior and perception. Our research supports Maccoby and Jacklin's conclusion.

## Summary and Conclusions

In summary, then, we have found that females are more expressive of love, happiness, and sadness than males. There is no sex difference in the expressiveness of anger. While it had been thought that the two hypothesized intervening variables, interpersonal orientation and parental expressiveness, would explain a large part of the gender-expressiveness relationship, this was not found to be the case. Parental expressiveness, however, was found to have a strong, independent effect upon expressiveness. Controlling for gender and parental expressiveness revealed that the relationship between interpersonal orientation and expressiveness is spurious.

The fact that most of the time females are more expressive than males, regardless of the other two variables, leads us to speculate that other factors might possibly contribute to this difference in expressiveness. General sociological literature suggests that if there is a difference in behavior patterns it is because of differential societal expectations. Expectations for femininity may include emotional and expressive aspects that overcome differences in interpersonal orientation or parental expressiveness. While the presence of a highly expressive father may account for a boy's increased expressiveness (a finding which will be discussed in the following chapter), the lack of such a father—coupled with a general social expectation for male inexpressiveness—will probably hinder his expressiveness. From a social structural perspective, the beginning point in the explanation of male inexpressiveness is the father's low participation in the care of children. While nonactive fathering distorts the ego boundaries of both females and males, it can have an emotionally devastating effect upon males. Boys who develop warm close relationships with their mothers, but who are a part of a cooler distant relationship with their fathers, will grow up overconforming to the inexpressive dimension of the male sex role. Due to the changing definitions and expectations concerning the male sex role, such inexpressive behavior has increasingly resulted in sex role strain for the male. In the following chapter we will take a closer look at the effect of parental expressiveness on children's expressiveness.

# 7

# Parents' Effects on Children

In chapter 6, gender differences in expressiveness were established, using interpersonal orientation and perceived parental expressiveness as control variables. Interpersonal orientation as an explanation of expressiveness washed out when gender and perceived parental expressiveness were introduced as controls. Perceived parental expressiveness, however, proved to be independently related to expressiveness when gender and interpersonal orientation were applied as control variables. It seems fruitful now to examine in detail the potential effect of parental expressiveness on children's expressiveness.

As noted in chapter 3, sex role strain theory views sex roles as operationally defined by sex-role stereotypes and norms. To boys and girls who keenly search for clues to what it means to be male or female, parental sex role behavior can be powerful determinants of children's interpretations of their own sex roles. This is to say that to children, parents come to be bodily representations of societal sex-role stereotypes and norms.

If SRS theory is correct, parental representations of sex roles will often be contradictory and inconsistent. Many children are likely to perceive in their parents a mixture of the traditional and the modern definition of sex roles. Some parents will represent a fairly traditional image of sex roles, in which the father will model considerably less expression of feelings than the mother. Other parents will represent a fairly modern image in which the father and mother are nearly equal in the type and amount of affect they express. Our analysis will investigate the complexity of the possible effect of perceived expressiveness of fathers and mothers separately on sons and daughters.

Unlike the research reported in the previous chapter, the data to be reported here is based on a large sample (N = 1,245) of high school students.

---

Some of the findings reported in this chapter appeared in K. Slevin, 1975. *Some Effects of Perceived Parental Expressiveness On Child Expressiveness,* unpublished doctoral dissertation, University of Georgia.

Children of high school age should be in a good position to assess their parents' expressiveness. Both perceived verbal and physical parental expressions of feelings have been obtained in this study. The study uses parametric statistics, which, combined with the larger sample size, allows for a more sophisticated manipulation of the data. Important variables used as controls include race and social class.

## Literature Review and Theoretical Orientation

Numerous studies of the family and sex roles have been concerned, directly or indirectly, with the Parsons-Bales distinction between instrumental (task oriented) and expressive roles. Given the structures of the family and occupational system in this society, Parsons and Bales (1955) argue that instrumental responsibility is forced upon the adult male (father) and expressive responsibility upon the adult female (mother). The validity and acceptability (theoretical and empirical) of this distinction has been the subject of considerable debate among sociologists and feminist writers. A core concern in the debate, more often implicit than explicit, centers upon the fact that in this society instrumentality is given greater formal prestige.

The above distinction, often wrongly interpreted as a dichotomy, is best understood and most useful as a tool when seen as a continuum. As Johnson, et al. (1975) point out, "Clearly both sexes perform both types of activities and any given role has both instrumental and expressive components." A point worth noting here is that there are sex differences in parent-child interaction.

The literature on sex-role socialization generally points out that females are encouraged to cultivate expressiveness while males are encouraged to adopt a more instrumental approach to life (Belsky, Lerner, and Spanier 1984). Based upon the analysis of responses of over one thousand parents, Block (1982) found that parents reported they encouraged sons more than daughters to be competitive and achievement-striving, independent, and in control of their feelings, while girls were encouraged to be physically and emotionally expressive. Other studies have found that boys more often than girls were socialized to be more dominant (Baumrind 1979), and that girls more often than boys were encouraged to talk about their concerns and feelings and to engage in interpersonal activities (Block 1973; Block, Block, and Harrigton 1974).

There has been a recent accumulation of research on how mothers and fathers differ in relationship to their children. There is evidence that differences between mother-child and father-child interaction begin very early and continue throughout childrearing. By observing parents with their children at one month, three months, and nine months, Belsky, Gilstrap, and Rovine

(1984) concluded that mothers were more engaging, response stimulating, and positively affectionate, while fathers engaged in more reading and watching television with their infants. In a study of Swedish parents, Lamb, Frodi, Hwang, Frodi, and Steinberg (1982) found that mothers were more likely to hold, tend to, display affection toward, smile at, and vocalize with their infants than were fathers. They also found that the more involved fathers engaged in *more* play than the less involved fathers. The reverse was true for mothers, as the most involved mothers played least with their infants. Parental differences in engagement in play with children was also found in a study of Mexican families, where fathers were more playful with children than were mothers (Bronstein 1984).

Parents, but especially fathers, have been found to practice sex typing in relating to their sons and daughters. Sex typing has been found to exist in the preschool years, but Snow, Jacklin, and Maccoby (1983) present evidence indicating that it may begin much earlier. They report that the boundaries of sex-appropriate play that are set by fathers are narrower for twelve-month-old boys than girls.

Recent research suggests that parental sex typing is affected by the interpersonal structure of family interaction. In a study of parent-adolescent interaction, Gjerde (1986) found that the presence of the spouse influenced the extent to which girls and boys were treated differently. For instance, a mother differentiates more between girls and boys in the *presence* of her husband, while a father differentiates more between girls and boys in the *absence* of his wife. Gjerde also found that a father was more responsive and more egalitarian-oriented when he was alone with his son than when his wife was present. In their study of toddler development in the family, Easterbrooks and Goldberg (1984) documented the importance of the father's active involvement with his children. They found that high father involvement related to optimal toddler development.

Two studies relevant to the research are reported in this chapter because they conceptualize parent-child relationships in terms of role theory. In their study of the perceptions of parental role responsibilities, Gilbert, Hanson, and Davis (1982) found that although fathers and mothers more often than not agreed on the relative importance of various parenting responsibilities, they did differ on one significant point: while mothers tended to perceive their role toward their male and female children the same, fathers endorsed differential patterns for male and female children. Mothers and fathers may begin by relating to their children in a certain way, but in the process their children come to expect them to play a given role toward them. Thus, in Dino, Barnett, and Howard's (1984) study of eight- to twelve-year-olds' perceptions of their parents' responses to an interpersonal problem, children indicated that they expected parents to respond in expressive ways to daughters and in instrumental ways to sons.

Role theory, as a theoretical offspring of symbolic interaction, is useful in supplementing SRS theory in our analysis of the effect of childrens' perceptions of parental expressiveness on their own expressiveness. Symbolic interactionism considers social interaction to be of vital importance in its own right: it sees this interaction as a *process that forms* human conduct rather than a means of or setting for the expression on release of human conduct (Stryker 1985). Interpretation then, is a key variable. As Blumer (1969) points out, it should not be regarded as a mere automatic application of established meanings but rather as a formative process in which meanings are used and revised as instruments for the guidance of action.

Symbolic interactionism stresses the necessity of referring to interpersonal relationship when using the term "role." This means an emphasis reciprocity between roles: "The idea of role-taking shifts emphases away from the simple process of enacting a prescribed role to devising a performance on the basis of an "inputed other role" (Lindesmith, Strauss, and Denzin 1974, 395). Thus, each actor adjusts his or her behavior and interactions to what he or she thinks the other is going to do. This idea of reciprocity is crucial in understanding masculine and feminine behavior because one is defined and considered in relation to all the others. The symbolic interaction approach to role is, therefore, to view it "not as a neat package of behavior wrapped up in a set of roles, but rather a relationship between what we do and what others do" (Lindesmith, Strauss, and Denzin 1974, 395).

In considering role from this perspective, we see the importance of communication in social interaction. Communication can be physical (gestures) or verbal, a distinction we have also made in this study. In differentiating between physical and verbal expressiveness, we recognize the importance of gestures to the development of expressiveness, and also see that a gesture may serve as a stimulus to the actor. Expressive behavior can exist at the overt physical level when, for example, two people embrace, and/or it can be at the verbal level, such as talking about a particular feeling.

Proposition Seven of the SRS theory of male inexpressiveness, as presented in chapter 3, is especially relevant to the research reported in this chapter. Proposition Seven states that "violating norms of inexpressivity has more severe consequences for males than females." Udry (1974, 52) has suggested that there is more pressure on boys than on girls to learn behavior appropriate to their sex during the earliest period. Girls have the advantage of learning appropriate sex-role behavior in a face-to-face, intimate relationship with their mothers, but boys are not as fortunate because they are characteristically separated from their fathers, and thus must learn appropriate masculine behavior from their mothers or from societal sex role stereotypes (Chodorow 1978). Turner states, "The boy typically lacks an adequate role model whose successful approach to the requirements of masculinity he can observe and emulate easily" (1979, 296). In following a culturally defined masculine role, males more than females fear social condemnation for violating norms of inexpressivity.

Proposition Six of the SRS theory of male inexpressiveness states that "actual or imagined violation of (not living up to) the traditional sex role leads males to overconform to this role, as exemplified by extreme inexpressiveness. . . . " This overcompensation is a result of the boy's development of self being contingent upon negative sanctions much more so than is the girl's. When males have trouble demonstrating role adequacy according to traditional sex-role definitions, they resort to merely defining the male role in terms of what is not specifically defined as a "female role." For example, if the female role is seen as expressive, then the male who is having problems defining his role adequacy in positive ways may resort to defining it negatively, by being inexpressive.

Based on our review of the literature and theoretical reasoning, the following hypotheses and corrollaries are proposed for testing:

1. *Fathers will be perceived to be less expressive than mothers.*

2. *The less physical expression perceived to exist from the parents to the child, the more inexpressive the child will be.*

    Corollary A: The less physical expression perceived to exist from the father to the son, the more inexpressive the son will be.

    Corollary B: The less physical expression perceived to exist from the father to the daughter, the more inexpressive the daughter will be.

    Corollary C: The less physical expression perceived to exist from the mother to the son, the more inexpressive the son will be.

    Corollary D: The less physical expression perceived to exist from the mother to the daughter, the more inexpressive the daughter will be.

3. *The less affective verbal communication perceived to exist from the parents to the child, the more expressive the child will be.*

    Corollary A: The less effective verbal communication perceived to exist from the father to the son, the more inexpressive the son will be.

    Corollary B: The less affective verbal communication perceived to exist from the father to the daughter, the more inexpressive the daughter will be.

    Corollary C: The less affective verbal communication perceived to exist from the mother to the son, the more inexpressive the son will be.

    Corollary D: The less affective verbal communication perceived to exist from the mother to the daughter, the more inexpressive the daughter will be.

4. *The amount of expressiveness (physical and verbal) perceived to exist from the same-sex parent to the child will be a greater predictor of the child's expressiveness.*

Corollary A: 1. The amount of physical expression perceived to exist from the father to the son will be a greater predictor of the son's expressiveness than the amount of physical expression perceived to exist from the mother to the son.

          2. The amount of physical expression perceived to exist from the mother to the daughter will be a greater predictor of the daughter's expressiveness than the amount of physical expression perceived to exist from the father to the daughter.

Corollary B: 1. The amount of affective verbal communication perceived to exist from the father to the son will be a greater predictor of the son's expressiveness than the amount of affective verbal communication perceived to exist from the mother to the son.

          2. The amount of affective verbal communication perceived to exist from the mother to the daughter will be a greater predictor of the daughter's expressiveness than the amount of affective verbal communication perceived to exist from the father to the daughter.

## Methodology

### Sample

The data in this study are based on responses to questionnaires generated by a nonprobability sample of 1,245 students from social science classes in eleven Georgia high schools. Although the sample is not random, consideration was given to selecting high schools that would be representative of all Georgia high schools, with an attempt to obtain respondents from both rural and urban schools. The sex percentage breakdown for this sample was 47 percent (578) males and 53 percent (656), females which adequately corresponds to the male-female ratio for adolescents in the general population. Demographic characteristics of the sample include: a mean age of 16.76 and a racial breakdown of 80.47 percent (933) white, 18.6 percent (230) black, and .89 percent (eleven) others.

### Instituting Concepts

*Perceived expressiveness of parents* was determined from responses to the question, "When your parents felt certain emotions, how often did they either tell you or physically express them to you?" Four types of emotions were categorized in a chart in which the respondents were asked to state whether father or mother verbally or physically expressed these emotions to them (see chapter 5).

*Expressiveness* was operationally based on the *Expression of Emotion Scale* (see chapter 5). *Social Class* was based on Hollingshead's two-factor index, but for our purposes we simply divided these as white collar (executive positions, business and independent business positions, and clerk sales), and blue collar (skilled, semi-skilled, and unskilled laborers).

A one-tailed single sample t-test for mean difference was used to test Hypothesis One, given that the direction of the difference was predicted. For Hypotheses Two and Three, correlation coefficients were used and a one-tailed t-test was used to determine the significance of coefficients. Hypothesis Four was tested by a comparison of two correlations within the same sample using a t-test to determine significance. For comparisons of correlation coefficients across subgroups the standard normal (Z) statistic was used, and since direction of difference was not predicted for differences between subgroups, two tailed significance tests were used. For the treatment of the control variables race and social class, both of which we operationalized as dichotomies, the two-sample t-test was used. The 5 percent level of significance was used to define the critical region in all significance tests in this study.

## Analysis of Data

### Expressive Differences between Mothers and Fathers

Hypothesis One predicts fathers will be perceived to be less expressive than mothers. The data in table 7–1 support this hypothesis, showing that fathers

**Table 7–1**
**Perceived Differences between Mothers' and Fathers' Expressiveness**

| | Difference of Means (Mother-Father) | | |
|---|---|---|---|
| | *Physical* | *Verbal* | *Total* |
| Total sample | 0.782*** | 1.423*** | 2.210*** |
| Sons | 0.680*** | 1.312*** | 2.002*** |
| Daughters | 0.880*** | 1.509*** | 2.388*** |

***$p < 0.001$

Note: For this and the following seven tables, the numbers in the tables represent means of scores for perceived mothers' expressiveness minus the means of perceived fathers' expressiveness.

are perceived to be less expressive than mothers for all measures of parental expressiveness. This perception is true for sons and daughters as well as for the total sample. Table 7–2 exhibits data on the specifics of these differences by examining expression of the emotions anger, love, sorrow, and happiness. These data display three tendencies: first, it is these youths' perception of their mothers as more expressive of love, sorrow, and happiness that accounts for the general association shown in table 7–1. The difference between mothers' and fathers' perceived verbal expression of anger, while statistically significant, is not nearly as great; fathers are viewed as being even slightly more expressive of physical anger than mothers. The second tendency is for the general associations to be stronger for verbal than physical expressiveness. Finally, for both verbal and physical expressiveness, the differences between mother and father are greatest in the emotion these youths define as "love."

Controls for race do not alter support for this hypothesis but do change slightly the specifics of this support. While mothers are still perceived as being more expressive than fathers among both black and white youths, for black youths the expression of happiness distinguishes between parents the most, while white youths perceive mother and father as most differentiated in the expression of love. In fact, for all but the expression of physical anger, black youths perceive their mothers as more expressive than do white youths. Controlling by social class alone and by social class and race simultaneously doesn't alter the findings.

### Table 7–2
**Perceived Differences between Mothers' and Fathers' Expression of Anger, Love, Sorrow, and Happiness**

| Type of Parentally Expressed Emotion | Difference of Means (Mother-Father) |
| --- | --- |
| *Physical* | |
| Anger | −0.093** |
| Love | 0.350*** |
| Sorrow | 0.269*** |
| Happiness | 0.252*** |
| *Verbal* | |
| Anger | 0.098*** |
| Love | 0.455*** |
| Sorrow | 0.448*** |
| Happiness | 0.418*** |

** = p<0.01
*** = p<0.001

Our explanation for this finding rests on the fact that in this society the definition of the male role is one that places great emphasis upon masculine stereotypes, with a resulting de-emphasis on expressiveness. This may be further complicated by the fact that in playing the role of father, the male may often be expected by his wife to adopt a more instrumental approach than he might choose toward his children, particularly in discipline. Children are also subject to viewing masculine and feminine roles in a stereotypic fashion, and it is quite possible their perceptions of their fathers as less expressive than their mothers is somewhat biased by these stereotypes rather than based upon the actual behavior of the fathers.

A second finding of some import is that in terms of separate emotions, fathers (both white and black) were perceived as more physically expressive of anger than mothers. This finding is supported by what the literature suggests (Spence, Deaux, and Helmreich 1985). Stereotypically speaking, emotions can be separated into those characterized as typically feminine and typically masculine, anger being seen as typically masculine. The definition of the female role in society, especially in terms of physical expression, is one in which we do not expect women to express anger. As Turner points out, " . . . a woman is more likely to lose feminine self-respect by *action* than by inaction . . . " (1970,295). Men, on the other hand, are allowed (indeed, often expected) to physically express anger. In terms of the division of parental roles, this finding may suggest that it is still true that when it comes to physical punishment of the children, mothers still tell their children, "Wait until Daddy gets home."

In terms of racial differences in perceived parental expressiveness, we further found that the black mother-father difference was considerably greater than that for white mothers and fathers. One possible explanation for this finding may be that the relationship parents have with each other will be reflected in their relationships to their children. The literature generally suggests a lesser interaction between black married couples than between white (Blood and Wolfe 1969; Staples 1974). This finding was especially true of perceived verbal expressiveness, and several explanations may apply here. First, Polansky (1970) has argued that blacks are more verbally inaccessible than whites, a trait he attributes to a subcultural phenomenon. Secondly, black fathers, given their overall job insecurity and low occupational status (in this sample 82 percent fell into blue-collar status), may overemphasize the male role by being inexpressive. Also these fathers may be absent from the home a considerable amount of time (Liebow 1967; McAdoo 1981), and may therefore play a much more minor role in their children's lives than do black mothers. It should further be noted that the questionnaire used for these data was perhaps biased toward white middle-class respondents (operationalized in this study as white collar) who certainly made up most of the sample. It is, therefore, possible that we did not tap unique aspects of black expressiveness.

*Children's Expressiveness
and Parents' Physical Expressiveness*

Hypothesis Two predicts that the perceived physical expressiveness of the parents and the total expressiveness of the child will be positively correlated. Results reported in table 7–3 demonstrate that there is a positive correlation in each case (i.e., father-son, father-daughter, mother-son, mother-daughter), and that each correlation is statistically significant.

These data exhibit two tendencies: First, the mother's perceived physical expressiveness yields greater correlations for both sons and daughters than does the fathers'. Second, the son-parent relationship is somewhat stronger than the daughter-parent relationship. Table 7–4 presents the specifics of these differences by examining the expression of the emotions anger, love, sorrow, and happiness. These data indicate that for the physical expression of anger, both sons and daughters (particularly sons) view their mothers as having a greater influence than their fathers on their own expression of anger. It should be remembered that this is *not* to suggest that mothers are perceived to be more physically expressive of anger than fathers, but rather that their influence on the youths' own expression of that emotion is viewed as somewhat greater. For the emotion of sorrow, these youth see their mothers' expression of sorrow as a greater influence on their own expression of it than their fathers'. Finally, the father-son relationship for the emotion of love yields the greatest correlation.

When race is used as a control, the most striking change is a low correlation between perceived parental expressiveness and black sons' physical expressiveness. In terms of emotions, there is a negative relationship between black youths' expression of love and their fathers' perceived physical expression of love. Also, black fathers are much more influential on their daughters' expression of sorrow than are white fathers. Controls for social class do not alter support for this hypothesis, but the data display a tendency for the white-collar sons to view mothers as somewhat more influential on their expressiveness than fathers; the opposite tendency was displayed for blue-collar sons.

**Table 7–3
Correlation Coefficients between Perceived Parental
Physical Expressiveness and Subject Expressiveness**

|  | *Father* | *Mother* |
|---|---|---|
| Son | 0.171*** | 0.181*** |
| Daughter | 0.143*** | 0.152*** |

***p<0.001

Table 7–4
Correlation Coefficients between Perceived Parental Physical Expression of Emotions, and Subjects' Expression of Emotions

|  | Anger | Love | Sorrow | Happiness |
|---|---|---|---|---|
|  |  | Father |  |  |
| Son | 0.118** | 0.212*** | 0.070 | 0.155*** |
| Daughter | 0.098* | 0.161*** | 0.050 | 0.200*** |
|  | Anger | Love | Sorrow | Happiness |
|  |  | Mother |  |  |
| Son | 0.188*** | 0.161*** | 0.093* | 0.131** |
| Daughter | 0.116** | 0.163*** | 0.153*** | 0.170*** |

*Note:* For this table and any following tables which give breakdowns by types of emotions, the measurement of the child's expressiveness is congruent with the parents' perceived expression of that emotion (i.e., anger-anger, etc.).
*p < 0.05
**p < 0.01
***p < 0.001

As key socializers, parents would be expected to be influential on their childrens' expressiveness. Especially in the case of males, it would seem that if parents are expressive in the home it will influence quite considerably the male child's ability to learn expressive behavior, thus possibly counteracting the influences on expressiveness from sources outside the family. It seems that for the majority of these male youths, parents' perceived physical expressiveness is somewhat more important to their own expressiveness than is the case for these female youths. Perhaps this is because the female in this society is allowed to be physically expressive and her own expressiveness in this dimension may be less precariously related to that of parents than is the case for males. Females more often than males receive physical expressiveness from sources other than parents; therefore, parents are one of the very few sources of physical expressiveness for male children.

It is interesting that the mothers' physical expression of anger appears to be somewhat more predictive of these youths' expression of anger than is the fathers'. Mothers, then, seem to be more positive role models for these youths' expression of anger. This finding makes sense if we remember that in the mother-child relationship, the child in any given day is likely to see the mother express many emotions. Being more in touch with her children and, therefore, more constantly expressive of the gamut of emotions, the mother will exhibit a tendency to express anger both more frequently and at lesser levels than the father. Given male stereotypes, we would expect that when men become angry they become *"really* angry," and these youths may perceive the consequences of their fathers' anger as being more serious. This finding also suggests that the male child is capable, at least in these instances, of role-taking across sex lines.

In examining racial differences, we found that for these black male youths the parents' perceived physical expressiveness was only a marginal predictor of their expressiveness. Any explanation for this finding would be precarious because the sample of black male youths was very small. Certainly this sample's finding that fathers are influential on black female youths' expressions of sorrow is one that could be worth future investigation, given that overall the black mother-daughter relationship is considerably stronger than the black father-daughter relationship.

*Children's Expressiveness*
*and Parents' Verbal Expressiveness*

The third hypothesis predicts that the perceived verbal expressiveness of the parents will be positively correlated with the total expressiveness of the child. The data presented in table 7–5 support this hypothesis and also indicate that the daughter-parent relationship is somewhat stronger than the son-parent relationship. In comparing the results of this hypothesis with those of Hypothesis Two regarding perceived parental *physical* expressiveness, it should be noted that while the verbal correlation coefficients are greater than the physical correlation coefficients (see table 7–3), the chief explanation for this lies in that the measure of total subject expressiveness is essentially verbal. Therefore, we would expect the present correlation coefficients to be greater.

Table 7–6 exhibits data on the specifics of these differences by examining the expression of the four emotions. The data display two major tendencies: First, these youth perceive their mothers' expression of anger as being of greater import to their own expression of anger than their fathers' perceived expression of anger. In Hypothesis One, the data indicate that fathers, rather than mothers, were seen as both physically and verbally more expressive of

**Table 7–5**
**Correlation Coefficients between Perceived Parental**
**Verbal Expressiveness and Subject Expressiveness**

|          | *Father*   | *Mother*   |
| -------- | ---------- | ---------- |
| Son      | 0.205***   | 0.198***   |
| Daughter | 0.258***   | 0.362***   |

***p < 0.001

Table 7–6
Correlation Coefficients between Perceived Parental Verbal Expressiveness
of Emotions and Subjects' Expression of Emotions

|  | Anger | Love | Sorrow | Happiness |
|---|---|---|---|---|
|  |  | *Father* |  |  |
| Son | 0.149*** | 0.260*** | 0.156*** | 0.206*** |
| Daughter | 0.119** | 0.232*** | 0.139*** | 0.241*** |
|  | Anger | Love | Sorrow | Happiness |
|  |  | *Mother* |  |  |
| Son | 0.169*** | 0.142** | 0.211*** | 0.235*** |
| Daughter | 0.159*** | 0.261*** | 0.208*** | 0.275*** |

**p<0.01
***p<0.001

anger. While this is true, the findings related to Hypotheses Two and Three further indicate that the mothers' perceived expression of anger is a greater predictor of the youths' own expression of anger than is the fathers'. Second, with the exception of the father-son relationship for the emotion of love, the mother-child relationship yields greater correlation coefficients for both sons and daughters.

While we found no significant social class differences, we do find some interesting racial differences. Black fathers' perceived verbal expressiveness to considerably less important to these black youths' expressiveness than is the mothers'. This is most noticeable for the black father-son relationship. Also, the black mother-daughter relationship is noticeably strong in this area.

Our explanation for these findings is similar to the previous hypothesis. Given that parents are key socializers for their children, we would expect there to be a positive relationship between parents' perceived expressiveness (whether physical or verbal) and these youths' expressiveness. That the mothers' verbal expressiveness was viewed as somewhat more influential on the various emotions is again most easily explained by the fact that not only is she generally more verbally expressive than the father, but also the children will see her exhibit a wide range of emotions in any given day. One possible explanation for the finding that for the emotion of love, fathers are more influential on their sons' expression of love, could be that males males and females differ in their conception of this emotion; thus, male youth, in learning the male role, tend to identify more strongy with their fathers' conception of love.

That the black mother is of more expressive dominance overall for these black youth is not too surprising. A higher rate of father absenteeism and a generally low and insecure job status are some factors that would lead us to suggest that the black father will have more difficulty defining his male role adequacy and of thus being of expressive import to his child, particularly his son. Blood and Wolfe (1969), among others (McAdoo 1981), have noted the absence of any high level of interaction between black husbands and wives. Irelan (1967, 20) points out that among lower-class families (the majority of this black sample is blue collar), "The passive role of the father in the house seems to strengthen the dependence of children on the mother." He further notes a greater emotional attachment to children on the part of these mothers as compensation for the emotional distance and lack of communication with their husbands.

### Children's Expressiveness and Gender of Parent

Hypothesis Four predicts that the correlations of expressiveness between the child and the same-sex parent will be greater than those between the child and the opposite-sex parent. Table 7–7 presents data for this hypothesis. Two tendencies are displayed in these results: First, contrary to our prediction, the mother-son relationship on physical expressiveness is *greater* than the father-son. Second, except for verbal expressiveness between mother and daughter, there are no significant differences between the same-sex or opposite-sex parent being a greater predictor of these youths' expressiveness. Table 7–8 presents the specifics of these differences by examining the expression of the four emotions. These data qualify the above findings and we note four trends: First, the mothers' physical expression rather than the fathers' is seen as a greater predictor of the sons' expression of anger and sorrow. Second, the fathers' perceived physical expression of happiness is more predictive of

Table 7–7
Correlation Coefficients between Perceived Parental Physical and Verbal Expressiveness for Same-Sex and Opposite-Sex Parents

|  | Father-Son minus Mother-Son | | Difference |
|---|---|---|---|
| Physical: | 0.171*** | 0.181*** | −0.010 |
| Verbal: | 0.205*** | 0.198*** | 0.007 |
|  | Mother-Daughter minus Father-Daughter | | Difference |
| Physical: | 0.152*** | 0.143*** | 0.009 |
| Verbal: | 0.362*** | 0.198*** | 0.104** |

**p<0.01
***p<0.001

Table 7–8
Differences in Correlation Coefficients between Perceived Parental Physical
and Verbal Expressiveness of Emotion for Same-Sex and Opposite-sex
Parents and Subjects' Expression of Emotions*

|  | Father-Son minus Mother-Son | | | |
|  | Anger | Love | Sorrow | Happiness |
|---|---|---|---|---|
| Physical | −0.070 | 0.051 | −0.023 | 0.024 |
| Verbal | −0.020 | 0.118** | −0.055 | −0.029 |

|  | Mother-Daughter minus Father-Daughter | | | |
|  | Anger | Love | Sorrow | Happiness |
|---|---|---|---|---|
| Physical | 0.018 | 0.002 | 0.103** | −0.030 |
| Verbal | 0.040 | 0.029 | 0.069 | 0.034 |

*The figures in the above table and all following tables represent *differences* between correlations.
**$p < 0.01$

the daughters' expression of that emotion than is the mothers'. Third, contrary to what was predicted, mothers are seen (in terms of verbal expressiveness) as greater predictors of their sons' expression of anger, sorrow, and happiness. Lastly, while the data do not reject the prediction that mothers' perceived verbal expressiveness will be a greater predictor of daughters' expressiveness of the various emotions, we can see that the correlation coefficients are not significant.

In terms of social class the data do display some differences. There appears to be a greater tendency for blue-collar youths to have a stronger relationship with the same-sex parent than do the white-collar youths. Radial differences are found and the tendency remains for the mothers' expressive influence over these black youths to be considerably stronger than fathers'.

The sample results as a whole reflect, to some extent, contradictions in the literature as to which parent will have the greater influence on the child. It is also possible, given our findings on social class differences, that these data reflect that the white-collar family structure places less emphasis on rigid sex-role differentiation. There is an indication, however, that these blue-collar youths were related somewhat stronger to same-sex parents when it came to expressiveness. We have discussed the relationship between male role adequacy and social class and it appears plausible, given our findings, that the white-collar father has fewer problems defining his male role adequacy and can, therefore, be of more significant expressive import to *both* his sons and daughters. The findings related to racial differences are relatively consistent.

Some possible explanations have already been offered for these findings and will be further discussed in the next chapter.

## Conclusions

Overall, it seems true there exists a clear relationship between perceived parental expressiveness and these youths' expressiveness. In this conclusion we will consider these findings in general and discuss them in terms of our theoretical orientation and the relevant literature.

### Differences between Fathers and Mothers

Our first finding that fathers were perceived on all measures, except for the physical expression of anger, to be less expressive than mothers indicates the extent to which parents are perceived to be functioning according to the traditional rather than the modern sex role. Given the traditional sex role stereotypes for males in society, and in particular for the fathers' generation as opposed to the sons' generation, we would expect the father to be seen as more inexpressive. If, as Mead (1934) contends, a fully developed self is contingent upon the incorporation of the "generalized other" (i.e., the inclusion of the attitudes of the organized group to which one belongs), then surely the male in this society will in many instances adopt the stereotypes of the male role which, until recently, placed a greater emphasis on inexpressiveness rather than expressiveness. That the finding held over race and social class is a further indication of the strength of the traditional stereotype, whether in terms of actual behavior or perceptions. Our evidence suggests that parental definitions of sex roles have changed little from what they were when Johnson (1963) found that children of both sexes perceived their mothers as much higher on expressiveness dimensions (using the semantic differential scale) than their fathers.

We found that the black youth in this study perceived an even greater difference between mothers' and fathers' expressiveness, and that black fathers were in general of much less import to their children's expressiveness than were mothers. This finding receives some support in the literature. Blood and Wolfe (1969) found that black husbands were rated low by their wives as providers, and also that they did not satisfy their wives' needs for understanding. Communication was also found to be poor between black husbands and wives. On this basis, we contend that the relationship parents have with each other will reflect that which they have with their children. As mothers are seen as more expressive, and as black fathers (most of whom in this study were blue collar) have the added problem of being black and blue-collar, it is not surprising that black children see greater differences between mothers' and fathers' expressiveness than do white children. The burden on lower-class black males in this society, most especially in terms of male status, has been such that perhaps Turner best describes it when he says, " . . . when people cannot prove themselves by what they can do, the fall back on the assertion of what they cannot do" (1970, 229); hence, the black father may resort to defining the male role in terms of what it is *not,* i.e., female and expressive. Aldous' (1969) findings strengthen this argument. She suggests that when the black wife is employed outside the home and shares the provider function, the husband may become more unsure of his status in the family and withdraw from family tasks and decisions. A further consideration that relates to helps explain this can be found in the work of the black sociologist Frazier (1939), who argued that even in the post-slavery era, the black male subordination to menial and subservient status had made the female the dominant person in the black family. Bell (1967), in a study of 202 black mothers in the Philadelphia area, showed that although the lower-class black male considered his marital and parental roles to be of little importance, the lower-class black woman believed that her role as mother was highly significant.

It is of considerable interest that fathers, overall, were seen as more expressive of physical anger than mothers. In discussing male and female stereotypes, several authors (Bardwick and Douvan 1971; Chafetz 1974) have pointed out that certain emotions are more typically masculine; Balswick and Peek (1970) argue that this is specifically true for anger. Our findings, then, are not surprising, given that in this society, anger is one of the few emotions males are allowed and even often expected to demonstrate. However, when it comes to which parent is most predictive of the child's expression of anger, we find, interestingly enough, it is the mother rather than the father in most cases (for perceived physical and verbal parental expressiveness). What this certainly indicates is that the mother's expression of anger is seen as a more acceptable model of behavior for these youths to imitate. It would seem then that when it comes to their expression of anger, sons are quite capable of role-taking across sex lines. Whether this is most true toward "significant-others" (such as mothers), it would be of interest to see whether expressiveness in general is an area where we find less rigidity in males (especially the present generation) in terms of their ability to role-take across sex lines.

We did find an exception to the above general finding in that black daughters perceived their fathers' *physical* expression of anger as having more influence on their own expression of anger. This was also true in daughters' perceptions of fathers' physical and verbal expression of sorrow and daughters' expression of sorrow. One possible explanation for this finding may lie in the fact that the anger subscale is made up of anger, hate, resentment, and rage items, and the black daughter may be empathizing to some extent with the overall black male status (particularly that of her father's generation) in this society, and she perhaps not only recognizes his frustrations but also considers them realistic enough to model her own behavior upon them. After all, in relation to stereotypes between blacks and whites, it would seem that it indeed may be more acceptable for black females to be more expressive of anger than for white females.

## Verbal and Physical Expressiveness

We also found a positive relationship between perceived parental physical and verbal expressiveness and the child's total expressiveness. There were, however, notable qualifications. In the relationship between perceived parental physical expressiveness and the youths' expressiveness, we found the mother to be *slightly* more predictive of the child's expressiveness than the father, which is not unexpected. It is of interest to note, however, that in the case of black sons, perceived parental physical expressiveness has little impact on the son's total expressiveness. In terms of perceived parental *verbal* expressiveness, the data indicate a negative relationship between the black father and son, but a positive relationship between the black mother and son. It seems, then, that black sons differentiate much more between perceived parental physical and verbal expressiveness than any others in the sample. While this finding is of significant interest to require further study, one possible explanation may be that, in this study, the black sons may be at an age where they are so rebellious toward their parents that they do not consider them significant influences. This suggestion gains further weight when we note that Staples suggests, "While the family is usually prime mediator of cultural values, there appears to be a greater amount of peer group socialization among blacks and lower-class whites" (1974, 550). In the mother-son relationship, what we may be finding is that because mothers are considered more verbally expressive than fathers (and this would be particularly true for blacks), the black son may be under some pressure from his mother to react to her verbal expressiveness. In general, these data indicate that the black mother is much more influential on her sons' and daughters' expressiveness than is the father, and certainly the gap is much greater than it is for the white children.

## Same- and Opposite-Sex Parents

In the sample as a whole, we found no great difference between the mother's and father's relationships to the children except between the mother's perceived verbal expressiveness and her daughter's total expressiveness. Some years ago, Johnson (1963) argued that the division of parental roles into those of father as disciplinarian and mother as emotional supporter is gradually being replaced by more similar role expectations for both mothers and fathers. Our findings do, then, support arguments against the Parsons-Bales dichotomy of parental roles (1955), and support that, at least in parenting, the traditional sex role is being redefined by modern sex roles.

## Social Class

In the blue-collar sample, indications are of a greater sex role rigidity than held for the white-collar sample. We found indications that the same-sex parent-to-child relationship was stronger for blue-collar children than it was for white-collar children, especially in the blue-collar mother-daughter relationship. This general trend is supported in the literature. Udry (1974) points out that there is less sex segregation in general activities among middle-class families. Other studies note that, comparatively, middle-class fathers devote more time to childrearing (Davis and Havighurst 1946; Spinley 1953). Our findings on blue-collar child-parent relationships would seem to indicate that as yet, there does not appear to be any significant lessening in the more rigid adherence to sex role stereotypes.

## Parents As Role Models

Overall, our data indicate that in role theory terms the parents are key socializers and serve as role models in their children's developments of expressive selves. Interestingly, there appears to be more evidence of role taking, in its most general sense, across sex lines than we would have predicted—at least in terms of "significant others."

# 8

# Situational Factors

Two studies particularly relevant to ours have examined emotional expressiveness in a situational context. Highlen and Gillis (1978) probed the effects of the participant's sex and situation (initiator, respondent), type of feeling (positive, negative), and sex of best friend in affective self-disclosure with male and female single undergraduates in dyadic interactions. They found that females disclosed significantly more feelings than did males, whereas across sex, participants disclosed significantly more positive than negative feelings to same-sex rather than opposite-sex best friends. Highlen and Gillis concluded: "It can be stated that affective self-disclosure is a complex variable which seems to be sex-linked and situation specific" (1978, 276).

Highlen and Johnston (1979) replicated the Highlen and Gillis (1978) study using the acquaintance-target intimacy level rather than the best-friend target. As in the original study, they found that females disclosed significantly more feelings than did males, whereas across sex, subjects disclosed significantly more positive than negative feelings as respondents rather than initiators.

Although not as directly relevant as Highlen's work, a number of recent studies have attempted to assess the situational context of affective self-disclosure. Several have revealed that women's friendships involve personal concern, intimate sharing, and other emotional interactions, and men's friendships are more likely to involve status, power, and shared activities (Bell 1981a; Caldwell and Peplau 1982; Peretti 1980). Women friends communicate on a wider variety of topics than do male friends, and emphasize emotional sharing and talking more than male friends (Caldwell and Peplau 1982; Davidson and Duberman 1982).

Most studies have found a tendency for males to avoid intimacy (Stokes,

---

Some of the findings reported in this chapter appeared in D. Dosser, 1981. *Sex Differences and Situational Factors In Emotional Expressiveness: A Reconsideration of Male Inexpressiveness*, unpublished doctoral dissertation, University of Georgia.

Fuehrer, and Childs 1980; Hunter and Touniss 1982; Franco, Malloy, and Gonzalez 1984; Aries and Johnson 1983; Wheeler, Reis, and Neylek 1983; Williams 1985). Aries and Johnson (1983), for instance, found that although males talk at greater depth with each other on the topic of sports, females talk more frequently and at greater depth on intimate topics like personal and family matters. However, in several studies of cross-sex interactions between college student dyads, males were found to disclose more than females (Derleaga, Windstead, Wong, and Hunter 1985; Hacker 1981). Other studies have suggested that males can disclose more to strangers and acquaintances than to intimates (Hansen and Schuldt 1982; Stokes, Fuehrer, and Childs 1980), that male expressiveness increases throughout the life cycle, reaching its peak at grandfatherhood (Feldman, Biringen, and Nash 1981), and that men having more romantic rather than rational attitudes toward love disclosed more to their mothers, fathers, male friends, and female friends (Lester, Brazil, Ellis and Guerin 1984). All these findings point to the need to understand the situational context of expressiveness.

Although most of the earlier work on general self-disclosure (Jourard 1961; Jourard and Lasakow 1958) treated it as a personality trait, more recent work has suggested that it also must be understood in a situational context. From a role theory perspective, Balswick and Balkwell stated that "Self-disclosure will be understood in terms of self's conception of himself, his perception of alter's (potential target person) role, and his perception of alter's expectation of him" (1978, 283). In a similar vein, Chelune stated that "to disclose the self implies that there is a self (a person) doing the disclosing and someone (a target) present to receive the disclosure. Furthermore, the disclosure (a topic) must occur within both a social context (a relationship) and an environmental setting (a situation)" (1979, 16).

Based on research of emotional expressiveness, affective self-disclosure, and general self-disclosure, it seems that to best understand emotional expressiveness one must take into account such situational variables as target person, size of group, type of feeling, participant role, and sex of best friend. The primary objective of our study was to use a combination of the different assessment methods developed by Balswick and Highlen to look more closely at emotional expressiveness by exploring how it is affected by the situational variables just mentioned.

Based upon findings from previous research, the following hypotheses were tested:

1. Across other situational factors, females will be more expressive than males.

2. Across other situational factors, subjects will be more expressive in situations requiring positive emotions than in those requiring negative emotions.

3. Across other situational factors, subjects will be more expressive in the respondent role than in the initiator role.

4. Across other situational factors, subjects will be: (a) more expressive to female rather than male best friends and (b) more expressive to same-sex than opposite-sex best friends.

5. Across other situational factors and when looking at specific feelings: (a) females will be more expressive of love, happiness and sadness and (b) males will be more expressive of anger.

6. Across other situational factors, subjects will be more expressive alone with a person than in a small group and more expressive in a small group than in a large group.

## Method

### Subjects

Questionnaires were administered to 331 (142 male and 189 female) university students. These volunteers came from introductory level classes (e.g., classes in child and family development, psychology, sociology, geography) at a large Southeastern university. Some of the male subjects were friends of the female subjects who volunteered to complete the questionnaire at the request of their female subject friends. Each subject who completed the questionnaire was also asked to volunteer for the second phase of the study. From this subsample of 185 (sixty-one male and 124 female) volunteers, a random sample of forty-eight subjects (twenty-four male and twenty-four female) was selected for the behavioral observation phase of the study. Analyses revealed no significant differences in self-reported expressiveness between a randomly selected sample of volunteers and a randomly selected sample of those who did not volunteer.

Demographic characteristics of the sample indicated that: (a) the mean age was 20.4 years; (b) 13.3 percent of the students were freshmen, 31.4 percent were sophomores, 30.2 percent were juniors, 18.7 percent were seniors, 4.2 percent were graduate students, and 2.2 percent did not respond on this item; (c) 91.8 percent of the sample were single, 7.9 percent were married, and .3 percent were separated or divorced; and (d) 92.1 percent of the sample were white, 5.4 percent were black, 1.8 percent selected "other," and .7 percent failed to respond to this item.

### Dependent Measures

The instruments used to measure the dependent variables are described in detail in chapter 6. These instruments consisted of the sixteen-item *Expres-*

*sion of Emotions Scale,* the sixteen-item *Emotion Scale,* the four-item *Pretend Expressiveness Scale,* the sixteen affective self-disclosure situation *Self-Report Performance Test, The Expression of Feeling Scale, Varied By Target Person* (father, mother, female friend, male friend, female stranger, and male stranger), *The Expression of Feeling Scale, Varied by Size of Group* (alone with the person, in a small group, and in a large group), the twenty-five-item *Self-Monitoring Scale,* and the sixteen affective self-disclosure *Behavioral Performance Test.* Together these scales measure an individual's general expressiveness and various specific types of situational expressiveness. Each of these measurements yields interval-type data.

*Observational Setting*
*for the Behavioral Performance Test*

**Setting and Equipment.** The second phase of the study took place in an experimental room where the furniture was removed to enable the subjects and actors to move freely. The videotape was placed in an observation booth with a two-way mirror to minimize distraction. All subjects knew they were being videotaped and were shown the observation booth and equipment to allay any anxiety about who or what might be behind the mirror.

All videotaping was done with the subject and actor standing so that the subject was free to gesture or move as desired. Subjects were, however, confined to an area one square meter in size (one meter by one meter) marked on the floor with tape. The actor stood just outside this marked area facing the subject to be sure that both subject and actor could be seen on videotape, while at the same time allowing the subject some freedom of movement for gesturing and other body movements. The camera recorded a subject frontal view from the waist up, and an actor rear-view from the waist up. The actor was positioned so that the distance between him or her and the subject could be regulated by the subject to insure that the subject's comfortable distance for interaction was not an intervening variable.

Videotape equipment required for the study included: a camera on tripod, a videotape deck, a video monitor, a microphone, and video tapes. An audiotape was also made using a cassette tape recorder to insure ease in transcribing for content rating.

**Actor Training.** The actors were trained to play the role of best male and best female friend in a consistent manner from one subject to the next. These efforts included an attempt by the actors to deliver their responses to the subjects consistently. Actors also attempted to present consistent facial expressions to subjects. These efforts were made to ensure that, to the greatest extent possible, the actors' differential behaviors between subjects was not an uncontrolled intervening variable. Actor training continued with practice of their responses videotaped and reviewed until actors were able to peform satisfactorily and felt comfortable in their roles.

**Procedure.** During spring quarter 1980, students in several introductory level classes were approached toward the end of their regular class meeting period and asked to volunteer to participate in a research study. They were told the study dealt with the expression of emotion and was being conducted for a dissertation under the direction of Dr. Balswick of the Child and Family Development Department. The questionnaire was explained briefly, including requests that answers be made without undue thought and that every question be answered. Subjects were told the questionnaire had taken other individuals approximately thirty minutes to complete but, since they would be allowed to carry the questionnaire home to complete, there would be no time limit. Time was allotted for volunteers to examine the questionnaire briefly. Any questions that arose were answered.

Specific instructions for completing each section of the questionnaire preceded the sections and since these instructions were believed to be self-explanatory, they were not explained further. Volunteers were asked, however, to turn to the last page of the questionnaire to review the instructions found there. They were told the second phase of the experiment was also very important and were encouraged to volunteer by supplying the information requested and returning that page. Further, they were told that if they completed the last page and turned it in, they might be contacted later in the quarter to arrange an appointment for the second phase of the study and that at that time the remainder of the study would be explained, but that they could decide not to participate further in the study for any reason and without penalty. Females who volunteered to complete the questionnaire were asked to deliver an additional copy of the questionnaire to one or more males whom they knew on campus, to encourage these males to complete it, and then to return the completed questionnaire with their own. This approach was required because so few males were enrolled in most of the classes available for recruiting volunteers. Questionnaires were completed at the subjects' convenience and returned to the class instructor or to the researchers.

About six weeks later, forty-eight subjects (twenty-four male and twenty-four female) were randomly selected from the larger group of volunteers to participate in the second phase of the study and were contacted by phone. At this time, the second phase was explained further and any questions they had were answered. An appointment to meet with the researcher at the Child and Family Development Center was arranged for those subjects who agreed to participate. For every subject who refused to participate, a name was randomly selected from the available pool of same-sex volunteers and this individual was contacted to ascertain his or her willingness to participate. This process was continued until appointments were made for the appropriate number of subjects. If subjects missed their scheduled appointment, a new appointment was arranged. Appointments were scheduled at thirty-minute intervals from 6:00 to 10:00 P.M. on week nights for two consecutive weeks.

When subjects arrived at the Child and Family Development Center for their scheduled appointment, they were greeted and ushered into a comfortably furnished lobby area. They were told the study dealt with the expression of emotion and was very similar to the questionnaire filled out earlier. They were informed that, during the study, they would be asked to respond to a male and female actor in sixteen different "everyday" situations. Subjects understood that their behavior would be videotaped and they were told how the videotape would be used.

When subjects had signed the consent form and had any questions answered to their satisfaction, they were asked to be seated and told that they would be called in a few minutes to the experimental room upstairs. They were given a card to review while they waited which contained the following instructions:

> *In this study, you will be asked to respond to typical situations which arise in people's lives. It is important that you try to imagine that you are actually in the situations, and are interacting with your best male or best female friend. It is also important that you try to express your true feelings that you would experience if you were in that particular situation with your best friend. Take a few seconds now to think of the name of your best female friend and your best male friend to help you keep in mind the people you are imagining you are with in these situations. Try throughout this experience to imagine the actor as your best male friend and the actress as your best female friend. In order to better imagine the situations that will be described, you could think about what it would feel like to be in the situation, where it would occur, and what you would see, hear, and smell. Then, when you are certain that you understand the situation and can imagine it, you may proceed to respond to the actor or actress. Try to respond just as you would to your best friend. Remember, express your feelings as well as you can. After each situation, I will explain the next situation and you will have time to get ready. In some of the situations, you will respond first, and, in others, you will respond after the actor or actress speaks to you.*

At this point the researcher left the subject in the lobby and returned to the experimental room upstairs.

After a brief time, the researcher returned to the lobby and requested that the subject move to the experimental room. After subjects had reached the experimental room, an effort was made to help them feel comfortable prior to starting the session. This included allowing the subjects an opportunity to relax and explore the experimental room and the observation booth. When the subject was relaxed and ready to proceed, the study began. The instructions that the subject had been reading were reviewed verbally by the researcher and any additional questions were answered. Finally, the instructions for subjects to behave as "realistically" as they could and to express their feelings as best they could were reiterated. When the subject demonstrated an understanding of the instructions, a description of the first situation was presented to the subject on a card. After the subject had a chance to understand and imagine the situation, a male or female actor entered the room and the subject responded. The situations were presented to the subjects in a random order to control for any order effects response bias and proceeded from one situation to another until all sixteen situations had been presented and responses to each had been obtained. Although subjects' responses were not limited by time, each response ended with their first response, and did not include any further interaction between the subject and the male or female actor.

No practice situations were provided for subjects because it was believed they would be sufficiently familiar with the situations and the procedure from their experiences in completing the questionnaire. If, however, a subject momentarily did feel confused or appeared overly anxious or nervous, an effort was made to calm the subject and the situation was repeated. This procedure was required for only three subjects during the course of the study.

Videotaping began at the end of the introduction to the situation and when the first words were spoken by either the actor or the subject. For identification purposes, the actor stated the number of the situation for the videotape and audiotape at the end of the subject's response to each situation.

Following each response to the situation each subject was asked to rate the anxiety he or she would actually feel if he or she had made that response to his or her best male or female friend. A one-to-seven Likert scale, ranging from "very calm and relaxed" to "extremely nervous" was used to report anxiety for each situation (following Highlen and Gillis 1978).

At the end of all sixteen situations, subjects were given a further explanation of the study, a presentation of specific hypotheses, a brief summary of previous research, etc. Any questions were answered and subjects were told when and where they could request, if interested, information on the results of the study. In lieu of any type of payment, reprints and a bibliography of articles on the inexpressive male were provided for those subjects who were interested. Subjects were asked not to describe the study to any of their friends until it was completed so as to avoid excessive demand characteristics. Subjects were then thanked and excused.

An effort was made during debriefing to ascertain if any subjects were upset by their participation in the study. As expected, none was. Furthermore, subjects reported no difficulty with the instructions and procedures and not being overly anxious or nervous. Most subjects said they enjoyed participating.

*Design and Data Analyses*

Analyses used for this study included unweighted means repeated measures analysis of variance and appropriate analyses of simple effects to clarify the relation among the variables in the significant interactions. Tests of simple effects included, where appropriate, the Newman-Keuls procedure, the Bonferroni-Dunn's procedure, univariate analyses of variance and paired t-tests. The repeated measures analysis of variance design was required because the same subjects responded to all the situational variables. Not all the data were analyzed because of the extent of the data and the focus of this particular study.

Balswick's *Expression of Emotion Scale* was analyzed using a two-by-four unweighted means repeated measures analysis of variance (ANOVA) design. Sex of subject was the between-subjects factor, while type of feeling (love, happiness, sadness, anger) was the within-subjects factor.

Balswick's *Expression of Emotion Scale* varied by target person was analyzed using a two-by-four-by-four unweighted means repeated measures ANOVA design. Sex of subject was the between-subjects factor, while target person (father, mother, female friend, male friend) and type of feeling (love, happiness, sadness, anger) were within-subjects factors. The stranger targets were not analyzed in this study.

Balswick's *Expression of Emotion Scale* varied by size of group was analyzed using a two-by-three-by-four unweighted means repeated measures ANOVA design. Sex of subject was the between-subjects factor, while size of group (alone with the person, in a small group, in a large group) and type of feeling (love, happiness, sadness, anger) were the within-subject factors.

The self-report performance test and the behavioral performance test were both analyzed using a two-by-four-by-two-by-two unweighted means repeated measures ANOVA design. For each, sex of subject was the between-subjects factor, while type of feeling (love, happiness, sadness, anger), subject role (initiator, respondent), and sex of best friend (male, female) were the within-subjects factors.

Additional analyses on all measures were completed for type of feeling (positive or negative). A positive-feeling score combined the happiness and love scores; the negative-feeling score combined the sadness and anger scores. This procedure allowed a more direct comparison to the findings of Highlen and Gillis (1978) and Highlen and Johnston (1979) and to determine if there was an advantage in considering specific feelings when exploring sex differences and situational variability in expressiveness. The sex-of-subject factor was analyzed as same- and opposite-sex as well as male and female best friend to more closely match previous research. For all analyses, an a priori alpha level of .01 was used to control for spurious findings resulting from the numerous texts conducted on the data.

# Results

In this study, expressiveness was assessed by four self-report methods and one behavioral method. Subjects' self-reported expressiveness scores were obtained from the *Expression of Emotion Scale,* the *Expression of Emotion Scale* varied by target person, the *Expression of Emotion Scale* varied by size of group, and the self-report performance test. A behavioral measure of subjects' expressiveness was obtained from the behavioral performance test that required subjects to express their feelings in role-play situations. To simplify the presentation of results from so many sources, the results that pertain directly to the six specific hypotheses of the study will be presented first. Next, the results that pertain to the general research questions that guided the study will be presented. Finally, those results that were most salient and persistent—those that were consistent across the different methodological approaches—will be reviewed.

*Hypothesis One. Across other situational factors, females will be more expressive than males.*

In general, this was supported by the data. As can be seen in table 8–1, the main effect for sex of subject was significant with females being more expressive than males when using four of the five methodological approaches for assessing expressiveness.

### Table 8–1
### Analysis of Variance *F* Values for Sex Differences in Total Expressiveness across Other Situational Factors

| Method | Total Expressiveness |
| --- | --- |
| Expression of Emotion (*EOE*) Scale | 16.22\*\*\*[a] (.05) |
| *EOE* Scale by Target Person | 21.88\*\*\*[a] (.07) |
| *EOE* Scale by Size of Group | 4.72[a] (———) |
| Self-Report Performance Test | 95.10\*\*\*[a] (.24) |
| Behavioral Performance Test | 8.76\*[a] (.16) |

\**p* .005
\*\**p* .001
\*\*\**p* .0001
[a]females more expressive than males

The one exception occurred with the *Expression of Emotion Scale* varied by size of group. This main effect, while not significant, demonstrated a trend in the expected direction such that females expressed slightly more feelings across size of group and type of feeling than did males.

*Hypothesis Two. Across other situational factors,*
*subjects will be more expressive in situations requiring*
*positive emotions than in those requiring negative*
*emotions.*

This was supported by the data from all five methodological approaches for assessing expressiveness. For these analyses, positive-feeling scores added the love and happiness scores and negative-feeling scores added the sadness and anger scores. As can be seen in table 8–2, significant main effects for type of feeling were found across all methods with subjects being more expressive in the situations requiring the expression of positive feelings than in those requiring negative feelings.

*Hypothesis Three. Across other situational factors,*
*subjects will be more expressive in the respondent role*
*than in the initiator role.*

This was not supported by the data from the self-report performance test or the behavioral performance test. In fact, the reverse was found: subjects were more expressive in the initiator role. The two performance tests were the only approaches to assessing expressiveness in this study that considered sub-

**Table 8–2**
**Analysis of Variance *F* Values for Type**
**of Feeling Main Effect (Positive-Negative)**

| Method | Type of Feeling Positive-Negative |
| --- | --- |
| Expression of Emotion (EOE) Scale | 543.95***[a] |
| EOE Scale by Target Person | 394.31***[a] |
| EOE Scale by Size of Group | 467.83***[a] |
| Self-Report Performance Test | 449.32***[a] |
| Behavioral Performance Test | 124.38***[a] |

*p .005
**p .001
***p .0001
[a]Subjects more expressive of positive feelings than of negative feelings

ject role as an independent variable. Analysis of the self-report performance test revealed a significant main effect for subject role, $F(1,297)=11.18$, $p<.001$. Across sex of subject, type of feeling, and sex of best friend, subjects were significantly more expressive in the initiator role ($M=3.15$) than in the respondent role ($M=3.05$). No significant main effect for subject role was found, however, for the behavioral performance test, $F(1,46)=1.26$, $p<.267$. Subjects were only slightly more expressive in the initiator role ($M=3.47$) than in the respondent role ($M=3.36$) across the other situational factors.

*Hypothesis Four. Across other situational factors, subjects will be: (a) more expressive to female rather than male best friends and (b) more expressive to same-sex rather than opposite-sex best friends.*

The sex of best friend variable was considered primarily using data from the self-report performance test and the behavioral performance test. Sex of subject was analyzed within the repeated measures ANOVA design in terms of female and male best friend. It is possible, however, using computed means for same- and opposite-sex best friend, to determine general trends when the data are considered in this manner. The data provided only slightly more support for part (a) of this hypothesis and a consistent lack of support for part (b). In fact, the reverse was found: Subjects were more expressive to their opposite-sex best friends.

In general, across sex of subject, type of feeling, and subject role, there were no significant differences between subjects' expressiveness scores with female and male best friends. There was, however, a trend for subjects to be more expressive with their opposite-sex best friends than with their same-sex best friends. Also, these general findings were apparent with the *Expression of Emotion Scale* varied by target person.

Specifically, in the self-report performance test the main effect for sex of subject was not significant, $F(1,297)=4.53$, $p<.034$. As expected, across sex of subject, type of feeling, and subject role, subjects were slightly more expressive to female best friends ($M=3.10$) than to male best friends ($M=3.08$). Another analysis indicated that across other situational factors, subjects were more expressive to opposite-sex best friends ($M=3.17$) than to same-sex best friends ($M=3.02$), which was unexpected.

Likewise, no significant main effect was found for sex of subject, $F(1,46)=.002$, $p<.966$, using the behavioral performance test. In fact, across other situational factors, subjects expressed the same amount of feelings to female ($M=3.41$) as to male ($M=3.41$) best friends. In terms of same-sex or opposite-sex best friends, the results were compatible with the self-report performance test, such that across other situational factors, subjects expressed more feelings to opposite-sex best friends ($M = 3.48$) than to same-sex best friends ($M = 3.34$).

In addition, analysis of the *Expression of Emotion Scale* varied by target person indicated no significant difference between subjects' expressions of feelings to female friends and male friends. As expected, however, across sex of subject and type of feeling, subjects were slightly more expressive of feelings to female friends ($M = 11.46$) than to male friends ($M = 11.13$). When sex of subject for this scale was viewed in terms of same- or opposite-sex friend, across sex of subject, subjects expressed more feelings to an opposite-sex friend ($M = 11.79$) than to a same-sex friend ($M = 10.79$).

*Hypothesis Five. Across other situational factors, and when looking at specific feelings: (a) females will be more expressive than males of love, happiness, and sadness, and (b) males will be more expressive than females of anger.*

Univariate ANOVAs were computed using all five methods of assessing expressiveness for each type of feeling to check for sex differences. The results (see table 8–3) support part (a) of the hypothesis but did not support part (b). Females were found to be significantly more expressive of love and happiness than males across other situational factors and using all five assessment methods. With four out of five methods, females were significantly more expressive of sadness than were males. For anger, the results from the three methods using the *Expression of Emotion Scale* indicated no significant sex differences. Males were, however, slightly more expressive than females of anger with two of the three methods. With the self-report performance test, females were significantly more expressive of anger across other situational factors than males. Finally, females were slightly more expressive of anger than males across other situational factors using the behavioral performance test.

*Hypothesis Six. Across other situational factors, subjects will be more expressive alone with a person than in a small group and more expressive in a small group than in a large group.*

This was supported by data from the *Expression of Emotion Scale* varied by size of group. The significant main effect for size of group, $F(2,596) = 999.15$, $p < .000$, indicated that across sex of subject and type of feeling, subjects expressed the most feelings when alone with a person ($M = 12.40$), followed by when in a small group ($M = 9.19$) and, finally, when in a large group ($M = 7.37$). Multiple comparison tests of every one of

**Table 8–3**
**Analysis of Variance *F* Values for Sex Difference in Expressiveness for Specific Feelings**

| Method | Love | Happiness | Sadness | Anger |
|---|---|---|---|---|
| Expression of Emotion (*EOE*) Scale | 10.95** (.03) | 29.28*** (.08) | 16.40*** (.05) | 2.28[a] (——) |
| EOE Scale by Target Person | 31.98*** (.09) | 22.62*** (.07) | 9.78* (.03) | 1.78 (——) |
| EOE Scale by Size of Group | 9.92* (.03) | 13.48** (.04) | 2.54 (——) | 2.18[a] (——) |
| Self-Report Performance Test | 42.90*** (.12) | 57.24*** (.15) | 70.73*** (.18) | 19.30*** (.06) |
| Behavioral Performance Test | 12.28** (.21) | .933 (——) | 5.79* (.11) | 1.23 (——) |

*Note:* Numbers in parentheses indicate *eta²*.
*p .005
**p .001
***p .0001
[a]Males more expressive than females

these means with every other one indicated that expression of feeling when alone with a person is significantly ($p < .01$) different from expression when in a small group, which in turn is significantly ($p < .01$) different from expression when in a large group.

### Interaction between Factors in Their Effect upon Expressiveness

A number of significant interactions were found that provide additional information on the effect of situational variables on sex differences in the expression of emotion. Also, interpretation of these interactions provided information on a number of the general research questions that guided this study. To clarify the relations among the variables in the interactions, additional analyses of the simple effects for each interaction were conducted. Whenever possible, similar interactions across methodological approaches are discussed together to simplify the presentation of the interactions.

A significant sex-of-subject by type-of-feeling interaction was a frequent finding, appearing in four of five methodological approaches. The one exception was the behavioral performance test. As seen in table 8–3, these interactions were due primarily to anger. On the *Expression of Emotion Scale* and the *Expression of Emotion Scale* varied by target person, females scored significantly higher than males in expression of love, happiness, and sadness across other situational factors. With anger, however, no significant sex difference was found. Similarly, across other situational factors, females scored significantly higher than males in expression of happiness and love, but no significant sex differences were found for sadness and anger using the *Expression of Emotion Scale* varied by size of group. Finally, females were significantly more expressive than males across other situational factors for all four feelings using the self-report performance test, but magnitude-of-effect computations indicated the sex difference was least for anger.

Three more significant interactions were found using the *Expression of Emotion Scale* varied by target person. Analysis of the sex of subject by target person interaction indicated that the interaction was primarily due to the female-friend target. Across type of feeling, females had significantly ($p = < .01$) higher expressiveness scores than did males to the mother, father, and male friend targets. For the female-friend target, however, there was no significant difference between the expressiveness scores of males and females.

A visual inspection of the data graphically presented in figure 8–1 indicates that the target-person by type-of-feeling interaction was apparently due to the male-friend target and anger. The feelings were expressed consistently across the targets with happiness expressed the most, followed by love and sadness expressed in about the same amount, and finally, anger, expressed least. The expression of feelings to targets were consistent across love and

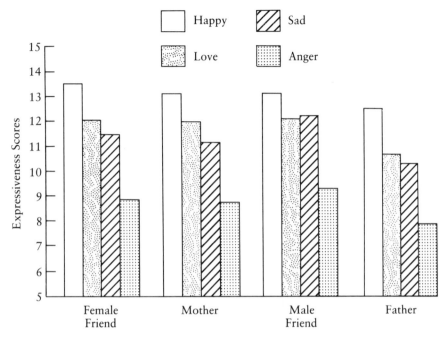

**Figure 8–1.** Target Person by Type-of-Feeling Interaction for Expressiveness Scores Using the Expression of Emotion Scale Varied by Target Person

happiness, with the female friend expressed to the most, followed by the mother, the male friend, and finally the father targets. This order changed a little with sadness, when the male friend was expressed to more than the mother. The biggest difference, however, was with anger, where the male friend was expressed to the most.

The sex-of-subject by target-person by type-of-feeling triple interaction appeared to be due to the differential way in which male and female subjects expressed feelings, particularly love, to their same-sex friend targets. Male subjects expressed feelings consistently with happiness expressed the most followed by love, sadness, and anger to all targets except those of the male friend to whom they expressed more anger than love. Females expressed the four feelings the same for all target persons except those of the female friend to whom they expressed more sadness than love. When love is considered alone (see figure 8–2), analysis revealed that males' and females' expressiveness scores were significantly different to the same-sex best-friend target. In addition, magnitude-of-effect computations indicated that while males' and females' love expressiveness scores were significantly different with both male and female friends, the sex difference was greater for the male-friend target.

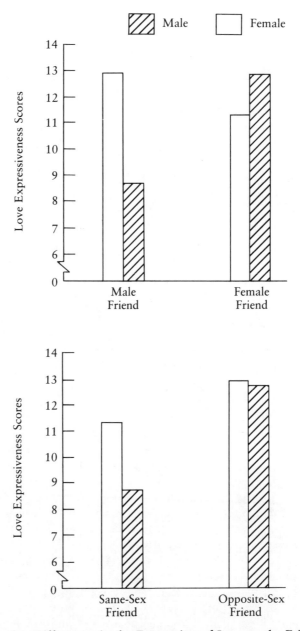

**Figure 8–2. Sex Differences in the Expression of Love to the Friend Targets Using the Expression of Emotion Scale Varied by Target Person**

Three additional significant interactions were also found, using the *Expression of Emotion Scale* varied by size of group. Analysis of the sex-of-subject by size-of-group interaction revealed that as the size of the group increased, the differences between females' and males' scores decreased. In other words, the difference between the females' and males' scores was the greatest in the alone condition ($D = .78$), followed by the small-group condition ($D = .41$), and finally by the large-group condition ($D = .19$). In addition, male and female scores were significantly ($p < .01$) different in the alone condition but were not significantly different in the small-group or large-group conditions.

Figure 8–3 indicates that in the size-of-group by type-of-feeling interaction, happiness was apparently affected less by the size of the group than were love, sadness, and anger. Moreover, figure 8–4 indicates that the triple interaction between sex-of-subject by size-of-group by type-of-feeling was primarily because females apparently differentiated between size of groups in their expression more than males did.

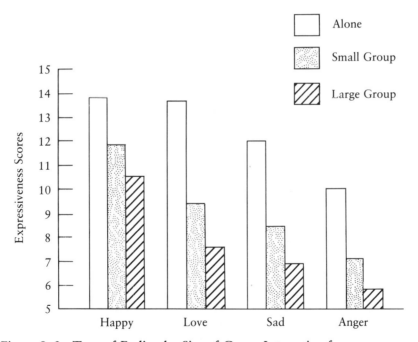

Figure 8–3. Type-of-Feeling by Size-of-Group Interaction for Expressiveness Scores Using the Expression of Emotion Scale Varied by Size of Group

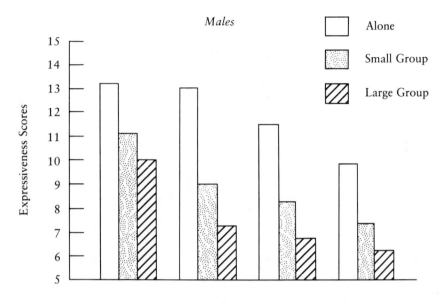

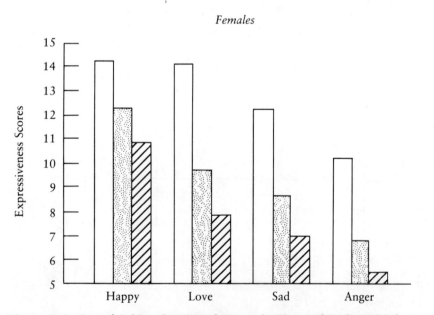

**Figure 8–4.** Sex-of-Subject by Size-of-Group by Type-of-Feeling Triple Interaction for Expressiveness Scores Using the Expression of Emotion Scale Varied by Size of Group

The self-report performance test and the behavioral performance test methods had two interactions in common that can be interpreted together for both methods. The significant type-of-feeling by subject-role interaction found in both tests was anger. For both methods across other situational factors for happiness, love and sadness, subjects either did not discriminate between roles or were more expressive in the initiator role. With anger, however, subjects in both methods were significantly more expressive in the respondent role.

The significant sex-of-subject by sex-of-best-friend interaction found for the self-report performance test (and the similar trend found with the behavioral performance test) was primarily because while females, across other situational factors, were more expressive than males to both male and female best friends, the sex difference was greater for the male best friend than for the female best friend. Another way of viewing this interaction is to consider the sex-of-best-friend condition in terms of same- or opposite-sex best friend. Viewed this way, females and males expressed more feelings to opposite-sex best friends, but males differentiated between same- and opposite-sex slightly more than females did.

In the self-report performance test, two more interactions were significant. Analysis of the sex-of-subject by type-of-feeling by subject-role triple interaction indicated that males differentiated between the respondent and initiator roles for expressing love and happiness, but not for sadness and anger. Females, on the other hand, differentiated between the respondent and initiator roles for expressing sadness and anger, but not for happiness and love. Also, males were significantly ($p < .01$) more expressive in the initiator role than in the respondent role for love and happiness. For sadness and anger, males were slightly more expressive in the respondent role. Females were significantly ($p < .01$) more expressive in the initiator role for feeling sadness and slightly more expressive in this role for love. They were also significantly more expressive in the respondent role for feeling anger and slightly more expressive in this role for feeling happiness.

Analysis of the sex-of-subject by type-of-feeling by sex-of-best-friend triple interaction indicated that across subject role, males differentiated between male and female best-friend targets for feelings love, happiness, and anger but did not for sadness. Females made this differentiation only for feeling love. Males expressed significantly ($p < .01$) more love and slightly ($p < .05$) more happiness and anger to opposite-sex best friends than to same-sex best friends. Likewise, females expressed significantly ($p < .01$) more love to opposite-sex best friends than to same-sex best friends. Females also expressed slightly more anger to same-sex best friends than they did to opposite-sex best friends.

Finally, the behavioral performance test had one additional significant interaction. The sex-of-subject by type-of-feeling by subject-role triple inter-action appeared to be caused by the differential way males and females distin-guished between the respondent and initiator roles. Males were slightly more expressive of love, happiness, and sadness in the initiator role and slightly more expressive of anger in the respondent role, but the differences between roles were slight. Females were slightly more expressive of happiness and significantly ($p < .01$) more expressive of sadness in the initiator role. Females also were slightly more expressive of love and anger in the respondent role.

In summary, the interaction seems primarily caused by females' being significantly ($p < .01$) more expressive of sadness in the iniatiator role, while neither sex differentiated between the roles for any of the other feelings.

The general research questions dealt with specific types of feelings and those feelings that would be expressed the most across other situational fac-tors. For the three methods using the *Expression of Emotion Scale,* the order of expression of feelings was consistent, with happiness expressed across other situational factors the most followed by love, sadness, and anger. With the *Expression of Emotion Scale,* multiple comparison tests indicated that all of these feelings were significantly different from each other. With the *Expression of Emotion Scale* varied by target person and the *Expression of Emotion Scale* varied by size of group, multiple comparison tests indicated that all of the feelings were significantly ($p < .01$) different from each other except for love and sadness.

Feelings were expressed in a slightly different order of frequency in the self-report performance test and the behavioral performance test. With both of these methods across other situational factors, subjects expressed love the most, followed by happiness, sadness, and anger. Multiple comparison tests on the self-report performance test indicated that all feelings were signifi-cantly ($p < .01$) different from each other except for happiness and sadness. Multiple comparison tests on the behavioral performance test indicated from the expression of love was significantly ($p < .01$) greater from the expression of happiness, sadness, and anger. Expression of happiness was significantly ($p < .01$) greater than the expression of anger. Expression of happiness was not statistically different from expression of sadness, and expression of sad-ness was not statistically different from expression of anger.

Another general research question addressed the question of which target would be expressed to the most. The *Expression of Emotion Scale* varied by target person revealed a significant main effect for target person, $F(3,864) = 39.55$, $p < .000$, which indicated that across sex-of-subject and type-of-feeling, subject expressed the most feelings to female friends, then to mothers, then to male friends, and finally to fathers. Multiple comparison tests demonstrated that the female friend, mother, and male friend targets were all significantly ($p < .01$) different from the father target but were not significantly different from each other.

*Hypotheses Supported by Alternative Methods*

A final research question addressed the identification of those results that were consistent across methods. As seen in table 8–4, Hypothesis Two (across other situational factors, subjects will be more expressive in those situations requiring positive emotions than in those requiring negative emotions) was supported across all five methods. Hypothesis Five (a) (across other situational factors, and when looking at specific feelings: (a) females will be more expressive than males of love, happiness, and sadness) was supported by all five methods. Hypothesis Six (across other situational factors, subjects will be more expressive when in a small group than when in a large group) was supported. Finally, Hypothesis One (across other situational factors, females will be more expressive than males) was supported by four out of five methods.

In summary, females were generally more expressive than males—particularly of happiness, love, and sadness. Also, subjects were most expressive of positive feelings when in the initiator role and when alone with their opposite-sex best friend.

## Discussion

The primary purpose of this study was to examine the construct of male inexpressiveness in terms of the situational effects on sex differences in emotional expressiveness. The results can be summarized by the following statements: First, sex of subject, type of feeling, subject role, sex of best friend, target person, and size of group are all potent factors that influence verbal expressiveness as measured by self-report and behavioral methods. Second, significant statistical interactions suggest that expressiveness is a complex variable, sex-linked and situation-specific, and therefore cannot be viewed as a personality trait. Third, females are generally more expressive than males, especially when females are in the initiator role expressing positive feelings to their male best friend.

*Comparison of Findings to Previous Research*

Some of the major findings support previous research, while others do not. Those confirming previous findings are: (a) females express more feelings than males (Balkwell, Balswick, and Balkwell 1978; Balswick and Averett 1977; Highlen and Gillis 1978; Highlen and Johnston 1979); (b) positive feelings are more readily expressed than negative ones (Highlen and Gillis 1978; Highlen and Johnston 1979); (c) females are more expressive than males of love, happiness, and sadness (Balkwell, Balswick, and Balkwell

# Table 8–4
## Summary of Results

| Hypothesis | Expression of Emotion (EOE) Scale | EOE Scale Varied by Target | EOE Scale Varied by Size of Group | Self-Report Performance Test | Behavioral Performance Test |
|---|---|---|---|---|---|
| 1. | Supported | Supported | Not Supported | Supported | Supported |
| 2. | Supported | Supported | Supported | Supported | Supported |
| 3. | N/A | N/A | N/A | Not Supported | Not Supported |
| 4(a). | N/A | Not Supported | N/A | Not Supported | Not Supported |
| (b). | N/A | Not Supported | N/A | Not Supported | Not Supported |
| 5(a). | Supported | Supported | Supported | Supported | Supported |
| (b). | Not Supported | Not Supported | Not Supported | Not Supported | Not Supported |
| 6. | N/A | N/A | Supported | N/A | N/A |

N/A = Method did not address hypothesis.

*Hypotheses*

1. Across other situational factors, females will be more expressive than males.

2. Across other situational factors, subjects will be more expressive in situations requiring positive emotions than in those requiring negative emotions.

3. Across other situational factors, subjects will be more expressive in the respondent role than in the initiator role.

4. Across other situational factors, subjects will be: (a) more expressive to female rather than male best friends and (b) more expressive to same-sex rather than opposite-sex best friends.

5. Across other situational factors, and when looking at specific feelings: (a) females will be more expressive than males of love, happiness and sadness, and (b) males will be more expressive than females of anger.

6. Across other situational factors, subjects will be more expressive alone with a person than in a small group, and more expressive in a small group than in a large group.

1978; Balswick and Averett 1977); and (d) subjects are more expressive alone with the target person than in a group (Rosenfeld, Civikly, and Herron 1979). Furthermore, expressiveness as measured by self-report and behavioral methods was most significantly affected by the type-of-feeling variable, which supported previous research (Highlen and Gillis 1978; Highlen and Johnston 1979). This was true whether the four feelings were considered separately or were combined into positive and negative feelings.

Results concerning the variables of subject role and sex of best friend are not consistent with results from previous research. In this study, subjects were more expressive in the initiator role than in the respondent role. They also were more expressive to their opposite-sex best friend than to their same-sex best friend. Both of these findings oppose predictions based on previous research (Highlen and Gillis 1978; Highlen and Johnston 1979). Differences in methodology between this and previous studies may explain the discrepancies. Although this study was patterned after one by Highlen and Gillis (1978), there were several important improvements, first, in assessment of expressiveness. Highlen and Gillis had subjects listen to and verbally respond to eight stimulus situations. Responses were audiotaped and later rated using a three-point scale. In this study, the self-report performance test required subjects to write their responses to sixteen stimulus situations; the behavioral performance test required subjects to respond on videotape to the same sixteen situations with a male or female actor playing the role of their best male or female friend. Both performance tests were later rated using a six-point scale. The differences between the two studies (the number of situations used, how the situations were presented, how subjects responded, and how subjects' responses were recorded and scored) may have contributed to the different findings. In addition, while the situations are similar, both having been adapted from the same larger set of situations (Highlen 1976), they do not contain the exact same subset of situations. Subset differences include changes in the wording of several of the original situations to make them more appropriate to this study and the addition of a new situation designed to elicit the feeling of sadness. It is impossible within the scope of this study to tell exactly how any of these differences might have affected the results.

Specifically, discrepancies in the sex-of-best-friend variable is most likely caused by the difference in the number of situations used for each study. Highlen and Gillis used eight, varied by type of feeling, subject role, and sex of best friend. To compare same-sex and opposite-sex expressiveness, they had to equate different situations requiring the expression of different feelings. For example, to consider the sex-of-best-friend variable, a situation requiring a negative response (sadness) to a *male* best friend had to be compared to another situation requiring a negative response (anger) to a *female* best friend. This was necessary because Highlen and Gillis only considered feelings as either positive or negative. This analysis may be problematic since it was assumed these different situations elecit similar negative feelings. Further, this procedure did not allow for a direct comparison between expression of the same emotion to same- and opposite-sex best friends.

In our study we tried to overcome these problems by (a) using eight situations adapted from Highlen (1976) to consider four types of feeling (happiness, love, sadness, and anger) rather than a global category of positive or negative, and (b) repeating each of the eight situations twice, once for the male best friend and once for the female best friend, to allow for a direct comparison between expressiveness to same- and opposite-sex best friends. There is little doubt these changes were substantial enough to produce differences in the results. In fact, when analyses used positive feelings (happiness and love) and negative feelings (sadness and anger), it was evident there was an advantage in considering each feeling separately. Specifically, direct comparisons between the two approaches for the self-report and behavioral performance tests revealed that combining the four feelings into positive and negative feelings eliminated significant sex-of-subject by type-of-feeling and type-of-feeling by subject-role interactions. In other words, combining the feelings apparently oversimplifies the effect of the type-of-feeling variable on expressiveness when this variable is considered by itself or with other situational variables.

Contrary to prediction, the results of our study indicated that subjects were more expressive in the initiator role than they were in the respondent role. This finding may also be caused by methodological differences (described previously) between this and previous studies. In addition, the previous findings concerning the subject-role variable, upon which the prediction was made, have not been consistent. Highlen and Gillis (1978) did not find the predicted effects for subject role, finding subjects being slightly more expressive in the initiator role instead. Highlen and Gillis pointed out that the effect of subject role on self-disclosure had been studied only once previously (Weigel, Weigel, and Chadwick 1969), finding that subjects were willing to disclose in greater depth when they were responders rather than initiators. They attributed their null findings to the simulated nature of their study and to the fact that Weigel et al. (1969) examined general self-disclosure, while they focused only on affective self-disclosure. In a subsequent study using similar procedures, however, Highlen and Johnston (1979) found a significant main effect for subject role: subjects were more expressive to acquaintances when in the respondent role. The prediction for our study that subjects would be more expressive in the respondent role than in the initiator role was made after considering all three of these studies. Although it did not seem to be an especially consistent finding or certain expectation, it did have intuitive appeal.

In summary, the discrepancy in the findings between this study and previous ones concerning the subject role variable would seem to be due not only to the methodological differences between the various studies, but also to the apparent inconsistency of the previous findings, which suggests that the effect of the subject role on expressiveness may not be clear or consistent. In fact, the findings of this study concerning subject role were not even consistent across the self-report and the behavioral performance tests. The main effect for subject role was significant using the self-report performance test, with subjects more expressive in the initiator role, while there was only a slight trend in this direction using the behavioral performance test. Apparently subject role is not a good variable to use because it is so highly sensitive to methodological and situational influences. It is also possible that the distinction between subject roles (initiator and respondent) is sufficiently blurred using the procedures of this study to lead to spurious results. It is important to note this study found a significant subject role effect when subjects were asked to imagine they were either initiating or responding with feeling, but no significant effect was found when subjects *actually* initiated or responded with feeling. This seems to suggest that any subject-role effect is more a result of methodological and situational influences than of the subject's discrimination between the two roles.

The intimacy level at the best-friend level for the performance tests is another source of methodological confusion that, no doubt, affected the results in this study. Highlen and Johnston (1979) attributed great importance to intimacy level. They believed that in more intimate relationships (e.g., best-friend target), the sex of the target is an important factor, whereas in less intimate relationships (e.g., acquaintance target), subject role assumes prominence. This is how Highlen and Johnston explained the discrepancies in the findings between their study (significant subject-role effect and no significant sex-of-target effect) and the Highlen and Gillis (1978) study (significant sex-of-target effect and no significant subject-role effect). This explanation did not hold up with our study, however, since, at least with the self-report performance test, there were significant main effects for both the subject-role and the sex-of-best-friend variables.

Apparently more than just intimacy level affects these variables. Another explanation is the difficulty in effecting actual intimacy. For example, there are questions concerning the intimacy level that subjects attributed to this study's targets. Although subjects were requested to imagine they were actually in the described situations and talking to their male or female friend, there was some anecdotal information suggesting they might have had difficulty doing this. Several reported that the situations were unrealistic for their best friends. Others reported that statements made by best-friend actors would not have been said by their actual best friends. Several subjects said they found it difficult to imagine the actors as their best friends. It may have been, then, that subjects did not consistently consider the target of the expression to be their best friend; this would also have affected the results and, no doubt, contributed to the discrepancies between study results.

### Complex Nature of Emotional Expressiveness

Although it is important and necessary to try to explain the discrepancies between the study findings, the methodological dissimilarities limit the possibility of simple, direct, and meaningful explanations for incongruent results. Perhaps it is advantageous to focus instead on the consistent findings.

The consistent findings across approaches used in this and other studies appear strong and durable and seem to offer the most useful information on the effects of situational factors on emotional expressiveness. The strongest and most consistent findings have been, (a) females are more emotionally expressive than males and (b) subjects are more expressive of positive feelings than of negative feelings.

This study supports previous findings that males are less emotionally expressive than females and supports the concept of the inexpressive male. It has been said that the relationship between sex and self-disclosure is complex (Archer 1979; Rosenfeld, Civikly, and Herron 1979). The same could also be said for emotional expressiveness. In other words, it is oversimplifying matters to say only that males are less expressive. We must also consider situational influences. Evidence of the complexity of sex differences in emotional expressiveness can be seen in the numerous significant interactions that were found between sex-of-subject and the situational factors. A significant sex-of-subject by type-of-feeling interaction was a frequent finding, appearing in four out of five methodological approaches used in this study. This indicated that the type of feeling must be considered in exploring sex differences in emotional expressiveness. These interactions were caused primarily in anger, in which little or no sex differences or between males' and females' expressiveness scores were obtained. There might well be other emotions (not considered in this study) of which males and females are equally expressive or of which males are more expressive.

This study also found that the nature of the target person affects sex differences in expressiveness. There were significant sex-of-subject by target-person and sex-of-subject by type-of-feeling by target-person interactions. With both types, the female-friend target was salient, since females were more expressive than males to the mother, father, and male-friend targets but not to the female-friend target. Again, there might well be targets not considered in this study to whom males and females are equally expressive or even to whom males are more expressive. An example of the way target-person and type-of-feeling interacted to affect sex differences is seen in this study in that males were more expressive of love to the female-friend target than females were. This is one example of a situation in which sexual politics may have triggered the males' attempts to establish close affectional ties with females. In other words, perhaps males learn that expressing positive feelings to females is the appropriate way to gain eventual power in relationships (cf. Sattel 1976). Or perhaps homophobia prevents females from expressing too much love and affection to their same-sex best friend (cf. Weinberg 1972). At the very least, it is more socially appropriate for females to express love and affection to males than to other females.

Size of group is another variable that interacts with sex-of-subject to affect expressiveness. As the size of the group increased, the difference between male and female expressiveness decreased. In fact, there were no significant differences between male and female expressiveness scores in the small group and large group conditions. Male expressiveness is less affected by size of group probably because they are less expressive generally and less sensitive to situational influences. The additional finding of a significant sex-of-subject by type-of-feeling by size-of-group triple interaction is another example of the complex way that size of group alone and in combination with type of feeling affects sex differences in the expression of emotion. Finally, the numerous significant interactions that were found using the self-report and behavioral performance tests are further evidence of the complexity of sex differences in the expression of emotion. These interactions clearly indicate that subject role, type of feeling, and sex of best friend all affect sex differences in expressiveness.

The number of situational variables we considered were by necessity limited; there are others that, no doubt, affect sex differences in expressiveness and should be studied. Additional research is needed to clarify the complex relationships between these situational variables. This study has, however, supported the belief that a concept like expressiveness cannot be studied as though it were a personality trait (Archer 1979; Chelune 1979). There can be no doubt that expressiveness is a complex human behavior multiply determined through the interaction of person and situational variables.

The second consistent finding in the literature is that positive feelings are more readily expressed than negative feelings. This study supports that generalization but also suggests it is an oversimplification. This study provided evidence that there is more to be learned about the effect of the type-of-feeling variable on emotional expressiveness. The significant interactions found between type-of-feeling and other variables when the four feelings were considered separately were not found when summarized as positive or negative. This suggests the four feelings are operating in different ways than merely positive and negative. Specifically, anger and sadness operate very differently from each other, alone and with other variables. When combined to create negative feelings, important information is missed about the different way in which subjects express these feelings.

While sadness and anger are clearly both negative feelings, combining them is probably a mistake because the results indicate subjects' expressions of the two feelings are very different. It would make even more sense from this study to combine happiness, love, and sadness and to let anger stand alone, because the difference between anger and the other three feelings was a major part of the explanation for most of the significant interactions between the type-of-feeling variable and other variables. For example, anger was the only feeling with which there were not consistent sex differences, and anger was the only feeling with which subjects were more expressive in the respondent role than in the initiator role. Also, across four of five methods and across other situational factors, anger was expressed significantly less than the other three feelings. The one exception was in the behavioral performance test, where sadness and anger were not significantly different (although anger was expressed the least across other situational factors).

In summary, this study supports the necessity of considering specific feelings rather than groups of feelings when exploring the effects of type of feeling on emotional expressiveness. Also, the number of feelings should be expanded in future research to provide more information on this topic. Certainly, one important feeling that was not included in this study is fear. No doubt it would have changed the results.

## Implications of Findings

This study had implications not only for future research on sex differences in emotional expressiveness but also for counselors interested in increasing their clients' expressiveness. Research has indicated that many men desire to be more expressive and that there are intrapersonal and interpersonal problems associated with inexpressiveness (Balswick 1982b; Phillips 1978). Knowledge about situations that facilitate or inhibit emotional expressiveness is critical for designing treatment programs to help men become more expressive. Counselors also can use this study's assessment procedures to identify inexpressive clients and to evaluate the efficacy of treatment programs (Dosser 1982).

This study is further evidence of the need for treatment programs to increase expressiveness, particularly if subjects' expressiveness scores are interpreted within the context of the procedures and criteria used to measure expressiveness. In the self-report performance test, the highest possible score for sex of subject was eighty; however, the average female and male scores were 53.28 and 44.32, respectively. The average female and male scores were 57.76 and 51.36, respectively, out of a possible score of eighty for sex of subject on the behavioral performance test. This appears to be a low level of expressiveness for subjects. Remember that the procedures of the study included explicit and repeated instructions for subjects to be as expressive as they could, to elicit subjects' maximal performance. Maximal performance under conditions designed to elicit it to the greatest degree has been distinguished from typical performance on one's usual or average behavior (Klein and Willerman 1979). Research has demonstrated that procedures that elicit maximal performance can lead to greater homogeneity in subjects' motivational level and create an experimental context within which socially undesirable or inappropriate behaviors can be made more socially desirable, consequently diminishing sex-role stereotypes (Klein and Willerman 1979). If efforts were successful to elicit subjects' maximal performance, the results are even more indicative of expressiveness difficulties for this sample, at least when compared to the criteria used to assess expressiveness in this study. Subjects' relative inexpressiveness suggests that perhaps they did not know how to express their feelings in appropriate ways. This possible behavioral deficit suggests the need for further research to confirm the relative inexpressiveness of this population of university students and to determine whether inexpressiveness is a problem intrapersonally or interpersonally for them.

## Summary

The primary objective of this study was to examine emotional expressiveness more closely by exploring how it is affected by sex of subject and these situational variables: target person, size of group, type of feeling, subject role, and sex of best friend. The results indicated that sex of subject and the situational factors, separately and in combination, were potent factors affecting expressiveness. Although it was found that females are generally more expressive than males, the results support the belief that sex differences in emotional expressiveness are complex and influenced by situational factors. In other words, this study supports the concept of the inexpressive male and the belief that inexpression should not be treated as though it were simply a personality trait. This study also contained several methodological improvements over previous research, thus enhancing the understanding of sex differences and situational factors in emotional expressiveness. Finally, the study demonstrated the usefulness of the self-report and behavioral assessment procedures to assess expressiveness.

# 9
# Marriage

Although much has been written concerning communication in marriage, little empirical analysis has been directed toward emotional expressiveness in marriage. What has been done is couched in terms of the relationship between affective self-disclosure and marital adjustment. Therefore, to be consistent with the reported literature, the term "affective self-disclosure" will be used in this and the following chapter interchangeably with the term "emotional expressiveness."

## Literature Review and Theory

The data in this chapter most directly test propositions nine and ten, proposed in chapter 3. Proposition nine states: "Inexpressiveness results in males experiencing strain in both their paid work and family roles." Proposition nine incorporates a temporal perspective into the source of this role strain: "Changing expectations of expressiveness has caused males to experience sex role strain." A primary life role to married men is husband. In the past, when the dominant form of marriage could be characterized as institutionally oriented, emotional expressiveness was not expected in marriage. In the change toward a companionship-type marriage, open and honest sharing of feelings has come to be expected. In this new definition of marriage, and resultant marital role expectation, inexpressiveness probably will cause role strain.

Jourard (1971) suggested that a primary function of marriage is to serve the individual's need to reveal his or her private self to another person. In an earlier study of self-disclosure to various target persons, Jourard and Lasakow (1958) reported that the most consistent intimate disclosure occurs in

Some of the findings reported in this chapter appeared in b. Davidson, 1980. *The Relations Between Partners' Levels of Affective Self-Disclosure and Marital Adjustment,* unpublished doctoral dissertation, University of Georgia.

marriage. More recent research also consistently identifies marriage as the setting in which the most intimate disclosure occurs, with the greater levels of positive disclosure positively related to marital satisfaction (Burke, Weir, and Harrison 1976; Chelune, Waring, Vost, and Sultan 1984; Hansen and Schuldt 1984; Hendrick 1981; Jorgensen and Gaudy 1980; Pascoe 1981; Schumm, Barnes, Bollman, Jurick, and Bregaighis 1986; Thomas Albrecht, and White 1984). Many of these studies further indicate that husbands disclose less than wives (Burke et al. 1976; Notarius and Johnson 1982; Levinger and Senn 1967; Pascoe 1981). In general, positive self-disclosure enhances satisfaction of marriage partners.

In attempting to play their role as husband, many men find it contradictory and inconsistent, succinctly stated in proposition two of the SRS theory of male inexpressiveness (see chapter 3): "Due to the current clash between the traditional and modern male role, male inexpressiveness is contradictory and inconsistent." In trying to clarify the inconsistencies, we will use equity theory.

The most direct test of the relationship between expressiveness and marital adjustment was based on a sample of ninety-six Colombian couples and 106 U.S. couples. Using the Emotional Expressiveness Scale (see chapter 5) and the Dyadic Adjustment Scale (Spanier 1976), Ingoldsby (1979) found that emotional expressiveness correlated positively with marital adjustment for the U.S. sample but not for the Colombian; that similarity in the expressiveness level between spouses correlated positively with marital adjustment for the Colombians; and that similarity in the level of expressiveness between spouses correlated positively with marital adjustment for the Colombian sample but not for the U.S. sample. Ingoldsby believes the differences are in the styles of marriage in the two countries. He argues that in a modern U.S.-type companionship marriage, a high level of expressiveness is conducive to good marital adjustment. In a culture (such as Colombia's) that stresses a traditional marriage and agreement between spouses, the key to good marital adjustment is the spouses' similarity to each other in their levels of emotional expressiveness, be it high, medium, or low.

As an offspring of social exchange theory, equity theory contains a refinement potentially important for understanding affective exchanges in marriage. Equity theory predicts that "when individuals find themselves participating in inequitable relationships, they will become distressed. The more inequitable the relationships, the more distressed individuals will feel" (Walster, Walster, and Berscheid 1978, 6). Even more important for our purposes is the implication that individuals may experience distress in relationships when they are either the overrewarded beneficiaries of inequity or the deprived victims of inequity. Thus, we must not only measure the absolute levels of self-disclosure but also assess the amount of self-disclosure. Equity theory forces us to examine overrewarded situations as well and to predict that overbenefited persons will be less satisfied in their marriages than those in an emotionally equal relationship.

A further refinement in equity theory is the prediction that "individuals who discover they are in inequitable relationships will attempt to eliminate their distress by restoring equity. The greater the inequity that exists, the more distress they will feel, and the harder they will try to restore equity" (Walster, Walster, and Berscheid 1978, 6).

There are only limited data on how people in inequitable intimate relationships attempt to restore equity. Walster, Traupman, and Walster (1978) found that underbenefited spouses were the most likely and quickest to engage in extramarital sexual activity. By actually changing the circumstances of the relationship, an individual may attempt to restore equity. When this is not feasible because of other impediments, participants probably will attempt to restore the "psychological" equity of the relationship (Walster, Walster, and Berscheid 1978, 183). Ways to do that range from simple denial of the inequity to an outright justification that the imbalance is deserved.

## Hypotheses and Methodology

Hypothesis One. For married individuals, the degree to which one's spouse indicates affective self-disclosure is positively related to one's reported marital adjustment.

Hypothesis Two. For married individuals, there is a positive relationship between the amount of affective self-disclosure that one perceives from the spouse and one's reported marital adjustment.

Hypothesis Three. Among married couples, as the difference between spouses in affective self-disclosure increases, marital adjustment decreases.

Hypothesis Four. For married individuals, as the differences between what one indicates affective self-discloser to the spouse is and what one perceives the spouse to discloser increases, one's reported marital adjustment will decrease.

Hypothesis Five. Among individuals who indicate high levels of marital adjustment: (a) individuals who indicate disclosing more to their spouses than their spouses indicate disclosing to them (underbenefited) will overestimate what their spouse indicate disclosing; and (b) individuals who indicate disclosing less to their spouses than their spouses indicate disclosing to them (overbenefited) will underestimate what their spouses indicate disclosing.

### Subjects

Two hundred sixty-six sets of questionnaires were distributed to married couples in the University Married Housing complexes of a large Southeastern university. Husbands and wives filled out questionnaires separately without discussing answers. One hundred sixty-two sets of the questionnaires (61 percent) were returned.

Demographic characteristics of this sample include: mean age of husbands (24.9), mean age of wives (23.7), mean number of years married (2.9), mean years of husband's education (16.6), mean years of wife's education (15.2), mean percentage of husband's contribution to total family income (51.9), and mean percentage of wife's contribution of total family income (40.4).

*Questionnaire and Measurements*

The two major measuring instruments upon which this study is based are the Expression of Feeling Scale for Couples (EFSC) and the Dyadic Adjustment Scale (DAS). The EFSC is presented and explained in Chapter Six. We would only note here that factor analysis of the scale gives us confidence in considering the self-disclosure of the specific emotions of love, happiness, anger, and sadness. The Dyadic Adjustment Scale (Spanier 1976) consists of thirty-two items that assess the quality of marital dyads.

The definition of variables which are measured within the EFSC are defined as follows: Output is defined as the disclosure an individual indicates giving to the spouse. Discrepancy in disclosure between spouses is defined as the difference in the output scores as indicated by both partners. This score is reported for couples and consists of the wife's output score minus the husband's output score. Input is defined as that disclosure which an individual perceives receiving from the spouse. An individual's perceived discrepancy in disclosure is defined as the difference between what one indicated disclosing to the spouse and what one perceived receiving from the spouse. Operationally defined for each individual, this was their output score minus their input score. A congruency estimate score of self-disclosure refers to the underestimate or overestimate an individual exhibits in describing how much disclosure was received from the spouse as compared to what the spouse indicated. For example, a congruency score for a husband was what his wife indicated disclosing to him minus what he indicated receiving. A negative congruency score indicates an overestimate of that disclosure by the individual while a positive score indicates an underestimate.

## Results and Discussion

*Hypothesis One*

The data in table 9–1 supports Hypothesis One, as for both husbands and wives significant positive relationships existed between the amount of love,

Table 9–1

Correlations between Partner's Affective Self-Disclosure Output and One's Dyadic Adjustment Score

| Dyadic Adjustment Scores | Partner's Disclosure Output | | | | |
|---|---|---|---|---|---|
| | Total | Love | Happiness | Anger | Sadness |
| Husbands | .18* | .19* | .25*** | −.01 | .14* |
| | (141) | (152) | (150) | (144) | (152) |
| Wives | .29*** | .37*** | .27*** | .03 | .19** |
| | (139) | (153) | (152) | (140) | (153) |

Note: Numbers in parentheses indicate the number of subjects used to compute correlations.

*$p < .05$

**$p < .008$

***$p < .001$

happiness, and sadness disclosure that one's spouse indicated disclosing and one's marital adjustment. In addition, this relationship was also significant for total disclosure. No relationship emerged between one's spouse's output of anger disclosure and one's marital adjustment, a finding that fits well with Levinger and Senn's (1967) account that the disclosure of pleasant feelings is more related to marital satisfaction than is the disclosure of unpleasant feelings.

Because it has been theorized that wives would be more concerned with receiving love disclosure than would husbands (see Balswick 1970; Balswick and Peek 1971), the correlations obtained for husbands and wives on the love output dimension were tested for significant differences. The correlations of .19 for husbands and .37 for wives were significantly different, $(z = 1.70, p < .0)$. This difference indicates that although it is significant for both spouses, the output of husbands' love disclosure appears more important for wives' marital adjustment than does the output of wives' love disclosure for husbands' marital adjustment.

Overall, the testing of Hypothesis One has provided strong support for viewing the actual exchange of affective disclosure as a reward. In line with the studies mentioned previously (Altman and Taylor 1973; Fitzgerald 1963; Halverson and Shore 1969; Worthy, Gary and Kahn 1969), the reception of affective self-disclosure appears to have a rewarding aspect that probably is related to an individual's adjustment within the marital dyad.

## Hypothesis Two

The data in table 9–2 support Hypothesis Two. For both husbands and wives, significant relationships existed between the amount of disclosure that

Table 9–2
Correlations between Perceived Affective Self-Disclosure and Dyadic Adjustment Scores

| Dyadic Adjustment Scores | Perceived Disclosure Input | | | | |
|---|---|---|---|---|---|
| | Total | Love | Happiness | Anger | Sadness |
| Total Sample | .27**** | .41**** | .32**** | −.03 | .19**** |
| | (285) | (307) | (301) | (291) | (305) |
| Husbands | .13 | .33**** | .23*** | −.20** | .06 |
| | (142) | (153) | (151) | (143) | (153) |
| Wives | .40**** | .48**** | .41**** | .14* | .33**** |
| | (143) | (154) | (150) | (148) | (152) |

Note: Numbers in parentheses indicate the number of subjects used to compute correlations.
*$p < .05$
**$p < .007$
***$p < .002$
****$p < .001$

one perceived receiving from one's spouse and one's marital adjustment. For both husbands and wives it can be seen that the perception of love and happiness input disclosure is positively related to marital adjustment. For husbands, however, the perception of anger input is negatively related to marital adjustment while the reverse is true for wives. This finding suggests that, for husbands, wives' disclosure of anger is dysfunctional for marital adjustment, while for wives the perception of husbands' disclosure of anger is functional. This differential finding is congruent with societal expectations concerning expressions of anger for the sexes. For women, the expectation is that their husbands will share their feelings of anger. For men, the expectation is that if their wives are angry, they should keep it to themselves. These correlations for anger were tested for significant differences. The correlations of −.20 for husbands and .14 for wives were significantly different, ($z = 2.95, p < .002$).

Perceived sadness input was related to wives' adjustment, suggesting that the more wives tended to perceive their husbands disclosing sadness, the greater was their marital adjustment. No relationship was obtained for husbands. For wives, it appears that the perception of receiving emotional disclosure of any kind is related to adjustment. For husbands, perceived anger input deviates from a prescribed norm and perceived sadness input bears no relation. It appears to affect husbands little whether they perceive wives disclosing sadness or not.

When compared to the findings of Hypothesis One, some interesting observations bear note. For husbands, as stated, perceived anger input from wives was inversely related to marital adjustment. From Hypothesis One, wives' stated outputs of anger were not related to husbands' adjustment. When comparing these findings from Hypothesis One and Two it becomes increasingly clear that the perceptions of one's spouse's affective disclosure frequently do not match what one's spouse perceives he or she is disclosing. In this case husbands do not always perceive the display of anger from their wives that matches what their wives say they show. Similarly, wives' perceptions of their own disclosure of anger were not related to their husbands' marital adjustment, but husbands' perceptions of their wives' disclosure of anger was a fairly strong indicator of husbands' adjustment.

As with Hypothesis One, the strongest relationships were observed between love and happiness disclosure and marital adjustment. When comparing the correlations from tables 9–1 and 9–2, we see that the perceived input correlations yield stronger predictors of adjustment. The relationship between the input one perceived and one's marital adjustment was stronger than the relationship between one's spouse's perceived output and one's marital adjustment. Wives' perceptions of love disclosure input were more strongly correlated with their marital adjustment than husbands' perceptions of love disclosure input were with their marital adjustment.

Overall, Hypothesis Two supports the idea that perceptions of receiving affective self-disclosure from one's spouse are rewarding and contributes to marital adjustment. Two exceptions to this generalization were the negative relationship observed between husbands' perceptions of wives' anger self-disclosure and husbands' marital adjustment, and the lack of a significant relationship between husbands' perceptions of wives' sadness self-disclosure and husbands' marital adjustment. In accord with equity theory, the perception of receiving rewards is seen as being a greater factor in determining reward value than the actual availability of such rewards. Although Hypothesis One confirmed the rewarding potential of receiving affective self-disclosure, Hypothesis Two confirmed that the perception of receiving such disclosure is more strongly related to marital adjustment.

*Hypothesis Three*

Hypothesis Three stated that as the differences between spouses in affective self-disclosure increase, marital adjustment decreases. For husbands and wives, few linear relations existed between the discrepancies in spouses' outputs and marital adjustment (table 9–3). Only two correlations were significant: love for husbands and happiness for wives. The significance of these can be understood by examining the separate correlations for overbenefited and underbenefited individuals. Overbenefited individuals were defined as those whose output scores indicated that they received greater or equal disclosure from their partners. Underbenefited individuals were defined as those who received less or equal disclosure from their partners. When examined in this way, it can be seen that for husbands who were overbenefited in love and happiness, the greater the overbenefiting, the less their marital adjustment. No such comparable relation emerged for the underbenefited husbands.

Similar results were obtained for overbenefited wives. Being overbenefited in love and happiness disclosure was related to decrements in marital adjustment. In addition, being underbenefited in love disclosure was inversely related to marital adjustment. The lack of relation for underbenefited husbands seems puzzling. That these individuals may not have perceived themselves as being underbenefited is an issue to be addressed in the analysis of Hypothesis Four.

The strongest findings summarized in table 9–3 concern the relationships between the discrepancies in love outputs and marital adjustment. With love disclosure the most rewarding of these four subscales of emotion, it follows that love disclosure would be the most likely area where an imbalance in exchange would be related to a decrease in levels of marital adjustment. Since the reception of love disclosure does possess a rewarding value, the correla-

Table 9–3
**Correlations between the Difference in Husband-Wife Output Scores and Dyadic Adjustment Scores**

| Dyadic Adjustment Scores | Differences in Outputs on Type of Disclosure | | | | |
| | Total | Love | Happiness | Anger | Sadness |
|---|---|---|---|---|---|
| Husbands | .12 | .20** | .04 | .05 | .06 |
| | (134) | (151) | (150) | (137) | (152) |
| Husbands overbenefited[a] | .20* | .28**** | .19* | .07 | −.01 |
| | (94) | (110) | (103) | (99) | (116) |
| Husbands underbenefited | −.01 | .01 | −.12 | .18 | .07 |
| | (46) | (80) | (82) | (55) | (57) |
| Wives | .07 | .03 | .15* | .06 | .11 |
| | (132) | (153) | (151) | (134) | (152) |
| Wives overbenefited[a] | .04 | .23* | .30*** | −.19 | −.08 |
| | (44) | (79) | (81) | (54) | (56) |
| Wives underbenefited | .07 | −.18* | −.08 | .16 | .18* |
| | (93) | (112) | (106) | (96) | (117) |

*Note:* Numbers in parentheses indicate the number of subjects used to compute correlations.
*$p < .03$
**$p < .006$
***$p < .003$
****$p < .001$
[a]For overbenefited individuals a positive correlation represents that the greater the difference in output scores is in one's favor, the less is one's marital adjustment.

tions between the discrepancies in love outputs and marital adjustment were computed with received love output partialed out to control for any effects that may be caused by the levels of love received. In other words, could the relations observed for the underbenefited and overbenefited individuals be spurious and due to the absolute levels of love disclosure received? For husbands, wives' levels of love disclosure were controlled and for wives, husbands' levels of love disclosure output were controlled. The new correlations followed the same pattern. The greater the extent of husbands being overbenefited and of wives being underbenefited or overbenefited, the less the marital adjustment as reported by these individuals. The respective correlations are .40, −.33, and .30, all significant at the $p < .001$ level.

The discrepancy in love disclosure outputs suggested the possibility of a curvilinear trend. To test for curvilinearity, an absolute value transformation was performed on the discrepancy scores and these transformed scores were correlated with marital adjustment. This permitted a test for absolute discrepancy in disclosure outputs being related to marital adjustment. As table 9–4 reveals, absolute discrepancies in love disclosure outputs were related to dyadic adjustment scores.

Overall, support was obtained for Hypothesis Three on love disclosure. As predicted within an equity theory context, discrepancies in love disclosure outputs were related to a decrement in marital adjustment. Of most interest in these findings is that being "overbenefited" in love disclosure is related to distress in one's relationship. This was found for both husbands and wives.

Table 9–4
Correlations between the Absolute Values of the Differences in Husband-Wife Output Scores and Dyadic Adjustment Scores

| Dyadic Adjustment Scores | Absolute Values of Differences in Spouses' Outputs on Type of Disclosure | | | | |
|---|---|---|---|---|---|
| | Total | Love | Happiness | Anger | Sadness |
| Husbands | −.14* | −.21***** | −.13ᵃ | .03 | −.02 |
| | (134) | (151) | (150) | (137) | (152) |
| Wives | .07 | −.17*** | −.13ᵃ | .20**** | .15** |
| | (132) | (153) | (151) | (134) | (152) |

Note: Numbers in parentheses indicate the number of subjects used to compute correlations.
*$p < .05$
**$p < .04$
***$p < .02$
****$p < .01$
*****$p < .005$
ᵃFor husbands and wives the correlations for happiness approached significance $p$ .06.

A strict social exchange framework would predict that the more love affective self-disclosure one receives, the more rewarded one would feel. The present findings necessitate a consideration of the amount of disclosure a spouse receives relative to what he/she provides. First, it is easy to see this relation holding for an underbenefited individual. Less apparent, but still important, is that this relation also holds for overbenefited individuals. These findings appear to complement and extend those of Daher and Banikiotes (1976), who observed that in addition to the reception of self-disclosure being a reward, the exchange of self-disclosure at similar levels of intimacy also is a reward. Further, there is support for the notion that well-adjusted couples may not be adequately characterized strictly by high levels of mutual self-disclosure but rather by similar levels of affective self-disclosure exchange.

*Hypothesis Four*

Hypothesis Four is central to an equity theory analysis of the perceived self-disclosure between marriage partners. This hypothesis differs from Hypothesis Three in that discrepancies in affective exchange were defined by each partner rather than by reported differences between partners. This analysis allowed for the possibility that individuals could perceive a discrepancy where none existed objectively. Coversely, a discrepancy could have existed objectively but not be perceived by individual partners.

The data in table 9–5 are for the total sample and separately for husbands and wives. It can be seen that positive relationships exist for the total sample and husbands between dyadic adjustment and perceived discrepancy in the total disclosure score as well as for anger and sadness disclosure.

**Table 9–5**
**Correlations between the Perceived Discrepancy in Affective Self-Disclosure and Dyadic Adjustment Scores for Total Sample, Husbands, and Wives**

| Dyadic Adjustment Scores | Perceived Discrepancies in Disclosure (Output-Input) | | | | |
|---|---|---|---|---|---|
| | *Total* | *Love* | *Happiness* | *Anger* | *Sadness* |
| Total Sample | .13* | .01 | .05 | .16** | .11* |
| | (279) | (306) | (301) | (285) | (304) |
| Husbands | .21** | .08 | 0.8 | .22** | .16* |
| | (141) | (153) | (151) | (142) | (153) |
| Wives | −.04 | −.08 | −.02 | .04 | −.05 |
| | (138) | (154) | (150) | (143) | (151) |

*Note:* Numbers in parentheses indicate the number of subjects used to compute correlations.
*$p < .04$
**$p < .007$

Examination of the table reveals that these relationships are entirely generated by husbands' relations for anger and sadness. The more husbands perceived their wives to self-disclose anger and sadness relative to themselves, the less adjusted they appeared to be in their marriage. To assert, however, that being overbenefited in anger and sadness disclosure causes distress tells us little concerning the equity of the relationship. Without further analysis, these results suggest only that as wives disclose more anger and sadness than do their husbands, their husbands' marital adjustment decreases. The insignificant relations between perceived discrepancies in love and happiness disclosure and dyadic adjustment scores suggested that a separate analysis for underbenefited and overbenefited spouses was needed. Hypothesis Four stated that for both underbenefited and overbenefited groups correlations would be obtained between the degree to which spouses were under- or overbenefited and marital adjustment. Since a significant negative correlation was expected for the underbenefited group and a significant positive correlation was expected for the overbenefited group, when both groups were combined it was expected that the opposing correlations would cancel out each other.

An examination of table 9–6 reveals that the data fit this expectation. For underbenefited individuals the extent of perceiving oneself as underbenefited in total disclosure as well as love, happiness, and sadness disclosure was inversely related to marital adjustment. For the overbenefited, the extent of perceiving oneself as being overbenefited in total disclosure as well as love, happiness, anger, and sadness disclosure was inversely related to marital adjustment. Data analyzed separately for husbands and wives generally replicate the findings based on the total sample.

With the exception of husbands who perceived themselves as underbenefited in anger disclosure, these relations confirmed the predictions derived from equity theory. Husbands who perceived themselves as underbenefited in anger disclosure were not distressed by this discrepancy, possibly because an imbalance of this sort fits with societal norms for anger self-disclosure in wives.

An examination of table 9–6 reveals curvilinear relationships between perceived discrepancy in self-disclosure (output-input) and marital adjustment. When this perceived discrepancy was positive, persons considered themselves underbenefited; when the discrepancy was negative, persons considered themselves overbenefited. The data in table 9–6 suggest that regardless of the direction of the discrepancy, the greater the discrepancy, the lower the marital adjustment. To test for curvilinearity, an absolute value transformation was performed on the perceived discrepancy in disclosure scores. An examination of table 9–7 provides support for curvilinearity. With the exception of the perceived discrepancy in anger self-disclosure for wives (which was in the predicted direction), all correlations between the absolute values of the perceived discrepancies in affective self-disclosure were significantly

## Table 9–6
## Correlations between the Perceived Discrepancy in Affective Self-Disclosure and Dyadic Adjustment Scores for Underbenefited and Overbenefited Spouses

| Dyadic Adjustment Scores | Perceived Discrepancies in Disclosure (Output-Input) | | | | |
|---|---|---|---|---|---|
| | Total | Love | Happiness | Anger | Sadness |
| Underbenefited | −.20*** | −.34**** | −.18*** | −.07 | −.12* |
| | (184) | (222) | (234) | (185) | (211) |
| Overbenefited[a] | .40**** | .43**** | .26**** | .29**** | .28**** |
| | (129) | (191) | (202) | (157) | (170) |
| Underbenefited husbands | −.28** | −.32**** | −.25*** | .00 | −.10 |
| | (75) | (109) | (112) | (81) | (84) |
| Overbenefited husbands[a] | .40**** | .44**** | .28*** | .31**** | .25*** |
| | (78) | (95) | (108) | (88) | (107) |
| Underbenefited wives | −.19* | −.37**** | −.16* | −.15 | −.18* |
| | (109) | (113) | (122) | (104) | (127) |
| Overbenefited wives[a] | .31** | .39**** | .21** | .19 | .28** |
| | (51) | (96) | (94) | (69) | (63) |

*Note:* Numbers in parentheses indicate the number of subjects used to compute correlations.
*$p < .05$
**$p < .03$
***$p < .005$
****$p < .001$
[a]For overbenefited individuals a positive correlation represents that the more one perceives oneself as receiving more disclosure than one gives, the less is one's marital adjustment.

## Table 9–7
## Correlations between the Absolute Values of the Perceived Discrepancy Scores in Affective Self-Disclosure and Dyadic Adjustment Scores

| Dyadic Adjustment Scores | Absolute Values of Perceived Discrepanices in Disclosures | | | | |
|---|---|---|---|---|---|
| | Total | Love | Happiness | Anger | Sadness |
| Total Sample | −.29*** | −.37*** | −.21*** | −.19*** | −.18*** |
| | (279) | (306) | (301) | (285) | (304) |
| Husbands | −.39*** | −.37*** | −.26*** | −.25*** | −.24** |
| | (141) | (152) | (151) | (142) | (153) |
| Wives | −.20** | −.37*** | −.20** | −.11 | −.14* |
| | (138) | (154) | (150) | (143) | (151) |

*Note:* Numbers in parentheses indicate the number of subjects used to compute correlations.
*$p < .05$
**$p < .01$
***$p < .001$

correlated with marital adjustment. This finding supports the contention that the extent of being either overbenefited or underbenefited in affective self-disclosure exchange was inversely related to marital adjustment.

That the knowledge of being underbenefited or overbenefited engenders distress within a relationship, however, does not reveal whether the same areas are of concern to the underbenefited as well as overbenefited individuals. The distress that each group experiences may be focused upon a different element of the inequity in the relationship. To examine further this possibility, the correlations between one's perceived discrepancies in disclosure and marital adjustment were computed again controlling separately for one's disclosure output and one's perceived disclosure input. Since the perceived discrepancies in disclosure scores are comprised of output minus input scores, controlling separately for these elements was thought to yield a more conservative test of the relations.

A careful inspection of table 9–8 reveals that the controlling of output and input measures had differential effects on the correlations for underbenefited and overbenefited individuals. When disclosure output was controlled for, the correlations increased for underbenefited individuals and decreased for overbenefited individuals. When perceived disclosure input was controlled, the original zero order correlations decreased for underbenefited individuals and increased for overbenefited individuals. Most important was the extent to which the controlling of input eliminated the observed relations for underbenefited individuals, while no change occurred for the overbenefited individuals.

From these findings it can be inferred that controlling output scores for underbenefited individuals increased the inverse relation between the degree of underbenefitedness and marital adjustment. This suggests that, for these individuals, the amount of disclosure they perceived receiving was of primary importance in determining marital adjustment. This finding is quite compatible with predictions from equity theory that state that if one is underbenefited, the most important consideration in determining that individual's marital adjustment would be *what* they were receiving. In contrast, for overbenefited individuals, when their perceived disclosure input received was held constant, the inverse relation between the degree of overbenefitedness and marital adjustment increased. This suggests that for these individuals the *amount* of disclosure they indicated giving was of primary importance in determining marital adjustment. This finding was also expected because if a person is overbenefited, she or he would be assumed to be most concerned with how much she or he could give back in order to achieve equity. As with the other hypotheses, the strongest relations between self-disclosure levels and marital adjustment occurred in the area of love disclosure, reaffirming the special importance that partners in a relationship place on the exchange of this affective resource.

Table 9–8

**Correlations between the Perceived Discrepancy in Affective Self-Disclosure and Dyadic Adjustment Scores for Underbenefited and Overbenefited Spouses, Controlling for Output and Perceived Input**

| Daydic Adjustment Scores | Perceived Discrepancies in Disclosure (Output-Input) | | | | |
|---|---|---|---|---|---|
| | Total | Love | Happiness | Anger | Sadness |
| *Controlling for Output* | | | | | |
| Underbenefited | −.27*** | −.40*** | −.19** | −.11 | −.20** |
| | (181) | (219) | (231) | (182) | (208) |
| Overbenefited[a] | .27*** | .21** | .10 | .27*** | .14* |
| | (126) | (188) | (199) | (154) | (167) |
| Underbenefited husbands | −.33** | −.38*** | −.27** | −.02 | −.15 |
| | (72) | (106) | (109) | (78) | (81) |
| Overbenefited husbands[a] | .28* | .23* | .18* | .37*** | .13 |
| | (75) | (92) | (105) | (85) | (104) |
| Underbenefited wives | −.25** | −.42*** | −.14 | −.17* | −.26** |
| | (106) | (110) | (119) | (101) | (124) |
| Overbenefited wives | .25* | .17* | −.01 | .11 | .20 |
| | (48) | (93) | (91) | (66) | (60) |
| *Controlling for Input* | | | | | |
| Underbenefited | .00 | −.01 | .08 | −.02 | .04 |
| | (181) | (219) | (231) | (182) | (208) |
| Overbenefited[a] | .51*** | .47*** | .30*** | .28*** | .33*** |
| | (126) | (188) | (199) | (154) | (167) |
| Underbenefited husbands | −.14 | .05 | −.09 | .01 | −.15 |
| | (72) | (106) | (109) | (78) | (81) |
| Overbenefited husbands[a] | .46*** | .50*** | .30*** | .12 | .29** |
| | (75) | (92) | (105) | (85) | (104) |
| Underbenefited wives | .04 | −.07 | .20* | −.05 | .06 |
| | (106) | (110) | (119) | (101) | (124) |
| Overbenefited wives[a] | .49*** | .40*** | .29** | .25* | .33** |
| | (48) | (93) | (91) | (66) | (60) |

*Note:* Numbers in parentheses indicate the number of subjects used to compute correlations.
*p < .05
**p < .005
***p < .001
[a]For overbenefited individuals a positive correlation represents less overbenefiting being positively related to dyadic adjustment.

Overall, Hypothesis Four was strongly supported. As predicted by equity theory, perceived discrepancies in affective self-disclosure were inversely related to marital adjustment. For underbenefited as well as overbenefited individuals, the degree to which a discrepancy in an equitable exchange of self-disclosure was perceived as negatively related to one's marital adjustment. The strongest relations were observed for discrepancies in the area of love exchange and were most pronounced for overbenefited individuals.

According to a strict social exchange perspective, individuals who perceive themselves as receiving more love disclosure than they give should not generate distress. The present data, however, do not support a strictly social exchange perspective. They can best be explained from an equity perspective because discrepancies in perceived equity engendered distress within the relationships.

Within an equity theory framework, fairness can be considered to be an internal, subjectively defined construct. Concerning the balance of affective self-disclosure between partners, the degree to which one perceived an imbalance, regardless of whether an imbalance actually existed, was clearly associated with marital adjustment. These results are also in accord with those of Daher and Banikiotes (1976) in that perception of similar levels of exchange by partners does appear to contain a rewarding value for participants as evidenced by increases in marital adjustment scores.

## Hypothesis Five

Hypothesis Five maintains that for individuals who indicate a high level of marital adjustment, those underbenefited in affective self-disclosure will tend to overestimate what their spouses indicate affectively sharing while those individuals who are overbenefited will tend to underestimate what their spouses indicate affectively sharing. This analysis assessed whether there was an internal equity restoration function which enabled individuals to "perceive" equity in their relationship and thereby maintain high levels of marital adjustment. Among individuals lower in marital adjustment, this type of psychological restoration of equity was predicted to not operate since "distortion" of perceptions would not be necessary to justify what has already been termed a lowly adjusted relationship.

Congruency estimation scores were computed to asses individuals' "over-" and "underestimates" of affective self-disclosure from their spouses. These scores were computed by subtracting what one perceived one's spouse to have disclosed to them from what one's spouse indicated that he/she disclosed. A negative congruency score indicated than an individual was overestimating the disclosure the spouse indicated giving while a positive congruency score indicated an underestimation. Table 9–9 presents the correlations between the differences in husband-wife output scores and one's congruency

Table 9–9

Correlations between the Differences in Husband-Wife Output Scores and
Congruency Estimation Scores of Other's Disclosure

| Congruency Estimation Scores | Differences in Outputs on Types of Disclosure | | | | |
|---|---|---|---|---|---|
| | Total | Love | Happiness | Anger | Sadness |
| Husbands | | | | | |
| Above Medium on Dyadic Adjustment | .82 (62) | .75 (77) | .84 (74) | .69 (64) | .75 (76) |
| Below Medium on Dyadic Adjustment | .55 (74) | .50 (83) | .82 (83) | .37 (77) | .62 (84) |
| Wives | | | | | |
| Above Medium on Dyadic Adjustment | .80 (57) | .87 (73) | .84 (72) | .80 (60) | .81 (71) |
| Below Medium on Dyadic Adjustment | .63 (79) | .62 (87) | .76 (86) | .51 (81) | .61 (87) |

*Note:* Numbers in parentheses indicate number of subjects used to compute correlations. All correlations significant $p < .001$.

estimation scores of one's spouse's disclosure. The data are presented for husbands and wives above and below the median on marital adjustment. For husbands, those with scores above the median (111.6) on the Spanier Dyadic Adjustment Scale were designated high in marital adjustment, while those below this figure were considered low in marital adjustment. For wives, a similar median split was performed at 114.5. The differences in output scores represented whether an individual was underbenefited or overbenefited in self-disclosure exchange with a negative score representing underbenefit and a positive score representing overbenefit. The positive correlations in table 9–9 demonstrate that underbenefited individuals tended to overestimate their spouses' disclosure and overbenefited individuals tended to underestimate their spouses' disclosure.

The data in table 9–9 partially support Hypothesis Five. As can be seen, all correlations were significant at the $p < .001$ level. Regardless of whether individuals were above or below the median on marital adjustment, those who were overbenefited tended to underestimate their partners' affective self-disclosure while those who were underbenefited tended to overestimate their partner's affective self-disclosure.

A comparison was undertaken of those above the median on adjustment with those below the median on adjustment. Correlations were transformed into z-scores and differences between correlations were computed. With the exception of the correlations between (a) congruency scores and differences in happiness outputs for husbands and wives, and (b) congruency scores and differences in sadness outputs for husbands, all differences in correlations for those individuals above and below the median on marital adjustment were significant at the $p < .02$ level or better. These findings support the contention that for those high in marital adjustment there was a greater need to "distort" the amount of disclosure received from one's spouse than for those who were low in marital adjustment.

To test for the interactive effects of marital adjustment and discrepancy in disclosure on congruency estimation scores, two-by-two (marital adjustment X discrepancy in disclosure outputs) fixed-design analyses of variance were performed. In order to accomplish this, absolute value transformations were performed on the discrepancy in disclosure output scores. Then, median splits were performed on the absolute discrepancies and Dyadic Adjustment Scores. This procedure resulted in the designation of high and low levels for the conditions of discrepancy in disclosure and marital adjustment, which, when crossed, yielded four groups in which to assess an interaction. The dependent measure was the absolute value of the congruency estimation scores. The use of absolute values for this variable enabled underestimation and overestimation scores to be treated as departures from congruency in estimation.

Based upon an application of analyses of variance statistical tests, it was found that the main effects of discrepancy in disclosure outputs were significant in every case. From this it may be concluded that for total disclosure of love, happiness, anger, and sadness, those individuals in the high discrepancy condition were more likely to overestimate or underestimate their partners' self-disclosure than those in the low discrepancy group. In addition, significant interactions were observed for husbands for the effects of dyadic adjustment and discrepancies in love disclosure, $F(1.147) = 6.2, p < .01$; happiness disclosure $F(1,146) = 5.8, p < .02$; and sadness disclosure, $F(1,148) = 3.8$, $p < .05$. For wives a significant interaction was observed for the effects of dyadic adjustment and discrepancy in love disclosure, $F(1,149) = 12.2$, $p < .001$. For purposes of brevity only the dyadic adjustment-by-discrepancy in love outputs interactions for husbands and wives will be discussed, as the others follow the same general pattern.

In figures 9–1 and 9–2 are graphic representations of the marital adjustment-by-discrepancy in love outputs interactions for husbands and wives. As these graphs demonstrate for both low and high marital adjustment groups, congruency estimation scores were greater in the high discrepancy in love outputs condition versus the low discrepancy condition, thus representing the main effects of discrepancy in love outputs. Examination of these figures reveals the interaction of these variables to be the differential effects of discrepancy in love outputs on marital adjustment. As can be observed, under the level of low discrepancy in love outputs, the low marital adjustment group was more likely to misestimate what spouses indicated disclos-

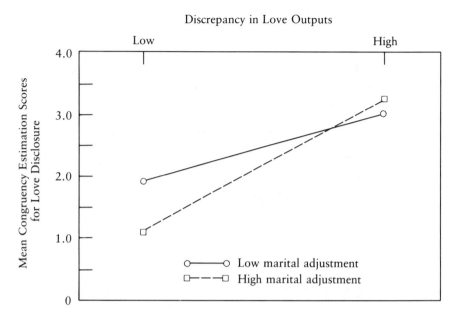

Figure 9–1. **Husbands' Mean Congruency Estimation Scores for Love Disclosure by Discrepancy in Love Outputs and by Marital Adjustment.**

ing, while under the level of high discrepancy in love outputs, the high marital adjustment group was most likely to misestimate spouses' self-disclosure. The differential effect of discrepancy in love outputs on marital adjustment was presumed to result in the high-marital-adjustment–high-discrepancy in outputs group being the one which would demonstrate the greatest misestimation, while the high-marital-adjustment–low-discrepancy in outputs group would show the least misestimation. This is precisely what was observed. For husbands, the mean congruency estimation score for the high-marital-adjustment–high-discrepancy in love outputs group was 3.3, while the mean score for the high-marital-adjustment–low-discrepancy in love outputs group was 1.1. For wives, the mean congruency estimation score for the high-marital-adjustment–high-discrepancy in love outputs group was 3.6, while the mean score for the high-marital-adjustment–low-discrepancy in love outputs group was 1.1.

Overall, support was obtained for Hypothesis Five. Testing demonstrated the most dramatic evidence supporting equity descriptions of the way participants account for imbalances in the exchange of affective self-disclosure. It may be that partners in a relationship may differentially per-

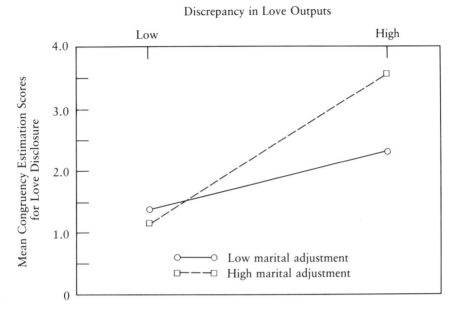

Figure 9–2. Wives' Congruency Estimation Scores for Love Disclosure by Discrepancy in Love Outputs and by Marital Adjustment.

ceive each others' emotional expressiveness. What may contribute to this "need to see" each others' affective self-disclosure in a specific way may be a function of the way in which partners react to imbalances in affective exchange. For those individuals who claim high levels of marital adjustment, the conscious perception of inequities in affective exchange would produce a "cognitive dissonance" that is discordant with their view of their relationship. For these individuals, evidence indicates that one way of restoring the perception of equity may be to overestimate or underestimate their partner's contribution of affective self-disclosure.

## Summary and Conclusions

This study supports equity theory notions about the relations between discrepancies in affective spousal self-disclosure and marital adjustment. As equity theory maintains, being underbenefited or overbenefited in resource exchange should cause distress for participants in a relationship. Our results suggested that imbalances or discrepancies in affective self-disclosure exchange were, in fact, related to lower levels of marital adjustment. What appears even more convincing were the findings that husbands' and wives' perceptions about the balance of affective self-disclosure exchange were even more strongly related to marital adjustment. Equity theory assumes that individuals' perceptions of the reward/cost factors involved in maintaining relationships will be a better predictor of distress (or happiness) than some external objective account of exchange. With reciprocity deemed an expected characteristic of self-disclosure (Davis 1976; Ehrich and Graeven 1971; Jourard 1959; Jourard and Landsman 1960; Jourard and Richman 1963; Levinger and Senn 1967; Tignoli 1969), deviations from this norm can be viewed as resulting in feelings of inequity for participants in a relationship.

Conversely, a balance, or lack of discrepancy, in levels of affective self-disclosure exchange between partners can be considered a stabilizer that produces feelings of equity. As Daher and Banikiotes (1976) have suggested, not only may the reception of self-disclosure be a reward but the exchange of disclosure at similar levels of intimacy may also be a reward.

The way individuals deal with discrepancies in affective self-disclosure in their relationships was also assessed. Walster, Walster, and Berschied (1978) have mentioned that individuals will attempt to restore equity and eliminate distress by either of two general manners, compensation or justification. When a discrepancy in disclosure between partners exists it is apparent that compensatory actions involving the increase or decrease of one's disclosure level to match the other's are not employed to restore equity. Whether individuals seek rewards or make sacrifices in other areas to restore equity is an issue not addressed in this study. However, as Turner et al. (1971) have demonstrated, people prefer to be rewarded with the same thing they give to another. This suggests that justification methods may be a likely manner in which participants in a relationship serve to restore the perception of equity. These psychological restoration techniques are assumed to be most operative for those individuals who claim to have a well-adjusted relationship, and also seem to be involved in discrepant disclosure exchange as evidenced by independent assessments of both partners' disclosure outputs.

The results of the present study support these contentions. When individuals are involved in inequitable relationships, one way they deal with inequity is to overestimate or underestimate one's spouse's contributions. The confirmation of this hypothesis shows the utility of implementing an equity theory analysis of affective self-disclosure exchange in relationships.

The findings reported in this chapter also have important implications for the sex role strain theory of male inexpressiveness. While the absolute levels of self-disclosure exchange do in fact seem to bear on the quality of relationships, what appears to exert a stronger influence is the similarity of partners' exchange, especially as perceived by the individual. It appears that regardless of the amount of self-disclosure exchanged, partners who are similar in their self-disclosure indicate better adjustment in their marriages than partners who are discrepant. Thus, it seems that partners who both indicate disclosing lesser amounts are about as well-adjusted as those disclosing greater amounts. Great dissatisfaction is likely to emerge when imbalances occur in the exchange.

The greatest imbalance in marital expressiveness is likely to take place in marriages in which the spouses have traditional definitions of sex roles. According to traditional sex role definitions husbands are to be less expressive than wives. However, if such expectations were actually internalized and accepted, then we should find that marital adjustment is not related to equity in marital expressive exchanges. Obviously, this is not the case.

The data illuminate how the complex nature of contemporary sex roles reflect the clash between traditional and modern definitions of the male role. Men may be expected to be both traditional (by not expressing their feelings in general) and "situationally modern" (by expressing their feelings within marriage). When confronted by this contradictory and inconsistent expectation, males experience strain in their marital role. Strain will begin to dissipate when males learn to accept the modern role that permits them to be expressive in a general sense—to their wives and children at home, as well as to their friends and acquaintances at work and at play.

At present there exists a cultural construction of masculinity which places contradictory demands on both men and women. These contradictory demands will disappear only when there is a return to consistency at the cultural and social structural level. Specifically, this would mean that male expressiveness would be valued in marriage, in fathering, *and* in the wider extrafamilial areas, such as work and play.

# 10
# Marriage and Friends

The findings in this chapter attempt to combine the topics of chapter 8, the effect of situational factors on expressiveness, and chapter 9, the effect of emotional inexpressiveness on marital adjustment. Specifically, this chapter will examine the relationships between sex role orientation, emotional expressiveness and self-disclosure to marital partner and friends, and marital adjustment. Except for sex-role orientation and self-disclosure to friends, a review of the literature for each of these variables can be found in chapters 8 and 9 and thus will not be repeated here.

Because of findings indicating that androgyny is positively related to self-disclosure, sex-role orientation was included as a potentially important variable in understanding emotional expressiveness. Bell (1981a) found that nonconventional men and women revealed more about themselves to their friends than conventional men and women, and that nonconventional women disclosed equally to male and female friends. Lombardo and Lavine (1981) and Lavine and Lombardo (1984) reported that androgynous respondents had more intimate disclosures across all target persons, including parents and friends. Sex-role orientation of both subject and target person have been found to influence disclosure, with androgynous individuals having higher disclosure (Gerdes, Gehling, and Rapp 1981; Rosenfield, Civikly, and Herron 1979).

Factors found to influence self-disclosure, then, include gender of respondent and target person, type of relationship, intimacy of topic, sex-role orientation, and marital status. Very little work has explored the relationships between disclosure patterns inside and outside of marriage and the effects of such on marital adjustment. Both developmental and systems theories recognize the semi-permeable boundaries that exist between family members and the outside social network, and acknowledge that exchange of resources with the social network can exert a strong influence on intra-family organization and functioning. In examining the functions of social networks, Barrera and Ainlay (1983) and Mitchell and Trickett (1980) have identified instrumental and affective components of social support provided by the network. Affective components include such aspects as expressing esteem, caring, and understanding; providing feedback about behavior, thoughts and feelings; and communication of expectations, evaluations, and shared world view. Self-disclosure behaviors can be viewed as being encompassed in these affective domains. How individuals may rely on different types of relationships, such as friendship and marriage, to meet their affective needs, is the focus of this chapter. In particular, we'll explore the relationship between intra-dyadic self-disclosure and extra-dyadic self-disclosure, and the effects of these disclosure patterns on marital adjustment, with an emphasis on the mediating effect of the contingency variable of sex-role orientation.

The relationship between disclosure to friends and disclosure to spouse has received limited attention. Bell has suggested that a common pattern regarding individual friendships for the married middle class is that each spouse may have some friends of the same sex, but "that any friendships with the opposite-sex will be within the context of married couples" (1981b, 131). Two studies may shed some light on expectations about and patterns of self-disclosure to friends and romantic partners. In a study of unmarried college women, Sollie and Fischer (1985) found that disclosure was highest to romantic partner, then to same-sex friend, and finally to opposite-sex friend, and that the romantic partner received the most intimate disclosure. Androgynous respondents demonstrated higher disclosure than sex-typed and undifferentiated respondents. Intimacy level, relationship type, and sex-role orientation were all related to self-disclosure, suggesting the complexity of self-disclosure patterns. Type of relationship was influential, accounting for 32 percent of the variance in self-disclosure, which indicates the existence of strong norms about the appropriateness of disclosure. Dickson-Markman (1983) examined the impact of self-disclosure to closest friend on marital satisfaction, and found that the quality of self-disclosure in friendships outside the marriage was a significant predictor of marital satisfaction. Results from this study indicate that friendships can be viewed as providing a support system for marriage.

Other related research points to the impact of marital status on self-disclosure behaviors. Booth and Hess (1974) found that unmarried persons of both sexes appeared to confide in opposite-sex friends more than same-sex friends, with married individuals showing a reduction in behavior exchange for all types of relationships. Together these studies point to the prevalence of norms about the appropriateness of self-disclosure to various target persons, depending on the relationship status of the individual and the gender of target persons outside the romantic or marital relationship.

A different set of literature suggests that dyadic interactions are influenced by the sex-role orientations of the members of the dyad. Ickes (1981) developed and tested a model of the influence of sex-role orientation on interpersonal interactions, with the basic premise that the presence of both instrumental and expressive capacities enhances interactions between individuals. That is, persons with androgynous sex-role orientation will be more effective in interpersonal relationships as a result of their wider repertoire of responses and their greater flexibility and adaptability. There is support for this premise. Shaver, Pullis, and Olds (1985) reported that married women in dyads where at least one partner was androgynous were more satisfied with their lives and marriages than were women in traditional "masculine man-feminine women" dyads. One limitation of this study was that data for only women were available. Antill (1983) had both partners of married couples in his study of the relationship between sex-role orientation and marital adjustment, and he reported that marital satisfaction was relatively high in dyads where both partners were androgynous, and relatively low in sex-role stereotyped pairs. Interestingly, both Antill (1983) and Shaver et al. (1980) found that high levels of satisfaction were consistently reported by women married to feminine-typed men, leading Antill to suggest that femininity of one's partner is directly related to marital satisfaction. Davidson and Sollie (1984) found that androgynous and sex-typed respondents were significantly higher in marital adjustment than undifferentiated respondents. Murstein and Williams (1983) found that androgynous husbands and wives reported greater marital adjustment than both cross-sex-typed and undifferentiated respondents; however, androgynous respondents were not significantly different from sex-typed respondents in marital adjustment. Results from these studies point to the importance of sex-role orientation as an influencing factor in relationship satisfaction, and further suggest that androgyny has a positive effect on relationship adjustment. Extrapolation from these studies to interpersonal aspects of dyadic relationships leads to the conclusion that androgyny is related to expressivity or self-disclosure, which in turn is related to relationship adjustment.

Based on the literature reviewed, the following hypotheses were derived and tested:

1. Spouses will show greater levels of self-disclosure to each other than to friends.

2. Spouses will show greater levels of self-disclosure to same-sex friends than to opposite-sex friends.

3. Sex-role orientation will be related to self-disclosure such that sex-role stereotyped as compared to androgynous individuals will show:
   a. a greater proportion of self-disclosure to same-sex rather than opposite-sex friends;
   b. a greater proportion of spousal rather than friend self-disclosure;
   c. a greater differentiation in disclosure patterns.

4. While levels of spousal self-disclosure will be positively related to marital adjustment for all spouses, sex-role stereotyped individuals as compared to androgynous individuals will show a greater decrement in marital adjustment as a function of their spouses' self-disclosure to "non-couple" opposite-sex friends.

## Method

The data in this chapter are based upon responses given by 112 sets of intact married couples (224 individuals) to questionnaires delivered to five hundred middle-class households (as identified through the use of 1980 census data) in a Southwestern city of two hundred thousand. Demographic characteristics of the subjects include a mean age of 42.3 for husband and 41.0 for wives, a mean level of 14.8 years of education for husbands and 14.1 years for wives, and a mean of 20.5 years married. In family placement, 5.4 percent of the subjects were under age thirty-five and childless, 2.5 percent were over thirty-five and childless, 53.2 percent had a youngest child under age six, 26.3 percent had a youngest child between ages six and eighteen, and 12.2 percent had a youngest child over age eighteen.

Husbands and wives were instructed to separately complete questionnaires containing the Bem Sex Role Inventory (BSRI) (Bem 1974), the Spanier Dyadic Adjustment Scale (DAS) (Spanier 1976), and modified forms of the Jourard Sixty-Item Self-Disclosure Questionnaire (JSDQ) (Jourard 1971) and the Expression of Emotion Scale (EOE). The BSRI is comprised of sixty self-descriptive items which employ a seven-point Likert-type response format that yields composite scores of masculine and feminine sex-role identity. Together, the masculinity and femininity scales can be combined to produce individual categories of androgynous, traditional male, traditional female, and undifferentiated. The JSDQ sixty-item Likert-type scale was modified to a twenty-one-item scale measuring self-disclosure in the general categories of attitudes and opinions, tasks and interests, work, money, personality, body, and sexuality. The EOE scale is described in chapter 5 and the DAS is described in chapter 9. For both the JSDQ and the EOE scales, subjects were asked to identify five targets of disclosure: spouse, a male friend who is *not* a friend of spouse, a female friend who is *not* a friend of spouse, and a male and female friend who as a couple are close to both the subject and spouse.

## Results and Discussion

A test of Hypothesis One was conducted by comparing the mean scores of individuals' self-disclosure and love disclosure to spouse and friends. Repeated measures analyses of variance were conducted separately for husbands and wives with self-disclosure and love disclosure to spouse and the four friend targets serving as the repeated dependent measure. All four ANOVAs were highly significant (p < .001), indicating differential disclosure levels to targets for both spouses. Of particular interest were the planned contrasts between disclosure to different targets. Table 10–1 presents the mean disclosure scores for husbands and wives to different targets. A graphic representation of this is shown in figure 10–1. All contrasts were in the predicted direction. For both husbands and wives, the contrasts between disclosure to spouse and friends were significant (p < .001). Table 10–2 summarizes these contrasts.

Hypothesis Two predicted greater same-sex versus opposite-sex friend disclosure. Planned contrasts were carried out between spousal disclosure to same-sex versus opposite-sex friends. Table 10–3 summarizes these contrasts. All differences were in the predicted direction and significant at the .001 level with the exception of love disclosure for husbands, which was significant at the .015 and .004 level for the two contrasts.

Figure 10–1 and the results of the planned contrasts demonstrate strong support for Hypotheses One and Two. That spouses should disclose more to each other than to their friends and to their same-sex friends versus their opposite-sex friends adds solid evidence to our conceptual reasoning. While past research has found the marital dyad to be a context for high levels of disclosure (Davidson et al. 1983a; Jorgensen and Gaudy 1980; Jourard and Lasakow 1958; Levinger and Senn 1967) little research has compared spousal disclosure within the dyad with disclosure to various friend targets outside the dyad. Jourard and Lasakow (1958) reported that spousal disclosure was

Table 10–1
Mean Self-Disclosure and Love Disclosure Scores to Spouse and Friend Targets for Husbands and Wives

| | | Target of Disclosure | | | |
|---|---|---|---|---|---|
| | *Spouse* | *Couple Male* | *Couple Female* | *Individual Male* | *Individual Female* |
| *Husbands* | | | | | |
| Self-disclosure | 28.75 | 18.70 | 15.96 | 18.09 | 15.96 |
| Love disclosure | 4.50 | 2.66 | 2.53 | 2.40 | 2.31 |
| *Wives* | | | | | |
| Self-disclosure | 29.58 | 16.90 | 20.40 | 16.50 | 20.72 |
| Love disclosure | 4.71 | 2.72 | 3.25 | 2.67 | 3.29 |

Table 10–2
Summary of Planned Contrasts (*t*-values) between Disclosure to Spouse and Friends

| | Husbands | | | |
|---|---|---|---|---|
| | Couple Male | Individual Male | Couple Female | Individual Female |
| Contrasts | | | | |
| Self-disclosure to wife versus | 22.57 (107) | 22.13 (100) | 30.24 (107) | 28.91 (94) |
| Love Disclosure to wife versus | 16.93 (109) | 20.19 (101) | 18.80 (109) | 20.97 (95) |
| | *Wives* | | | |
| Self-disclosure to husband versus | 27.60 (106) | 25.56 (90) | 19.54 (105) | 17.62 (106) |
| Love Disclosure to husband versus | 17.52 (108) | 15.81 (92) | 13.49 (108) | 12.71 (108) |

*Note:* All *t*-values significant at the .001 level. Degrees of freedom in parentheses.


Table 10–3
Summary of Planned Contrasts (*t*-values) between Spouses' Disclosure to Same- Versus Opposite-Sex Friends

| | Male Couple vs. Female Couple | Male Indiv. vs. Female Indiv. |
|---|---|---|
| *Husbands* | | |
| Self-disclosure | 9.26 (107) | 6.77 (92) |
| Love disclosure | 2.76[a] (110) | 2.20[b] (93) |
| *Wives* | | |
| Self-disclosure | −9.85 (105) | −8.84 (90) |
| Love disclosure | −6.75 (108) | −6.94 (92) |

*Note:* All *t*-values significant at the .001 level unless otherwise noted.
[a]p < .004
[b]p < .015

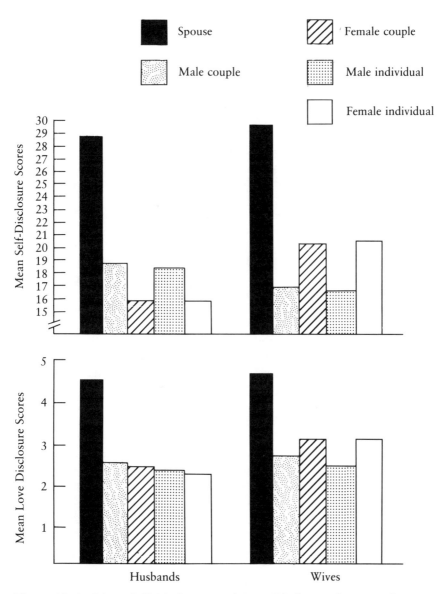

**Figure 10–1. Mean Self-Disclosure and Love Disclosure Scores to Spouse
and Friends**

greater than friend disclosure for married subjects. However, in their analyses, opposite-sex friend and spouse were treated as equivalent targets, thus obscuring a comparison between disclosure to types of friends. In addition, only a fraction of their sample were married, with the major emphasis of the study being concerned with disclosure patterns of undergraduate students.

In general, studies of sex differences in self-disclosure suggest either greater female disclosure or no difference at all (see Cozby 1973; Rosenfeld, Civikly, and Herron 1979 for reviews of this issue). Several studies also have reported that greater levels of self-disclosure are displayed to opposite-sex targets than to same-sex targets (Annicchiarico 1973; Brooks 1974; Hyink 1975; Inman 1978); however, these studies did not include marriage as a factor. Some contradictory findings are reported by Cash (1975), who found greater disclosure to female targets by males and females. That females should be greater receivers of disclosure is supported by the "norm of reciprocity," which specifies the reciprocal nature of disclosure as those who reveal more about themselves will be revealed to more, which isn't surprising, since females have generally been found to be higher disclosures.

Booth and Hess (1974) have found that unmarried people of both sexes appear to confide in opposite-sex friends more than same-sex friends, with married individuals showing reduced behavior exchange for all types of friendships. This is somewhat akin to Jourard and Lasakow's (1958) observation that for the twenty married people in their sample, overall self-disclosure was at a similar level as for unmarried individuals—however, it was distributed differentially so as to reveal a relative decrease to targets other than the spouse.

While no comparisons between married and unmarried individuals were made in this study, the results support the intervening effects of marriage on disclosure to those outside the marriage. For husbands and wives, not only was disclosure greater to each other than to friends (as previous studies lead us to believe) but also, spouses appeared to display greater amounts of disclosure to same-sex than to opposite-sex friends. It is this last finding that departs from much of the earlier research, mostly done with college students, and stresses the importance of considering the marital characteristics of the sample.

Hypothesis Three further addressed the influence of subject personality characteristics on spousal and friend disclosure. In predicting differences between sex role types on disclosure patterns it was expected that androgynous and sex-typed individuals would differ in their proportions of friend and spousal disclosure. Hypothesis Three(a) predicted that androgynous individuals would show greater relative levels of opposite-sex friend disclosure than same-sex disclosure as compared to sex-typed individuals. To assess this, proportion scores were computed by dividing opposite-sex friend disclosure by same-sex friend disclosure for all individuals. Table 10–4 displays the

Table 10–4
Mean Disclosure Scores to Targets by Sex Role Type for Husbands
and Wives

|  | Husbands | | |
|  | *Androgynous* | *Masculine* | *Undifferentiated* |
| --- | --- | --- | --- |
|  | *(25)* | *(53)* | *(28)* |
| *Targets* |  |  |  |
| Wives |  |  |  |
| (Self-dis.) | 29.51 | 29.08 | 26.97 |
| (Love dis.) | 4.78 | 4.48 | 4.23 |
| Couple | 19.71 | 19.19 | 17.05 |
| Male | 3.18 | 2.49 | 2.41 |
| Individual | 18.56 | 18.70 | 16.74 |
| Male | 3.00 | 2.23 | 2.22 |
| Couple | 17.26 | 15.99 | 14.60 |
| Female | 3.12 | 2.31 | 2.30 |
| Individual | 17.59 | 15.63 | 15.25 |
| Female | 2.95 | 2.09 | 2.25 |

|  | Wives | | |
|  | *Androgynous* | *Feminine* | *Undifferentiated* |
| --- | --- | --- | --- |
|  | *(24)* | *(53)* | *(23)* |
| Husbands | 29.16 | 30.45 | 27.62 |
|  | 4.70 | 4.76 | 4.58 |
| Couple | 18.59 | 16.12 | 16.61 |
| Male | 3.15 | 2.56 | 2.54 |
| Individual | 18.88 | 15.93 | 16.47 |
| Male | 3.21 | 2.73 | 2.31 |
| Couple | 19.96 | 20.48 | 20.70 |
| Female | 3.37 | 3.30 | 2.98 |
| Individual | 21.43 | 20.70 | 20.50 |
| Female | 3.65 | 3.32 | 2.88 |

mean levels of self-disclosure and love disclosure to the various targets by sex role types for husbands and wives.

Table 10–5 displays the mean porportion scores for opposite-sex to same-sex friend disclosure for androgynous and sex-typed spouses and the results of planned contracts assessing differences. An examination of table 10–5 reveals that while all of the differences were in the predicted direction,

Table 10–5
Mean Proportions of Opposite-Sex to Same-Sex Friend Disclosure for
Androgynous and Sex-Typed Spouses

|  | Husbands | | | |
|  | Androgynous | Masculine | t | sig. |
|---|---|---|---|---|
| Proportions of Disclosure |  |  |  |  |
| Self-disclosure | .903 | .836 | 2.23 | p < .02 |
| Love Disclosure | 1.01 | .957 | .93 | p > .22 |
|  | Wives | | | |
|  | Androgynous | Feminine | t | sig. |
| Proportions of |  |  |  |  |
| Self-disclosure | .924 | .782 | 3.89 | p < .001 |
| Love Disclosure | .936 | .806 | 2.31 | p < .02 |

*Note:* The higher the proportion score, the more relative disclosure to opposite-sex friends than same-sex friends.

three of the four contrasts were significant at the .02 level or better. Androgynous individuals showed higher proportions of opposite-sex to same-sex friend disclosure than did sex-typed individuals regarding self-disclosure and love disclosure for wives and regarding self-disclosure for husbands. While androgynous husbands showed a greater proportion of opposite-sex to same-sex friend love disclosure than did masculine husbands, the difference was not significant. Table 10–4 appears to explain this. Masculine hsubands' love disclosures to both male and female friends was low in comparison to their androgynous counterparts and did not differ much to male or female targets; hence their proportion scores would still remain quite high. This general tendency for masculine type males to suppress intimate disclosure, particularly outside the marital dyad, is in line with Balswick's observations concerning the lack of emotional expressivity for males (Balswick and Peek 1971; Balswick and Averett 1977). It has been suggested by Balswick that this lower expressivity should be particularly evident for men who display a more masculine-type orientation to the world. In a sense, this finding may be viewed as a result of a ceiling effect on masculine intimate disclosure outside the marital dyad.

The findings of self-disclosure for husbands and wives clearly support the hypothesis that sex-role type will influence or reflect one's distribution of disclosure to external targets. For wives, the difference between the proportions of love disclosure to opposite-sex and same-sex friends was also significant, though less so than was the case for self-disclosure. In table 10–4, a striking difference is found between feminine wives and masculine husbands. While the absolute levels of love disclosure to all friends appeared suppressed for masculine husbands, this appeared to only be so for feminine wives in their love disclosure to male friends, hence, their lower proportion scores as compared to husbands (.806 versus .957). Once again, this appears to be in line with general expectations for women to be greater disclosers of intimate material. In this case, it appears that for feminine wives, intimate disclosure to male friends goes against one's self-conception, while disclosure to female friends suffers no such stigma.

Hypothesis Three(b) predicted that androgynous individuals, as compared to sex-typed individuals, would show a greater relative proportion of disclosure to friend versus spouse. By dividing friend disclosure by spouse disclosure, an index of proportionate disclosure was created. In table 10–6 is an examination of these proportions and planned contrasts. All differences were in the predicted direction—however, only two were significant, with a marginal third. For wives, androgynous versus feminine individuals did show a significantly greater relative proportion of friend-to-spouse disclosure. For love disclosure this difference approached significance, which can be interpreted as supporting the hypothesis that greater relative amounts of external disclosure outside the marital dyad is more in line with androgynous womens' views of appropriate behavior. The findings were somewhat different for husbands. For self-disclosure, the difference in relative proportions was in the predicted direction but not significant. For love disclosure, a significant dif-

**Table 10–6**
**Mean Proportions of Friend-to-Spouse Disclosure for Androgynous and Sex-Typed Spouses**

|  | Husbands | | | |
|---|---|---|---|---|
|  | *Androgynous* | *Masculine* | *t* | *sig.* |
| *Proportions of Disclosure* | | | | |
| Self-disclosure | .626 | .599 | .866 | $p > .19$ |
| Love Disclosure | .628 | .506 | 2.29 | $p < .02$ |
|  | Wives | | | |
|  | *Androgynous* | *Feminine* | *t* | *sig.* |
| *Proportions of Disclosure* | | | | |
| Self-disclosure | .692 | .611 | 2.57 | $p < .01$ |
| Love Disclosure | .726 | .633 | 1.58 | $p < .06$ |

*Note:* The higher the proportion score, the more relative disclosure to friend than spouse.

ference was observed in the predicted direction. This means that androgynous husbands appeared more willing to disclose relative amounts of love outside of the marital dyad than did masculine husbands. Why this showed up for love disclosure but not for self-disclosure may have something to do with the intimate nature of the material disclosed. For masculine husbands it would appear that disclosure of an intimate affective nature is best suited to dyadic disclosure, which appears consistent with earlier studies of self-disclosure that indicate males maintain the most intimate disclosure with their spouses, while decreasing disclosure to other targets (Jourard and Lasakow 1958). However, our study demonstrates that sex role type is a mediating influence on this relation.

Hypothesis Three(c) predicted a greater differentiation in disclosure patterns for sex-typed individuals than for androgynous individuals. To test this, two sets of comparisons were conducted. Androgynous husbands were compared with androgynous wives on mean self-disclosure and love disclosure scores to various targets. A similar set of comparisons contrasted masculine husbands and feminine wives. We expected a greater number of differences would be evident in the second set of contrasts. Table 10–7 presents a summary of these contrasts. Between androgynous individuals, three significant

## Table 10–7
## Mean Scores and Comparisons for Androgynous and Sex-Typed Spouses on Disclosure to Targets

| | Androgynous Husbands versus Androgynous Wives | | | | Masculine Husbands versus Feminine Wives | | | |
|---|---|---|---|---|---|---|---|---|
| | Hus-bands | Wives | t | signif. | Hus-bands | Wives | t | signif. |
| *Target of Self-disclosure* | | | | | | | | |
| Spouse | 29.51 | 29.07 | 0.32 | p>.35 | 29.04 | 30.47 | −1.89 | p<.04 |
| Couple Male | 19.71 | 18.59 | 0.87 | p>.19 | 19.32 | 16.17 | 3.50 | p<.001 |
| Couple Female | 17.26 | 19.83 | −2.10 | p<.02 | 16.06 | 20.52 | −4.79 | p<.001 |
| Indiv. Male | 18.56 | 19.13 | −0.47 | p>.32 | 18.81 | 15.95 | 3.18 | p<.001 |
| Indiv. Female | 17.58 | 21.45 | −2.86 | p<.004 | 15.63 | 20.71 | −5.53 | p<.001 |
| *Target of Love Disclosure* | | | | | | | | |
| Spouse | 4.78 | 4.68 | 0.51 | p>.32 | 4.47 | 4.77 | −2.47 | p<.008 |
| Couple Male | 3.18 | 3.20 | −0.07 | p>.48 | 2.52 | 2.56 | −0.15 | p>.44 |
| Couple Female | 3.12 | 3.34 | −0.67 | p>.26 | 2.33 | 3.31 | −4.17 | p<.001 |
| Indiv. Male | 3.00 | 3.28 | −0.81 | p>.22 | 2.25 | 2.71 | −1.93 | p<.03 |
| Indiv. Female | 2.95 | 3.14 | −1.88 | p<.04 | 2.09 | 3.33 | −5.55 | p<.001 |

differences were noted, all related to disclosure to a female friend. Androgynous wives more than androgynous husbands disclosed to a female couple friend, and to a female individual friend. No differences were found for spousal disclosure or disclosure to male friends. All but one of the comparisons between masculine husbands and feminine wives were significant: Masculine husbands compared to feminine wives showed: (1) *less* spousal self-disclosure and spousal love disclosure; (2) *less* female friend (both couple and individual) self-disclosure and love disclosure; (3) *more* male couple friend and male individual friend self-disclosure; and (4) *less* male individual friend love disclosure. The only contrast in which no significant difference was noted was that which compared love disclosure to male couple friends. It appears safe to say that greater differentiation patterns in disclosure were observed for sex-typed versus androgynous individuals.

The differences found for androgynous individuals, in which wives disclosed more to female friends, are not surprising and are not nearly as great as those same differences for the sex-typed comparisons. One difference, which at first appeared contrary to what we expected, concerned the contrast between masculine friends and feminine wives with regard to love disclosure to a male individual friend. Wives showed a greater amount of this type of disclosure than husbands. The same comparison for the full self-disclosure scale was significant and in the predicted direction. What apparently is reflected in this data is the effect of the intimacy of material on disclosure to male targets. With love disclosure being the most intimate, it is not surprising to see masculine males revealing little of this type of disclosure to male targets. Such disclosure would be quite contrary to their sex role norms. Reinterpreted, it is not so much that feminine wives disclose high levels of love to male friends but rather that masculine males disclose very low levels. The information in table 10–7 reveals that next to love disclosure to female individual friends, masculine males' disclosure of love to male individual friends was the lowest of any love disclosure indicated for any of the four groups.

The findings of Hypothesis Three(c) support the differential impact of sex-role type on disclosure to spouse and friends. In line with other research on sex role orientation, our study supports the notion of greater flexibility and diversity in interpersonal orientation for androgynous versus traditionally typed individuals. This is not meant to imply that these individuals are necessarily more easily able to adjust to all social situations, but rather that the strategies that one enacts in interpersonal adjustment are in some way dependent upon one's view of self. With self-disclosure representing one such major process of interpersonal functioning, it is expected that one's self-concept in terms of sex role attributes would affect this aspect of communication.

Hypothesis Four predicted that while spousal disclosure will be related to marital adjustment, disclosure of an intimate nature to opposite-sex individual friends will be less so, and will be differentially related for androgynous and sex-typed individuals. In essence, it was expected that one's spouse's love disclosure to an opposite-sex individual friend would be more inversely related to one's marital adjustment for sex-typed individuals than for androgynous individuals. To test this hypothesis, Pearson correlation coefficients were computed between one's spouse's love disclosure to opposite-sex individual friends and one's marital adjustment, separately for sex-typed and androgynous individuals. To test for the significance of the difference between these coefficients, a $z$-score transformation was conducted, which allowed a test for the difference between independent correlations.

For androgynous wives, husbands' love disclosure to spouse was related to wives' marital adjustment, $r(24) = .62$, $p < .001$. For feminine wives, a similar relation (though not as strong) was observed, $r(54) = .37$, $p < .003$. For androgynous husbands, the correlation between spouse's love disclosure and one's marital adjustment was $r(25) = .52$, $p < .004$. For masculine husbands, this relation was $r(53) = .22$, $p < .056$. These data support the initial part of this hypothesis and demonstrate the importance of spousal disclosure to one's marital adjustment, and suggest a stronger relation for androgynous individuals of both sexes. In table 10–8 are the correlations between love disclosure to opposite-sex friends and spousal marital adjustment by sex role types. While we see that spousal love disclosure to opposite-sex friends did not negatively affect one's marital adjustment for androgynous and sex-typed individuals, there seems to be an apparent tendency for this relation to become more *positive* under the androgynous conditions. In fact, if one includes the undifferentiated in this comparison, further evidence for this trend appears. For wives, the $z$ test was significant between the correlations for

Table 10–8
Correlations between Spouse's Disclosure to Opposite-Sex
Friend and Marital Adjustment by Sex Role Types

| | Husbands | Wives |
|---|---|---|
| | $r$ | $r$ |
| *Self-disclosure* | | |
| Androgynous | .163 | .263 |
| Sex-typed | .090 | .026 |
| Undifferentiated | −.018 | −.333 |
| *Love Disclosure* | | |
| Androgynous | .270 | .202 |
| Sex-typed | .126 | 1.09 |
| Undifferentiated | −.312 | −.135 |

androgynous and undifferentiated individuals for self-disclosure, $z = 2.23$, $p < .03$; and for husbands between the correlations for androgynous and un-differentiated individuals for love disclosure, $z = 1.967$, $p < .05$. While these findings were not predicted, they are still of interest and may be suggestive of some differential tendencies that different sex role type individuals may experience in their partners' extradyadic disclosure.

None of the correlations between spouse's disclosure to opposite-sex friends and one's marital adjustment reached significance, although there was a tendency for androgynous individuals to show a slight positive relation, sex-typed individuals no relation, and undifferentiated individuals an inverse relation. This finding was replicated for both spouses, which suggests that it may be more than spurious. If so, what might it represent? A further look at table 10–4 shows that undifferentiated individuals, as compared to androgy-nous and sex-typed individuals, revealed the least amount of self-disclosure and love disclosure to spouses. This was further confirmed in significant dif-ferences between androgynous husbands and undifferentiated husbands for self-disclosure to spouse and for love disclosure to spouse ($t(106) = 2.36$, $p < .02$; $t(108) = 2.93$, $p < .004$) and masculine husbands and undifferenti-ated husbands on self-disclosure to spouse ($t(106) = 2.31$, $p < .03$). In addi-tion, feminine wives indicated more self-disclosure to husbands than did un-differentiated wives ($t(106) = 2.78$, $p < .006$). What this seems to indicate is that disclosure to spouse for undifferentiated individuals is relatively low compared to the other groups. If so, we may assume that when partners of these individuals disclose outside the dyad, a potential imbalance is created within the dyad which may violate a norm of reciprocity. In other words, undifferentiated individuals may be disclosing less because they are receiving less, hence their perceptions of external disclosure by their partners may en-gender jealousies that disturb their marital adjustment.

## Summary and Conclusions

Our analyses have generated support for including sex role orientation as a mediating variable when investigating self-disclosure to various targets inside and outside the marital dyad. In particular, we found that spouses demon-strate the greatest levels of disclosure to each other and to same-sex versus opposite-sex friends. This last finding is of particular interest in that previous research (Booth and Hess 1974; Jourard 1964) has found that unmarried individuals typically disclose more to opposite-sex acquaintances or to fe-males. That marriage serves as a contingency factor in establishing appropri-ate guidelines for extradyadic disclosure appears to be demonstrated by our findings. Also, we found that sex role orientation further mediates this rela-tionship. Androgynous individuals as compared to sex-typed individuals appear to distribute their extradyadic disclosure differentially. Androgynous individuals were seen to display greater *relative* proportions of opposite-sex to same-sex disclosure and friend disclosure to spouse disclosure than their sex-typed counterparts. Also, greater differences in disclosure patterns were seen when comparing sex-typed individuals as compared to androgynous individuals.

When the effect of spousal extradyadic intimate disclosure to an opposite-friend was examined in terms of its impact on marital adjustment, the results were not as clear-cut. For androgynous and sex-typed individuals, an inverse relationship between spousal extra-dyadic intimate disclosure to an opposite-sex friend and marital adjustment was not found and no significant differences in the strengths of correlations were observed. However, when undifferentiated individuals were included in the analysis, a tendency emerged suggesting that these individuals may be the ones most perturbed by this type of disclosure. This may reflect a violation of the norm of reciprocity, or an imbalance in disclosure patterns in these individuals' relationships, as these were the people most likely to indicate low levels of spousal disclosure.

Of direct relevance to the family practitioner or researcher are the mediating effects of sex-role orientation on the intradyadic and extradyadic disclosure patterns of married persons. Jourard (1971) and others (see Cozby 1973) have suggested that full, unlimited disclosure may be related to maximal adjustment, but others (Gilbert 1976) believe an optimal level of disclosure within marriage is most beneficial. Our study, while not resolving that issue, sheds light on some mitigating factors that may play into the full-versus optimal-disclosure level controversy. Certainly, it is apparent that the manner in which one defines himself or herself is related to what one considers appropriate disclosure. To prescribe an across-the-board ideal of disclosure for married couples without taking these other factors into consideration is to ignore information that may allow one to more accurately assess the private needs of particular individuals. Different couples and individuals probably have worked out strategies that work best and are well liked. It is perhaps these contingency factors that make up the context in which disclosure occurs that may in the long run unravel more about this central aspect of relationship formation and maintenance.

# 11
# The Need for Change

S table, nonchanging societies are characterized by cultural integration
and continuity. Rapidly changing societies inevitably pass through periods of cultural disintegration and discontinuity. In most societies the
question of what it means to be male or female would not be an issue. In
contemporary Western society however, there are few areas of cultural life
called into question more often during the past two decades than that of sex
roles. When traditional ways of thinking, living, and behaving are in the
process of change, change is rarely uniform (Ogburn 1920, 1955). This observation is no less true for the current redefinition of sex roles. The specific
contradictory form the current cultural discontinuity in the male sex role
takes includes: (1) the expectation that males are to become intimately involved in primary relationships that include the reciprocal verbal expression
of emotions; (2) a parental socialization structure that renders the male psychologically incapable of entering into such intimate relationships; and (3)
the expectation that males will preferentially participate in extrafamilial social institutions in which the expression of human emotions are devalued,
leaving the familial, emotionally laden roles to females.

This last chapter will examine alternative change strategies that might
effectively restore continuity in a society that defines men as expressing feelings too little. To highlight the need for change, I will begin by summarizing
some of the more recent popular writing on men's difficulty with intimacy.

## The Search for Male Intimacy
## in Current Popular Books

The popularity of several recent books is evidence of the current public interest in the inability of males to be intimate. *Women Who Love Too Much*
(Norwood 1985) describes the dilemma facing women who have emotionally
invested in a relationship with a man, only to find they are receiving very
little emotional support in return. It is significant that the subtitle to Nor-

wood's book is, *When You Keep Wishing and Hoping He'll Change.* Norwood believes that many women who are married to men who cannot fully love back are living with an illusion that if they will just love a little bit more, then surely their husbands will reciprocate such expressions of love. The tragedy, according to Norwood, is that there is little evidence that men can be expected to change.

*Men Who Hate Women and The Women Who Love Them* (Forward and Torres 1986) is another national best-seller that deals with emotional imbalance in female/male realtionships. Forward and Torres believe many women are caught up in relationships with men who love them, yet cause them tremendous pain. This pain is caused by men who intimidate by yelling or withdrawing into angry silence; switch from charm to anger without warning; belittle a woman's opinions, feelings, or accomplishments; withdraw love, money, approval, or sex as a form of punishment or control; or humiliate a woman in front of others. An ad targeted toward women readers says "Alone, he may not be able to help himself control his behavior. But *you can.* Because, of course, this is *not* the way love is supposed to feel. And understanding your man's destructive pattern, and the part you play in it, is the first step in breaking the pattern, healing the hurt, and regaining vital self-respect and confidence" *The Book Review,* Los Angeles Times, 21 September 1986, p. 7).

No fewer than three recent books have focused on the adverse effect upon relationships resulting from men's uneasiness with intimacy. *The McGill Report On Male Intimacy* (McGill 1985) is a qualitative analysis of the nature of the relationships between men and their wives, children, other women, and male friends. McGill's conclusions are not very encouraging. In marriage he finds, "Most wives live with and love men who are in some very fundamental ways strangers to them—men who withhold themselves and, in doing so, withhold their loving. These wives may be loved, but they do not feel loved because they do not know their husbands" (p. 74). Even in relationships with "other women," where a man can be "revealing without risk, caring without commitment or loss of control, honest without being hassled," McGill finds that "men are not completely self-disclosing. . . . As a result, rarely does anyone really know a man, rarely does anyone know his love and feel loved by him" (pp. 115–116). As a father, the average man is found to be more "phantom man" than "family man," for even "when he is present he is absent—there in body, but in every other respect removed from the family. Present or absent, the father is reliant on his spouse to relate to the children for him. Whatever closeness he has with his daughter is more likely to be based on imagery and illusion than on information about himself. His relationship with his son is circumscribed by competition, where proving oneself is more important than presenting oneself" (p. 155). Men do not fare much better in their relationships with other men, in which they are found to be "superficial, even shallow." Even the best of buddies "reveal so little of themselves to each other that they are little more than acquaintances. There is no intimacy in most male relationships and none in what intimacy offers: solace and support" (p. 184).

*In A Man's World: Father, Son, Brother, Friend and Other Roles Men Play* (Garfinkel 1985) offers another pessimistic analysis of the way men handle intimacy. In reflecting on what a boy can expect to gain from his father, Garfinkel states, "If he has learned well—about the importance of power, achievement, competition, and emotional inexpressiveness—he will enter relationships with other men with great caution and distrust" (p. 43). And what is the most important lesson a boy can learn from his brother? It is that " . . . rivalry rules. He who comes in first—who is born first, scores higher, earns more—is better. Like an endless game of one-upmanship from cradle to coffin. The lessons of competition and emotional inexpressiveness come through the brother bond as well" (p. 95). Men may join clubs as a retreat from the competitive nonnurturant society at large—"Once inside, however, they are faced with similar struggles and competitions for power and control. . . . A man comes away from his men's club and fraternity experience with mixed feelings. His need to belong is fulfilled but his need for closeness to men may not be" (p. 107). Although Garfinkel finds a lack of intimacy among men, he believes they should not be content in this condition. He summarizes that "men should talk to each other. Not the proverbial 'shoptalk,' but the deeper feelings about work, about love, about themselves, *about their feelings for each other*" (p. 180).

*Finding Our Fathers: the Unfinished Business of Manhood* (Osherson 1986) is the book most theoretically based of the recent qualitative analysis of men's struggle with intimacy. Osherson's thesis is that "boys grow into manhood with a *wounded father* within, a conflicted inner sense of masculinity rooted in men's experience of their fathers as rejecting, incompetent, or absent" (p. 3). In borrowing upon the works of Chodorow (1978), Osherson argues that the process of individuation is difficult for boys because they must first psychologically separate from their mother, and secondly identify and bond with their father. "The end result of the boys separation-individuation struggle is that men carry around as adults a burden of vulnerability, dependency, or emptiness within themselves, still grieving, reliving a time when going to mother for help as they wanted to was inappropriate, and they wouldn't or couldn't go to father with the confusion, anger, or sadness they felt. When men are put in touch with their pain today, they respond ambivalently—with rage or shame, attempting to prove their independence, as well as with curiosity and a desire to deal the wounds they feel" (pp. 6–7). All of this renders men distant, cool, and inexpressive in interpersonal relationships.

*Intimate Strangers: Men and Women Together* (Rubin 1983) represents an attempt to build upon psychoanalytic feminist views in explaining why men have so much trouble in meeting the intimacy needs of women. When boys, who have been raised by a woman, attempt to establish their gender identity, they find it necessary to renounce their connection with their mothers. As Rubin (pp. 55–56) argues, "He must renounce this connection with the first person outside self to be internalized into his inner psychic world—the one who has been so deeply embedded in his psychic life as to seem a part of himself—and seek instead a deeper attachment and identification with father. But this father with whom he is expected to identify has, until this time, been a secondary character in his internal life, often little more than a sometimes pleasurable, sometimes troublesome shadow on the consciousness of the developing child." As a reaction to the pain a boy experiences in this radical shift in his internal world, he begins to build defenses around his emotional expressiveness. Rubin describes this as "the development of ego boundaries that are fixed and firm—barriers that rigidly separate self from other, that circumscribe not only his relationships with others but his connection to his inner emotional life as well" (p. 56). Although males seem to show a contempt for women based upon arrogance, it is in reality a contempt born of fear, "the fear of a child who finds himself pressed to reject so powerful an inner presence as mother has been in his early life. It's a fear so great that he can live with it only by disempowering her—by convincing himself that she's a weak and puny creature whose lack of maleness must doom her forever to a subordinate and contemptible place in the world" (p. 57).

Strong mothering and weak fathering constitute an inversed socialization practice which builds into a male psychical structure an incapacity for emotional openness and sharing with another individual. Under such conditions males are deprived of the development of empathic capacities available to females. "The context within which separation takes place and identity is forged means that a girl never has to separate herself as completely and irrevocably as a boy must. Her sense of herself, therefore, is never as separate as his, she experiences herself always as more continuous with another; and the maintenance of close personal connections will continue to be one of life's essential themes for her as a result, she will preserve the capacity, born in the early symbiotic union, for participating in another's inner life, for sensing another's emotional states almost as if they were her own—the capacity that, in an adult, we call empathy" (Rubin p. 59).

Men and women reach adulthood with differing psychic structures and emotional needs. They exist together as "intimate strangers;" for women, intimacy means sharing of thoughts and feelings, and for men it means being in the same room. The implications of Rubin's position are clear. Although the source may be social-structural, the problem is perpetuated and recycled from one generation to the next because it resides within the psychic structure of men who are incapable of true intimacy. This incapacity perpetuates a cycle. Men are crippled as fathers from establishing bonds of intimacy with their children, and as husbands, of intimacy with their wives.

## Alternative Change Strategies

Male inexpressiveness can be best understood as a product of internal and external factors. Internally, male inexpressiveness can be seen as a product of personality traits or dispositions originating in a father-absent/mother-dominated socialization process that begins at birth and continues throughout the formative years. Externally, male inexpressiveness can be seen as a result of interpersonal, situational, and social-structural conditions existing in society. In contrast to a strict "medical" model that conceptualizes male inexpressiveness as internal to the individual, I have employed a more structural model casting inexpressiveness as behavior exhibited by men because it has been, or continues to be, at least partly functional within the social structures and systems within which it resides. The difficulty is that this inexpressive behavior is also partly dysfunctional, in light of the changing social and cultural structures and changing definitions and expectations of the male role.

Strategies for change in inexpressive males involve individual therapy and couple and family therapy. Men's groups, which focus on both male consciousness-raising and structural changes in male-female relationships, are also effective. Finally, structural change is required in the broader system of major social institutions—the family, the economy, the legal system, etc.

### Individual Therapy

When treating an inexpressive male alone, some effort will be made to investigate family background and past experiences. This exploration may uncover specific events that have triggered the blocking of emotional expression. Working through some of these painful experiences and recognizing dysfunctional interactional patterns may provide incentive for change. Reality testing can assist in discerning inappropriate affective expression. Once an awareness is established, and providing the individual wants to change his behavior, various treatments may be appropriate. Behavioral procedures such as desensitization and rehearsal, Gestalt techniques such as role playing and empty-chair confrontations, rational-emotive approaches such as restructuring belief systems, and relational approaches such as role modeling and improving communication skills are all treatment strategies that may be useful in helping an individual change inexpressive patterns.

## Marriage and Family Therapy

Conjoint therapy with a couple or family emphasizes a systems theory framework. The obvious advantage this approach has over individual therapy is that the therapist has firsthand experience in observing communication between couples or family members and can, therefore, detect dysfunctional patterns. The interactional material that emerges "in session" sets the stage for pointing out ways to improve interaction. When a cyclical response occurs between an overexpressive partner and inexpressive partner, each can begin to recognize his or her own part in the pattern and can be encouraged to concentrate on specific ways of breaking established patterns.

In conjoint family sessions, each member becomes aware of the negative effects of inexpressiveness, since it leads to erroneous assumptions and conclusions by other members. The more verbally expressive members, on the other hand, often err by not listening, interrupting, and speaking for others. Conjoint therapy provides a real-life situation in which each member can recognize how he or she contributes to the breakdown of the whole system. It becomes a dramatic way of experiencing the interconnectedness of patterns and the recognition of how important it is for all members to participate in the change process. It takes cooperative efforts to ensure permanent changes that will benefit the entire system.

In 1974 I wrote an article for *Woman's Day* entitled, "Why Husbands Can't Say 'I Love You'." This article was primarily addressed to wives, suggesting ways in which they might attempt to draw an inexpressive husband out of his shell. I believe there is a place for such an emphasis, for some males are better able to become expressive by means of an understanding wife. In a well-taken criticism of the *Woman's Day* article, Sattel (1976) points out the danger in burdening the wife with this additional "emotional work" at a time in history when she is probably struggling to define who she is. If I were to write another article to wives on this subject (the editor strongly suggested that few husbands would actually read the article), I would emphasize the need for a change in the amount of time spent in certain roles. I would suggest to wives that they encourage their husbands to assume more of the childrearing responsibilities in the home, which may be induced only if they themselves become more involved in activity outside the home.

## Men's Groups

Two types of men's group activities appear to be useful in increasing inexpressive males' ability to express feelings—consciousness-raising and cognitive-behavioral change. A neglected impetus for change involves making men aware of the potential gains of changed role relationships. One way of heightening this awareness has been through men's consciousness-raising groups. Such groups, in which males are able to open up to each other and exchange experiences related to their masculine identities, are undoubtedly enabling males to become more expressive. There is some evidence that such groups are effective in providing the needed impetus for change long after involvement in such a group has ceased. However, a selective factor may be involved in the formation of such groups. The males who are most aware of the stifling effects of our culture's "masculine" emphasis are most likely to be the ones to join such groups. Thus, those men who could benefit most from consciousness-raising group involvement are the ones who may never be a part of such a group.

Many inexpressive males are not good candidates for most types of therapy and would be extremely reluctant to enter personal, couple, or family therapy because to do so could be seen by themselves and others as an expression of weakness and vulnerability, feelings he has been taught to avoid. My finding has been that the least expressive men are the least likely to be interested in programs dealing with "feelings." There are several explanations for this, some of which were discussed previously in describing male socialization. Part of the problem, no doubt, arises from a fear of the unknown and of change. Other aspects involve exaggerated and irrational ideas that men might have about the nature of such programs, including the idea that they are run by "radicals" who want to "put them down" and who will try to get them to change their personalities and behavior drastically. Another exaggerated and irrational idea that men have expressed is that participating in such "men's groups" is tantamount to homosexual behavior and so they resist participating. This is an important reason for not only using a skills approach combined with cognitive restructuring to encourage changes in men's behavior and beliefs, but also for addressing primarily one specific element, expressive behavior, and doing so in a very systematic fashion. Expressiveness training is less threatening to inexpressive males since it affords the opportunity to improve expressiveness skills in an unthreatening, accepting environment. While addressing behavioral deficits, here they are also introduced to new skills with the use of reinforcement techniques encouraging more satisfying behavior. Even though the primary effort is focused on changes in behavior and skills, attitudes and beliefs are recognized and attention is paid to cognitive strategies and unstructured consciousness raising. Issues related to rigid sex-role stereotypes and the ways in which they limit men's behavior are addressed to provide new ways of behaving.

For those men with particularly intense or severe personal, couple, or family problems, the training serves to motivate them to take advantage of group or individual counseling or therapy. These therapies can make use of cognitive restructuring activities, challenging the beliefs that men must always be strong, tough, expert, and competent. Assessments made before, during, and after the training are used to evaluate progress. They also identify more serious problems that would require referral for more in-depth treatment techniques.

An additional advantage of the group training approach is the group's dynamics of cohesion and support and the increased opportunities for modeling. In addition, expressiveness training can be used as a preventive as well as a treatment program, thus increasing its potential efficacy with widely diverse groups. Finally, this program teaches specific skills that can be added to a male's behavioral repertoire of expressiveness in different situations. No assumption is made that males should always be expressive in every situation. Instead, the primary assumptions of expressiveness training are: (a) men can learn to be more expressive, (b) men can choose to be more expressive in a variety of situations with various individuals, and (c) many men can benefit intra- and interpersonally from becoming more expressive. Expressiveness training uses techniques and procedures borrowed from assertiveness training, communication skills training, and group dynamics, and is an effective means of increasing male expressiveness.

### Social Structural Change

Social psychological research indicates that it is much easier to bring about attitudinal change by changing behavior than it is to cause behavioral change by changing attitudes. In a similar vein, the most effective way to change inexpressive males may be to change their role commitments rather than their attitudes about expressiveness. Or, to put it another way, the most effective way to reduce male inexpressiveness may be to change the social structures that encourage inexpressiveness in males rather than to attempt to directly change their personalities.

If men are to become more expressive, social structural change is needed in two important areas: (1) their involvement in *parenting* within the home, and (2) the demands placed upon them to give high-priority involvement in *economic* activities outside of the home. At present most parenting is, in reality, mothering. Fathers need to be jointly involved in childbearing efforts. The father's contribution must be significant enough to enable "in-depth" emotional bonding to take place between him and his children. This structural change is especially important for the development of emotional expressiveness in sons. As Chodorow has theorized and Rubin's research has supported, the more exclusively a boy is parented by a mother, the greater his need to be superior to women and negate any behavior hinting at femininity. As my own research has shown, when sons view their fathers as being expressive, they too are expressive of their feelings.

A latent result of fathers becoming involved in the parenting process is the likelihood that they will become more expressive. In contrast to men in the world of work, where decisions are expected to be based on the rational rather than the emotional, men as caretakers of children will find themselves more inclined to consider personal and emotional issues. This will affect work roles as well.

It may very well be that, because of the separation of work and family brought about by the industrial revolution, fathers are less emotionally bonded with their children today than they were in the past. As men's roles are traditionally defined, men are expected to commit themselves to a lifetime of hard work and economic support of their family. This they could do. The modern definition of the male role however, includes the expectation that men establish and cultivate the emotional dimension of their relationship with their wives, their children, kin, and close friends in general. This they have trouble doing. "He can act out anger and frustration inside the family, it's true. But ask him to express his sadness, his fear, his dependency—all those feelings that would expose his vulnerability to himself or to another and he's likely to close down as if under some compulsion to protect himself" (Rubin 1983, 82).

Tragic, but true: we now live in a society in which cultural definitions of masculinity are not in harmony with the inner capacities of men. Men are expected to possess the emotional capacities that will enable them to tenderly nurture their children, and sympathetically listen to the frustrations and hurts of their wives, as well as share their own feelings of love, joy, disappointment, and sorrow. If we are to take seriously the evidence suggesting that modern society has become increasingly cold, heartless, and impersonal, then the need for the family to be intimate, nurturant, and caring becomes even more evident. Men must daily do battle in this impersonal and heartless society, and they often returned battered and bruised to the confines of their self-contained, somewhat fragile, emotionally isolated nuclear family. At the same time, wider social-structural supports for family members—extended families, neighborhood support networks, community embeddedness—largely have been eroded by the cultural move towards modernity. The result is that the nuclear family often becomes the sole potential source for meeting its members' emotional needs. Because of all of these social and cultural changes, men need and are emotionally needed by their family members more than ever.

However, family roles cannot be altered without altering work roles. Thus the second type of structural change needed is in the priority demands the economic institution makes on men. As Rubin states:

> Generally, men still are best at the cognitive, rational mode that work requires, so it's where they turn for validation. Usually, women still are more comfortable in the emotional and experimental mode that interpersonal connections require, so that's where they look for fulfillment. For men, therefore, it's still work that gets their first allegiance, if not in word, then in deed; for women it's still love. (p. 182)

There are several types of social-structural constraints which need to be changed in society at large to increase male expressiveness. Systemic linkage between the family and the economy is one area of needed change, and the legal system another.

That the father is usually the main link between the family and the economy means first that he is not around the home very much because his job generally is performed elsewhere. Hence, he has much less opportunity to be expressive toward his children even if he so desires because his job greatly reduces the time he can spend with them. He must usually crowd any attempts at expressiveness into a few hours at the end of a work day (when his emotional resources for doing so are probably lowest) or into increasingly busy weekends. He may thus attempt to telescope his emotional expressiveness into these limited time periods by inventing and improvising shorthand symbols of it, such as purchasing gifts, taking the family on a brief excursion for milkshakes after dinner, playing quick-ending games, making jokes, and telling bedtime stories.

That the father is the main link between the family and the economy also means that for approximately eight hours a day, he will likely be exposed through his job to an environment which, by stressing rationality and emotional control rather than emotional expression, will reinforce his initial tendencies not to be expressive. Societal norms regulating ties between the family and the economy recognize the father as that link by stressing the priority of his work role even when it involves hardships for the family (hence, making it more difficult for him to leave and thus remove a basic link between the family and the economy). If the family can possibly do without the income, a mother is expected to give up her job should it interfere with her relationship to her children, but the father is expected to give priority to his job over his role as a parent.

The legal system further discourages the father's development of expressive relations with his children by playing down the father-child relationship. Fatherhood, and thus the father-child relationship, is not a legally acceptable reason for being deferred from the military draft. Divorce laws have traditionally expressed preference for the mother-child relationship by usually giving the mother custody of the children and relegating the father to the position of having to seek legal permission to visit his own children. Fathers can be brought into court for not financially supporting their children; unless physical harm results to the children, as in the cases of battered or neglected children, the laws say little about the absence of emotional support from fathers. But the legal system is changing in response to the recognized importance of the father's role. An increase in male expressiveness will follow such structural change—an expectation one film writer has already attempted to illustrate in the movie Kramer vs Kramer.

The current structure of economic life and family life work together to keep men and women dependent upon each other. *While women are kept economically dependent upon men, men are kept emotionally dependent upon women.* What is most needed is a change in the amount of time males are asked to devote to emotion-laden roles. If men committed as much of their time to relating to their children as their wives do, it would undoubtedly be reflected in their own expressive ability, not to mention the effect it would have on their sons. Part of the needed structural changes have already been initiated by women's redefining their role in society; these changes will "force" men to commit greater amounts of their time to roles that carry higher expressive expectations.

For many men the current clash between the traditional and modern male role is experienced personally as contradictory and inconsistent. The resulting anxiety may tempt men to react defensively against the current redefinition of sex roles. But the challenge can also be viewed as an opportunity— an opportunity to become more fully developed human beings. The obvious benefits from such change will be to those involved personally with men; the less obvious, but no less real benefits, will be to the men themselves.

# Bibliography

Abbey, A. 1982. Sex differences in attributions for friendly behavior: do males misperceive females' friendliness? *Journal of Personality and Social Psychology* 42:830–38.

Abrahams, B., S. S. Feldman, and S. C. Nash. 1978. Sex-role self-concepts and sex-role attitudes: enduring personality characteristics or adaptations to changing life situations? *Developmental Pschology* 14:393–400.

Aldous, J. 1969. Wives' employment status and lower-class men as husband-fathers: support for the Moynihan thesis. *Journal of Marriage and the Family* 31 (3): 469–76.

Almeida, E. 1980. Factors related to changing sex-roles: a cross-national study of four countries. *Report to UNESCO.*

Altman, I., and D. Taylor. 1973. *Social Penetration: The Development of Interpersonal Relationships,* New York: Holt, Rinehart, and Winston.

Angrist, S. 1975. Social science research on women: an overview. *Signs* (Autumn): 175–83.

Annicchiarico, L. 1973. Sex differences in self-disclosure as related to sex and status of the interviewer. *Dissertation Abstracts International* 34 2296B.

Antill, J. K. 1983. Sex-role complementarity versus similarity in married couples. *Journal of Personality and Social Psychology* 45:145–55.

Archer, R. 1979. Role of personality and the social situation. In G. J. Chelune (ed.), *Self-disclosure: Origins, Patterns, and Implications of Openness in Interpersonal Relationships,* San Francisco: Jossey-Bass.

Aries, E. J., and F. L. Johnson. 1983. Close friendship in adulthood: conventional content between same-sex friends. *Sex Roles* 9:12, 1183–96.

Auerback, A. 1970. The cowboy syndrome. Summary of research contained in a personal letter from the author.

Balkwell, C., J. Balswick, and J. Balkwell. 1978. On black and white family patterns in America: their impact on the expressive aspect of sex-role socialization. *Journal of Marriage and the Family* 40:743–47.

Balswick, J. 1970a. The effect of spouse companionship support on employment success. *Journal of Marriage and the Family* 32:212–15.

Balswick, J. 1970b. Theology and political attitudes among clergymen. *Sociological Quarterly* 11 (Fall): 369–404.

———. 1974. Why husbands can't say I love you. *Woman's Day* (April).

———. 1975. The development of an emotion scale and an expression of emotion scale. American Sociological Association Meeting, San Francisco.

———. 1978. The effect of a broken home upon children's feelings and expression of feelings. *The Family Life Educator* 9 (2): 3–6.

———. 1979. The inexpressive male: functional-conflict and role theory as contrasting explanations. *The Family Coordinator* 28:331–36.

———. 1981a. Inexpressiveness as role behavior for men, in *Men in Difficult Times.* R. Lewis (ed.). New York: Random House.

———. 1981b. The expressive male, in *Forty-Nine Percent Majority: Readings on the Male Sex Role,* 2nd ed. D. David and R. Brannon (eds.). Addison-Wesley Publishing Co.

———. 1981c. Personality vs. strategy: a reply to Sattel, in *The Forty-Nine Percent Majority: Readings on the Male Sex Role,* 2nd ed. D. David and R. Brannon (eds.). Addison-Wesley Publishing Co.

———. 1982a. Strong men and virtuous women: changing male and female roles in Korea. *Royal Asiatic Society Transactions* (Spring).

———. 1982b. Male inexpressiveness: psychological and social aspects, in *Men in Transition: Theory and Therapy.* K. Solomon and N. Levy (eds.). New York: Plenum Publishing Co.

Balswick, J., T. Abernathy, C. Proctor, and P. Stover. 1974. Emotional feelings and expressiveness among married couples. Paper presented at the Annual Meeting of the National Council on Family Relations. St. Louis.

Balswick, J., and C. Averett. 1977. Differences in expressiveness: gender, interpersonal orientation, and perceived parental expressiveness as contributing factors. *Journal of Marriage and the Family* 39 (February): 121–27.

Balswick, J., and J. Balkwell. 1977. Self-disclosure to same- and opposite-sex parents: an empirical test of insights from role theory. *Sociometry* 40 (September): 282–86.

Balswick, J., and J. Balkwell. 1978. Religious orthodoxy and emotionality. *Review of Religious Research* 19:308–19.

Balswick, J., and C. Peek. The inexpressive male and family relationships during early adulthood. *Sociol Symp* 4:1–2.

Balswick, J., and C. Peek. 1971. The inexpressive male: a tragedy of American society. *The Family Coordinator* 20:363–68.

Balswick, J., D. Ward, and D. Carlson. 1975. Theological and socio-political belief change among religiously conservative students. *Review of Religious Research* 17 (Fall): 61–67.

Barclay, A., and D. Cusumano. 1967. Father-absence; cross-sex identity, and field-dependent behavior in male adolescents. *Child Development* 38 (1): 243–50.

Bardwick, J. 1971. *Psychology of Women: A Study of Bio-cultural Conflicts.* New York: Harper and Row.

Bardwick, J. 1973. Androgyny and humanistic goals. Mimeographed paper.

Bardwick, J., and E. Douvan. 1971. Ambivalence: the socialization of women, in V. Gornick and B. Moran (eds.) *Women in Sexist Society.* New York: New American Library.

Barrera, M., Jr., and S. Ainlay. 1983. The structure of social support; a conceptual and emperical analysis. *Journal of Community Psychology* 11:133–43.

Bartemeier, L. 1953. The contribution of the father to the mental health of the family. *American Journal of Psychiatry* 110:277–80.

Baumrind, D. 1979. Current patterns of parental authority. *Developmental Psychology Monographs* 41.

Bell, R. 1967. The related importance of mother and wife roles among negro lower-class women. *Groves Conference on the Family* San Juan, Puerto Rico.

Bell, R. 1981a. Friendships of women and of men. *Psychology of Women Quarterly* 5:402–17.

Bell, R. 1981b. *Worlds of Friendship.* Beverly Hills: Sage Publications.

Bellah, R. 1970. Christianity and symbolic realism. *Journal for the Scientific Study of Religion* 9 (Summer): 89–96, 112–15.

Belsky, J., G. Gilstrap, and M. Rovine. 1984. The Pennsylvania infant and family development, I: stability and change in mother-infant and father-infant interaction in a family setting at one, three and nine months. *Child Development* 55:692–705.

Belsky, J., R. Lerner, and G. Spanier. 1984. *The Child In The Family.* Reading, MA: Addison-Wesley Publishing.

Bem, S. 1975. Sex-role adaptability: one consequence of psychological androgyny. *Journal of Personality and Social Psychology* 31:634–43.

Bem, S. L. 1974. The measurement of psychological androgyny. *Journal of Consulting Clinical Psychologists* 42:155–62.

Benedict, R. 1938. Continuities and discontinuities in cultural conditioning. *Psychiatry* 1:161–67.

Benson, L. 1968. *Fatherhood: A Sociological Perspective.* New York: Random House.

Berger, P. 1974. Some second thoughts on substantive versus functional definitions of religion. *Journal for the Scientific Study of Religion* 13:125–33.

Bernard, J. M., and S. Nesbitt. 1981. Divorce: an unreliable predictor of children's emotional predispositions. *Journal of Divorce* 4:31–41.

Berscheid, E., E. Walster, and G. Bohrnstedt. 1973. The body image report. *Psychology Today* 7:119–31.

Bienvenu, M. 1970. Measurement of marital communication. *The Family Coordinator* 19:26–31.

Biller, H. 1971. *Father, Child, and Sex Role.* Lexington, Mass.: Lexington Books.

Biller, H. B. 1981. "Father Absence, Divorce and Personality Development. In M. Lamb (ed.) *The Role of the Father in Child Development.* New York: John Wiley.

Blackburn, T. 1971. Sensuous-intellectual complementarity in science. *Science* 172 (June 11): 1003–07.

Blalock, H. 1960. *Social Statistics.* New York: McGraw-Hill Co.

Block, J. 1982. Assimilation, accommodation, and dynamics of personality development. *Child Development* 53:281–94.

———. 1973. Conceptions of sex roles: some cross-cultural and longitudinal perspectives. *American Psychologist* 28:512–29.

Block, J., J. H. Block, and J. Harrington. 1974. Some misgivings about the matching familiar figures test as a measure of reflectuin-impulsivity. *Developmental Psychology* 10:611–32.

Blood, R., and D. Wolfe. 1960. *Husbands and Wives: The Dynamics of Married Living.* Glencoe: Free Press.

———. 1969. Negro-white differences in blue-collar marriage in a northern metropolis. *Social Forces* 48:59–64.

Blumer, H. 1969. *Symbolic Interactionism: Perspective and Method.* Englewood Cliffs: Prentice-Hall.

Booth, A., and E. Hess. 1974. Cross-sex friendship. *Journal of Marriage and the Family,* 36:38–47.

Boyd, L., and A. Roach. 1977. Interpersonal communication skills differentiating more satisfying from less satisfying marital relationships. *Journal of Counseling Psychology* 24:540–42.

Brenton, M. 1966. *The American Male.* New York: Coward-McCann.

Brody, Leslie R. 1985. Gender difference in emotional development: a review of theories and research. *Journal of Personality* 53:102–49.

Bronfenbrenner, U. 1961. Some familial antecedents of responsibility and leadership in adolescents. In Petrullo, L. and Bass, B. (eds.) *Leadership and Interpersonal Behavior.* New York: Holt, Rinehart, and Winston.

Bronstein, P. 1984. Differences in mother's and father's behavior toward children: a cross-cultural comparison. *Developmental Psychology* 20:995–1003.

Brooks, E. 1974. Interactive effects of sex and status on self-disclosure. *Journal of Counseling Psychology* 21:469–74.

Broverman, I. K., S. R. Vogel, D. M. Broverman, F. E. Clarkson, and P. S. Rosenkrantz. 1972. Sex-role stereotypes: a current appraisal. *Journal of Sociological Issues.* 28:59–78.

Brown, D. 1957. Masculinity-femininity development in children. *Journal of Counseling Psychology* 21:197–203.

Burgess, E., and H. Locke. 1955. *The Family.* New York: American Book.

Burgess, R. J., T. Weir, and D. Harrison. 1976. Disclosure of problems and tension experienced by marital partners. *Psychological Report* 38:531–42.

Byrne, D. 1971. *The Attraction Paradigm.* New York: Academic.

Caldwell, M. A., and L. A. Peplau. 1982. Sex differences in same-sex friendships. *Sex Roles* 2:149–60.

Cash, T. F. 1975. Self-disclosure in the acquaintance process: effects of sex, physical attractiveness, and approval motivation. *Dissertation Abstracts International* 35:3572B.

Chafetz, J. 1974. *Masculine/Feminine or Human,* Itasca, Ill.: F.E. Peacock Publishers, Inc.

Chelune, G. T., E. M.Waring, B. N. Vosk, F. E. Sultan, and T. K. Ogden. 1984. Self-disclosure and its relationship to marital intimacy. *Journal of Clinical Psychology* 40:216–19.

Chelune, G. 1979. Measuring openness in interpersonal communication, in Chelune, G. (ed.) *Self-Disclosure.* San Francisco: Jossey-Bass. 1–27.

Chodorow, N. 1978. *The Reproduction of Mothering.* Berkeley: University of California Press.

Ciminero, A., K. Calhoun, and H. Adams (eds.). 1977. *Handbook of Behavioral Assessment.* New York: John Wiley and Sons.

Clayton, R. 1975. *The Family Marriage, and Social Change,* Indianapolis, Ind.: DC Heath and Co.

Coleman, J. 1962. *The Adolescent Society.* New York: Free Press.

Coleman, K. H. 1980. Conjugal violence: what 33 men report. *Journal of Marital and Family Therapy* (April) 207–13.

Conger, R. D. 1976. Social control and social learning models of delinquent behavior: a synthesis. *Criminology* 14:17–40.

Cooley, C. 1922. *Human Nature and the Social Order.* New York: Shocken Books.

Cozby, P. 1973. Self disclosure: a literature review. *Psychology Bulletin* 79:73–92.

Cromwell, R. E., D. Olson, and D. G. Fournier. 1976. Diagnosis and evaluation in marital and family counseling. In *Treating Relationships* D. Olson (ed.) Lake Mills: Graphic Publishing. 517–62.

Cuber, J., and P. Harroff. 1965. *The Significant Americans: A Study of Sexual Behavior Among the Affluent.* New York: Appleton-Century-Crofts.

Daher, D. and P. Banikiotes. 1976. Interpersonal attraction and rewarding aspects of disclosure content and level. *Journal of Personality and Social Psychology* 33 (4): 492–96.

Damgaard, J. 1974. *Structured Versus Unstructured Procedures for Training Groups in the Expression of Feeling-Cause Relations.* Dissertation, Duke University, Durham, N.C. Abstracted, *Dissertation Abstracts Int* 1975. 35:499B.

Davidson, B., and D. L. Sollie. 1974. Sex-role orientation and marital adjustment. Paper presented at the *National Council on Family Relations* annual meeting. San Francisco.

Davidson, B., J. Balswick, and C. Halverson. 1983a. Affective self-disclosure and marital adjustment: a test of equity theory. *Journal of Marriage and Family* 45 (1): 93–102.

———. 1983b. The relationship between spousal affective self-disclosure and marital adjustment. *Home Economics Research Journal* 11 (4): 381–91.

Davidson, B., and D. Dosser. 1982. *Test-retest Reliabilities of the Expression of Emotion Scale.* Unpublished manuscript. (Available from B. Davidson, Department of Child and Family Development, University of Georgia, Athens, Ga.)

Davidson, L. R. and L. Duberman. 1982. Friendships: communication and interactional patterns in same-sex dyads. *Sex Roles* 8:809–22.

Davis, J. 1976. Self-disclosure in an acquaintance exercise: responsibility for level of intimacy. *Journal of Personality and Social Psychology* 33:787–92.

Davis, A., and R. Havighurst. 1946. Soial class and color differences in child-rearing. *American Sociological Review* 11:698–710.

Denzin, N. 1969. Symbolic interactionism and ethnomethodology: a proposed synthesis. *American Sociological Review* 34:922–34.

———. 1979. The interactionist study of social organization: a note on method. *Symbolic Interaction* 2:59–72.

Derleaga, V., B. A. Winstead, P. T. P. Wong, and S. Hunter. 1985. Gender effects in an initial encounter: a case where men exceed women in self-disclosure. *Journal of Social and Personal Relationships* 2:25–44.

Diaz-Loving, R., R. Diaz-Guerrero, R. L. Helmreich, and J. T. Spence. 1981. Comparacion transcultural y analysis psycometrico de una medida de ragos masculinos (instrumentales) y femeninos (expresivo). *Revista de La Associacion Latinamericana de Psicologia Social* 1:3–37.

Dickson-Markman, F. 1983. Self-disclosure among friends and lovers: an investigation of the role of friendship patterns and social support in marital satisfaction. *Dissertation Abstracts International* 43:7–B.

Dino, G. A., M. A. Barnett, and J. A. Howard. 1984. Children's expectations of sex differences in parent's responses to sons and daughters encountering interpersonal problems. *Sex Roles* 11(7/8): 709–17.

Dosser, D. 1982. Male inexpressiveness: behavioral intervention. In *Men In Transition: Theory and Therapy* K. Solomon and N. B. Levy (ed.). New York: Plenum Press. 343–437.

Dosser, D., J. Balswick, and C. Halverson. 1983. The situational context of emotional expressiveness. *Journal of Counseling Psychology* 30 (3): 375–87.

Downey, A. M. 1984. The relationship of sex-role orientation to self-perceived health status in middle-aged males. *Sex Roles* 11:211–25.

Easterbrooks, M. Ann, and W. A. Goldberg. 1984. Toddler development in the family: impact of father involvement and parenting characteristics. *Child Development* 55:740–52.

Edleson, J. L., Z. Eisikovits, and E. Guttman. 1985. Men who batter women: a critical review of the evidence. *Journal of Family Issues* 6:229–47.

Ehrich, H., and D. Graeven. 1971. Reciprocal self-disclosure in a dyad. *Journal of Experimental Social Psychology* 7 (4): 389–400.

Eisler, R.M., P. M. Miller, and M. Hersen. 1973. Components of assertive behavior. *Journal of Clinical Psychology* 29:295–99.

Eisler, R.M., M. Hersen, P. M. Miller, and et al. 1975. Situational determinants of assertive behaviors. *Journal of Consulting and Clinical Psychology* 43:330–40.

Erikson, E. 1968. *Identity: Youth and Crisis.* New York: Norton.

Farrell, M. P. 1986. Friendship between men. *Marriage and Family Review* 9:163–97.

Feldman, S. S., Z. C. Biringen, and S. C. Nash. 1981. Fluctuations of sex-related self-attributions as a function of stage of family life cycle. *Developmental Psychology* 17 (1): 24–35.

Fischer, T. L., and L. R. Narus, Jr. 1981. Sex roles and intimacy in same sex and other sex relationships. *Psychology of Women Quarterly* 5:445–55.

Fitzgerald, M. 1965. Self-disclosure and expressed self-esteem, social distance, and areas of the self revealed. *Journal of Psychology* 56:405–12.

Forward, S., and J. Torres. 1986. *Men Who Hate Women and the Women Who Love Them.* New York: Bantam.

Franco, J., T. Malloy, and R. Gonzalez. 1984. Ethnic and acculturation differences in self-disclosure. *The Journal of Social Psychology* 122:21–32.

Frazier, E. 1939. *The Negro Family in the United States.* Chicago: University of Chicago Press.

Frin, J. 1986. The relationship between sex role attitudes and attitudes supporting marital violence. *Sex Roles* 14:235–44.

Garfinkel, P. 1985. *In A Man's World: Father, Son, Brother, Friend and Other Roles Men Play.* New York: Norton.

Geertz, C. 1966. Religion as a cultural system, in Michael Banton (ed). *Anthropological Approaches to the Study of Religion.* New York: Praeger.

Gerdes, E. P., J. D. Gehling, and T. N. Rapp. 1981. The effects of sex and sex-role concept on self-disclosure. *Sex Roles* 7:989–98.

Gilbert, Lucia A., G. R. Hanson, and B. Davis. 1982. Perceptions of parental role responsibilities: differences between mothers and fathers. *Family Relations* 31:261–69.

Gilbert, L. A., C. J. Deutsch, and R. F. Strahan. 1975. Feminine and masculine dimensions of the typical desirable, and ideal woman and man. *Sex Roles* 4:767–77.

Gilbert, L. A., J. A. Waldroop, and C. J. Deutsch. 1981. Masculine and feminine stereotypes and adjustment: a reanalysis. *Psychology of Women Quarterly* 5:790–94.

Gilbert, S. 1976. Empirical and theoretical extensions of self-disclosure, in G. Miller (ed.) *Explorations in Interpersonal Communication.* Beverly Hills, Calif.: Sage.

Gilligan, C. 1982. *In a Different Voice: Psychological Theory and Women's Development.* Cambridge: Harvard University Press.

Gjerde, P. F. 1986. The interpersonal structure of family interaction settings: parent-adolescent relations in dyads and triads. *Developmental Psychology* 22:297–304.

Goldfried, M. and J. Friedman. 1982. Clinical behavior therapy and the male sex role, in K. Solomon and N. Levy (eds.) *Men in Transition: Theory and Therapy.* New York: Plenum.

Gray, S. 1957. Masculinity-femininity in relation to anxiety and social acceptance. *Child Development* 28:203–14.

Guttman, D. 1965. Women and the concept of ego strength. *Merrill-Palmer Quarterly* 11:229–40.

Hacker, H. 1957. The new burdens of masculinity. *Marriage and Family Living* 19:227–33.

Hacter, H. M. 1981. Blabbermouths and clams: sex differences in self-disclosure in same-sex and cross-sex friendship dyads. *Psychology of Women Quarterly* 5:385–401.

Hadden, J. 1977. Editor's introduction: review symposium, The New Religious Consciousness. *Journal for the Scientific Study of Religion* 16:305–309.

Hall, J. A., and A. G. Halberstadt. 1980. Masculinity and femininity in children: development of the children's personal attributes questionnaire. *Developmental Psychology* 16:270–80.

Hall, J. 1978. Assessment of assertiveness, in McReynolds, P. (ed.) *Advances in Psychological Assessment IV.* San Francisco: Jossey-Bass.

Halpern, T. 1977. Degree of client disclosure as a function of past disclosure, counselor disclosure and counselor facilitativeness. *Journal of Counseling Psychology* 24:42–47.

Halverson, C., and R. Shore. 1969. Self-disclosure and interpersonal functioning. *Journal of Counsulting Clinical Psychology* 33:213–19.

Hanford, J. 1975. A synoptic approach: resolving problems in empirical and phenomenological approaches to the psychology of religion. *Journal for the Scientific Study of Religion* 14:219–27.

Hannerz, U. 1969. *Soulside*. New York: Columbia University Press.

Hansen, J. E., and W. J. Schuldt. 1984. Marital self-disclosure and marital satisfaction. *Journal of Marriage and Family* 46:923–26.

———. 1982. Physical distance, sex, and intimacy in self-disclosure. *Psychological Rep.* 51:3–6.

Hargrove, B. 1973. Organization man on the frontier. *Journal for the Scientific Study of Religion* 12:461–66.

Harmon, H. 1976. *Modern Factor Analysis* (3rd ed.). Chicago: University of Chicago Press.

Harrison, J. 1978. Warning: the male sex role may be dangerous to your health. *Journal of Social Issues* 34:66–86.

Hartley, R. 1959. Sex-role pressures and the socialization of the male child. *Psychological Reports* 5:457–68.

Heimberg, R., D. Montgomery, C. Madsen et al. 1977. Assertion training: a review of the literature. *Behavior Therapy* 8:953–71.

Heiss, J. 1962. Degree of intimacy and male-female interaction. *Sociometry* 25:197–208.

Hendrick, S. S. 1981. Self-disclosure and material satisfaction. *Journal of Personality and Social Psychology* 40:1150–59.

Hersen, M., and A. Bellack. 1977. Assessment of social skills, in Ciminero, A., Calhoun, K. and Adams, H. (eds.) *Handbook of Behavioral Assessment*. New York: John Wiley and Sons.

Hess, B. B. 1981. Friendships and gender roles over the life course, in P. J. Stein (ed.) *Single Life*. New York: St Martin's Press.

Hetherington, E. 1972. Effects of father-absence on personality development in adolescent daughters. *Developmental Psychology* 7 (3): 313–26.

Highlen, P. 1976. Effects of social modeling and cognitive structuring strategies on affective self-disclosure of single, undergraduate males. Doctoral dissertation, Michigan State University. *Dissertation Abstracts International*. 1976. 36:5823A (University Microfilms No. 76–5571).

Highlen, P., and B. Johnston. 1979. Effects of situational variables on affective self-disclosure with acquaintances. *Journal of Counseling Psychology* 26:255–58.

Highlen, P., and N. Voight. 1978. Effects of social modeling, cognitive structuring, and self-management strategies on affective self-disclosure. *Journal of Counseling Psychology* 25:21–34.

Hirschi, T. 1969. *Causes of Delinquency*. Berkeley: University of California Press.

Hoffman, L. 1972. Early childhood experiences and women's achievement motives. *Journal of Social Issues* 28 (2): 129–55.

Hollandsworth, J., and K. Wall. 1977. Sex differences in assertive behavior: an empirical investigation. *Journal of Counseling Psychology* 24:217–22.

Hollingshead, A. 1949. *Elmstown's Youth*. New York: Wiley.

Hunter, F. T., and J. Touniss. 1982. Changes in functions of three relations during adolescence. *Developmental Psychology* 18 (6): 806–11.

Hurvitz, N. 1964. Marital strain in the blue-collar family, in A. Shostak and W. Gomberg (eds.) *Blue-Collar World*. Englewood Cliffs: Prentice-Hall.

Hyink, P. W. 1975. The influence of client ego strength, client sex and therapist sex on the frequency, depth, and focus of client self-disclosure. *Dissertation Abstracts International* 35:4652B

Ickes, W. 1981. Sex role influence in dyadic interaction: a theoretical model. In C. Mayo and N. M. Henley (ed.) *Gender and Noverbal Behavior* New York: Springer-Verlag.

Ilgengritz, M. 1961. Mothers on their own—widows and divorcees. *Marriage and Family Living* 23 (1): 38–41.

Ingoldsby, B. 1979. Emotional expressiveness and marital adjustment: a multi-method, cross-cultural analysis, Ph.D. dissertation, University of Georgia.

Inman, D. J. 1978. Self-disclosure and interviewer reciprocity. *Dissertation Abstracts International* 38:3398B.

Irelan, L. (ed.) 1967. *Low-Income Life Styles*. Washington, D.C.: U.S. Department of Health, Education, and Welfare.

Izard, C. 1971. *The Face of Emotion*. New York: Appleton-Century-Crofts.

———. 1972. *Human Emotions*. New York: Plenum Press.

Jackubowski, P., and P. Lacks. 1975. Assessment procedures in assertion training. *Counseling Psyhcology* 5 (4): 84–89.

Jenkins, J. 1971. Review of J. R. Earle, D. D. Knudsen, D. W. Shriver, "Spindles and Spires," *Journal for the Scientific Study of Religion* 16:421–22.

Johnson, M. 1963. Sex role learning in the nuclear family. *Child Development* 34:319–33.

Johnson, M., J. Stockard, J. Acker, and C. Naffziger. 1975. Expressiveness reevaluated. *School Review* 83:617–44.

Jorgensen, S. R., and T. C. Gaudy. 1980. Self-disclosure and satisfaction in marriage: the relation examined. Family relations examined. *Family Relations* 20:281–87.

Jourard, S. 1959. Self-disclosure and other-cathexis. *Journal of Abnormal and Social Psychology* 59:428–31.

———. 1961. Age trends in self-disclosure. *Merrill-Palmer Quarterly* 7:191–97.

———. 1964. *The Transparent Self*. Princeton: Van Nostrand.

———. 1971. *Self-Disclosure: An Experimental Analysis of the Transparent Self*. New York: John Wiley and Sons.

Jourard, S., and M. Landsman. 1960. Cognition, cathexis, and the dyadic effect in men's self-disclosing behavior. *Merrill-Palmer Quarterly* 6:178–86.

Jourard, S., and P. Lasakow. 1958. Some factors in self-disclosure. *Journal of Abnormal Social Psychology* 56:92–98.

Jourard, S., and P. Richman. 1963. Disclosure output and input in college students. *Merrill-Palmer Quarterly* 9:141–48.

Keiser, R. 1969. *The Vice Lords*. New York: Holt.

Kim, J. 1975. Factor analysis, in N. Nie, C. Hull, J. Jenkins, K. Steinbrenner, and D. Brent (ed.), *SPSS, Statistical Package for the Social Sciences*. New York: McGraw-Hill.

Kirkwood, J. 1973. *P. S., Your Cat Is Dead*. New York: Warner Publishing.

Klein, H., and L. Willerman. 1979. Psychological masculinity and femininity and typical and maximal dominance expression in women. *Journal of Personality and Social Psychology* 37:2059–70.

Komarovsky, M. 1962. *Blue-Collar Marriage*. New York: Random House.

Korda, M. 1973. *Male Chauvinism: How It Works*. New York: Random House.

Kuhn, T. 1962. *The Structure of Scientific Revolutions*. Chicago: University of Chicago Press.

Kulik, J. A., and H. Harackiewicz. 1979. Opposite-sex interpersonal attraction as a function of the sex roles of the perceiver and the perceived. *Sex Roles* 5:443–52.

L'Abate, L. 1980. Inexpressive males or overexressive females? A reply to Balswick. *Family Relations* 29:229–30.

Lamb, M. E., J. H. Pleck, E. L. Charnov, and J. A. Levine. 1986. A biosocial perspective on paternal behavior and involvement, in J. B. Lancaster, A. Rossi, J. Altmann, and L. R. Sherrod (eds.) *Parenting Across the Lifespan: Biosocial Perspectives*. Chicago: Aldine.

Lamb, M., P. J. Pleck, and J. Levine. 1986. Effects of increased paternal involvement on children in two-parent families. In R. Lewis and R. Salt (eds.) *Men In Families*. Beverly Hills: Sage.

Lamb, M. E., J. Pleck, and J. A. Levine. 1985. The role of the father in child development: the effects of increased paternal involvement. In B. B. Lanhey and A. E. Kazdin (eds.) *Advances in Clinical Child Psychology*. vol. 8. New York: Plenum.

Lamb, M. E., A. M. Frodi, C. P. Hwang, M. Frodi, and J. Steinberg. 1982. Mother and father-infant interaction involving play and holding in traditional and nontraditional Swedish families. *Developmental Psychology* 18:215–21.

Lamb, M. E. 1981. Fathers and child development: an intergrative overview. In M. E. Lamb, (rev. ed.) *The Role of the Father in Child Development*. New York: John Wiley.

Lamb, M. E., M. T., Owen, and L. Chase-Lansdale. 1979. The father-daughter relationship: past, present, and future. In C. B. Kopp and M. Kirkpatrick (eds.) *Becoming Female: Perspectives on Development*. New York: Plenum.

Lamb, M. E. 1977. The development of mother-infant and father-infant attachments in the second year of life. *Developmental Psychology* 13:637–48.

Landis, J. 1960. The trauma of children when parents divorce. *Marriage and Family Living* 22 (1): 7–13.

Lange, A., and P. Jackubowski. 1976. *Responsible Assertive Behavior: Cognitive/ Behavioral Procedures for Trainers*. New York: Research.

Lavine, L. D., and T. P. Lombardo. 1984. Self-disclosure: Intimate and nonintimate disclosures to parents and best friends as a function of Bem sex-role category. *Sex Roles* 11:735–44.

Leik, R. 1963. Instrumentality and emotionality in family interaction. *Sociometry* 26:131–45.

Lengermann, P., and R. Wallace. 1985. *Gender in America: Social Control and Social Change*. Englewood Cliffs: Prentice-Hall.

Lester, D., N. Brazil, C. Ellis, and T. Guerin. 1984. Correlates of romantic attitudes toward love: androgyny and self-disclosure. *Psychological Reports* 54:554.

Levinger, G., and D. Senn. 1967. Disclosure of feelings in marriage. *Merrill-Palmer Quarterly* 13:237–49.

Levinson, D. 1978. *The Seasons of A Man's Life*. New York: Ballantine.

Lewis, M. 1972. Parents and children: sex-role development. *School Review* 80:229–40.

Lewis, R., and R. Salt. 1986. *Men in Families*. Beverly Hills: Sage.

Lewis, R. 1978. Emotional intimacy among men. *Journal of Social Issues* 34:108–21.

———. 1981. *Men in Difficult Times.* New York: Random House.

Liebow, E. 1967. *Tally's Corner.* Boston: Little.

Lindesmith, A., A. Strauss, and N. Denzin. 1974. *Social Psychology* (4th ed.). New York: Holt, Rinehart, and Winston.

Lombardo, J. P., and L. Lavine. 1981. Sex-role stereotyping and patterns of self-disclosure. *Sex Roles* 2:161–66.

Luckmann, T. 1967. *The Invisible Religion.* New York: MacMillan.

Lynn, D. 1969. *Parental and Sex Role Identification: A Theoretical Formulation.* Berkeley, Calif.: McCutchan Publishing Co.

Maccoby, E., and C. Jacklin. 1971. Sex differences and their implications for sex roles. Paper presented at the annual meeting of the American Psychological Association. Washington, D.C.

———. 1974. *The Psychology of Sex Differences.* Stanford: Stanford University Press.

Major, B., P. J. Carnevale, and Deaux. 1981. A different perspective on androgyny: evaluations of masculine and feminine personality characteristics. *Journal of Personality and Social Psychology* 41:988–1001.

Manis, J. 1976. *Analyzing Social Problems.* New York: Praeger.

Maslow, A. 1966. *The Psychology of Science.* New York: Harper and Row.

Matson, F. 1966. *The Broken Image: Man, Science and Society.* Garden City: Anchor Books.

Mayo, P. 1968. Self disclosure and neuroses. *British Journal of Social and Clinical Psychology* 1:140–48.

McCready, W., and A. Greely 1976. *The Ultimate Values of the American Population.* Beverly Hills: Sage.

McGill, M. 1985. *The McGill Report on Male Intimacy.* New York: Harper and Row.

Mead, G. 1934. *Mind, Self, and Society.* Chicago: University of Chicago Press.

Means, R. 1970. Methodology for the sociology of religion: an historical and theoretical overview. *Sociological Analysis* 31 (Winter): 180–96.

Mehrabian, A. 1972. *Nonverbal Communication.* Chicago: Aldine-Atherton.

Miller, B. 1958. Lower class culture as a generation milieu of gang delinquency. *Journal of Social Issues.* 121:5–19.

Mischel, W. 1968. *Personality and Assessment.* New York: Wiley.

Mitchell, B. D., and E. Trickett. 1980. Social networks as mediators of social support. *Community Mental Health Journal* 14:27–44.

Moberg, D. 1978. Virtues for the sociology of religion. *Sociological Analysis* 39:1–18.

Morin, S., and E. Garfinkle. 1978. Male homophobia. *Journal of Social Issues* 34:29–45.

Morin, S., and L. Nungesser. 1981. Can homophobia be cured? in R. Lewis (ed.) *Men in Difficult Times: Masculinity Today and Tomorrow.* Englewood Cliffs: Prentice-Hall.

Moynihan, D. 1965. *The Negro Family: The Case for National Action.* Washington, D.C.: U.S. Department of Labor.

Murstein, B. D., and P. D. Williams. 1983. Sex roles and marital adjustment. *Small Group Behavior.* 14:77–94.

National Opinion Research Center. 1976. General Social Survey (Principal Investigator: James A. Davis). Distributed by the Roper Public Opinion Center, Williams College.

Newman, W. 1973. Glock as policy researcher. *Journal for the Scientific Study of Religion.* 12:469–73.

Norwood, S. 1985. *Women Who Love Too Much.* New York: Simon and Schuster.

Notarius, C., and J. Johnson. 1982. Emotional expression in husbands and wives. *Journal of Marriage and the Family.* 44:483–89.

Nowak, S. 1969. Observation and understanding of human behavior in the construction of sociological concepts and theories. *Revue Internationale de Sociologie.* 5:439–54.

Nunnally, J. 1967. *Psychometric Theory.* New York: McGraw-Hill.

O'Conner, K., D. W. Mann, and J. M. Bardwick. 1978. Androgyny and self-esteem in the upper-middle class: a replication of Spence. *Journal of Consulting Clinical Psychology.* 46:1168–69.

Oetzel, R. 1966. Annotated bibliography, in *Development of Sex Differences,* E. Maccoby (ed.) Stanford: Stanford University Press. 223–321.

Ogburn, W., and M. Nimkoff. 1955. *Technology and the Changing Family.* Boston: Houghton-Mifflin.

———. 1922. *Social Change.* New York: Viking Press.

Olsen, D. 1977. Insiders' and outsiders' views of relationships: research studies, in Levinger, G. and Rausch, H. (eds.) *Close Relationships.* Amherst: University of Massachusetts Press. 115–35.

O'Neil, J. 1982. Gender role conflict and strain in men's lives: implications for psychiatrists, psychologists, and other human-service providers, in K. Solomon and M. Levy (eds.) *Men in Transition: Theory and Therapy.* New York: Plenum.

Ornstein, R. 1977. *The Psychology of Consciousness* (2nd ed.) New York: Harcourt, Brace, Janovich.

Osherson, S. 1986. *Finding Our Fathers: The Unfinished Business of Manhood.* New York: Free Press.

Parsons, T. 1951. *The Social System.* Glencoe, Ill.: The Free Press.

Parsons, T., and R. Bales. 1955. *Family, Socialization, and Interaction Process.* Glencoe, Ill.: The Free Press.

Pascoe, A. W. 1981. Self-disclosure and marital satisfaction. *Dissertation Abstracts International.* 42 (3A): 1013.

Pederson, F.A., B. Anderson, and R. Cain. 1980. Parent-infant and husband-wife interactions observed at age five months. In F.A. Pederson (ed.) *The Father-Infant Relationship: Observational Studies in the Family Setting.* New York: Praeger.

Peretti, P. 1980. Perceived primary group criteria in the rational networks of closest friendships. *Adolescence.* 15:555–65.

Phillips, R. 1978. Men as lovers, husbands, and fathers: explorations of male socialization and the implications for marriage and family therapy, in C. Simpkinsen and J. Platt (eds.) *1978 Synopsis of Family Therapy Practice.* Olney, Md.: Family Therapy Practice Network.

Pleck, J. 1982. *The Myth of Masculinity.* Cambridge: MIT Press.

——. 1976. The male sex role: definitions, problems, and sources of change. *Journal of Social Issues.* 155–64.

Polansky, N. 1970. Social class and verbal accessibility. Unpublished manuscript.

Prager, E. 1986. Intimacy status: its relationship to locus of control, self disclosure, and anxiety in adults. *Personality and Social Psychology Bulletin.* 12(1): 91–109.

Proctor, A. 1975. Sex differences in expressiveness. Unpublished master's thesis. University of Georgia.

Rainwater, L. 1965. *Family Design: Marital Sexuality, Family Size and Contraception.* Chicago: Aldine Publishing Co.

Rich, A., and H. Schroeder. 1976. Research issues in assertiveness training. *Phychology Bulletin,* 83 (6): 1081–96.

Rimm, D., and J. Masters. 1974. *Behavior Therapy: Techniques and Empirical Findings.* New York: Academic Press.

Robinson, I., and D. Foster 1969. The modeling of society. Paper presented at the annual meeting of the American Sociological Association, San Francisco.

Romer, N., and D. Cherry. 1980. Ethnic and social class differences in children's sex-role concepts. *Sex Roles.* 6:246–63.

Rosenbaum, A., and K. D. O'Leary. 1981. Marital violence: characteristics of abusive couples. *Journal of Consulting and Clinical Psychology* 4:63–71.

Rosenberg, M. 1968. *The Logic of Survey Analysis.* New York: Basic Books.

Rosenberg, B., and H. Silverstein. 1969. *The Varieties of Delinquent Experience.* Waltham: Blaisdell.

Rosenfeld, L., J. Civikly, and J. Herron. 1979. Anatomical and psychological sex differences, in G. Chelune (ed.) *Self-disclosure: Origins, Patterns, and Implications of Openness in Interpersonal Relationships.* San Francisco: Jossey-Bass.

Rosenkrantz, R. S., S. R. Vogel, H. Bee, I. L. Brovermand and D. M. Broverman. 1968. Sex role stereotypes and self concepts in college students. *Journal of Consulting and Clinical Psychologists.* 32:287–95.

Rossi, A. 1984. Gender and parenthood. *American Sociological Review.* 49:1–19.

Rubin, L. 1983. *Intimate Strangers: Men and Women Together.* New York: Harper and Row.

Ruble, T. L. 1983. Sex stereotypes: issues of change in the 1970's. *Sex Roles.* 9:397–402.

Runge, T. E., D. Frey, P. M. Gollwitzer, R. L. Helmreich, and J. T. Spence. 1981. Masculine (instrumental) and feminine (expressive) traits: a comparison between students in the United States and West Germany. *Journal of Cross-Cultural Psychology.* 12:142–62.

Ryder, R. 1967. Computational remarks on a measure for comparing factors. *Educational and Psychological Measurement* 27:301–04.

Sackett, G. (ed.) 1978. *Observing Behavior, II: Data Collection and Analysis Methods.* Baltimore: University Park Press.

Saliba, J. 1974. The new ethnography and the study of religion. *Journal for the Scientific Study of Religion.* 13:145–59.

Sanday, P. 1981. *Female Power and Male Dominance: On the Origin of Sexual Inequality.* Cambridge: Cambridge University Press.

Sattel, J. 1976. The inexpressive male: tragedy or sexual politics? *Social Problems.* 23:469–77.

Schroeder, W. 1977. Measuring the muse: reflections on the use of survey methods in the study of religious phenomena. *Review of Religious Research.* 18:148–62.

Schumm, W. R., H. L. Barnes, S. R. Bollman, A. P. Jurich, and M. A. Bregaighis. 1986. Self-disclosure and marital satisfaction revisited. *Family Relations.* 34:241–7.

Schutz, A. 1970. *On Phenomenology and Social Relations.* Chicago: University of Chicago Press.

Shaver, P., C. Pullis, and D. Olds. 1985. Report on the LHJ "Intimacy Today" survey. In W. Ickes (ed.) *Compatible and Incompatible Relationships* New York: Springer-Verlag.

Sherman, J. 1971. *On the Psychology of Women, A Survey of Empirical Studies.* Springfield, Ill.: Charles C. Thomas.

Shichman, S., and E. Cooper. 1984. Life satisfaction and sex-role concept. *Sex Roles.* 11:227–40.

Short, J., and F. Strodtbeck. 1965. *Group Process and Gang Delinquency.* Chicago: University of Chicago Press.

Shriver, D., and D. Knudsen. 1978. Reply to J.C. Jenkins' book review. *Journal for the Scientific Study of Religion.* 17:89–90.

Simms, R. E., M. H. Davis, H. C. Foushee, C. K. Holahan, J. T. Spence, and R. L. Helreich. 1978. Psychological masculinity and femininity in children and their relationships to trait stereotypes and toy preferences. New Orleans: Paper presented at the meeting of the *Southwestern Psychological Association.*

Slevins, K., and J. Balswick. 1980. Sex differences in perceived parental expressiveness. *Sex Roles: A Journal of Research* 6(2):293–99.

Smith, K. 1974. Forming composite scales and estimating their validity through factor analysis. *Social Forces.* 53:168–80.

Snow, M. E., C. N. Jacklin, and E. E. Maccoby. 1983. Sex of child differences in father-child interaction at one year of age. *Child Development.* 54:227–32.

Snyder, M. 1974. Self-monitoring and expressive behavior. *Journal of Personality and Social Psychology.* 30:526–37.

Snyder, M. 1979. Self-monitoring progresses, in Berkowitz, L. (ed.) *Advances in Experimental Social Psychology.* (vol.12). New York: Academic Press.

Sollie, D. L., and J. L. Fischer. 1985. Sex role orientation, intimacy of topic, and target person differences in self-disclosure among women. *Sex Roles* 12:917–29.

Solomon, K., and N. Levy. 1982. *Men in Transition: Theory and Therapy.* New York: Plenum Press.

Spanier, G. 1976. Measuring dyadic adjustment: new scales for assessing the quality of marriage and similar dyads. *Journal of Marriage and the Family.* 38:15–28.

Spence, J. T., K. Deaux, and R. L. Helmreich. 1985. Sex roles in contemporary American society, in *The Handbook of Social Psychology: Volume II.* (3rd ed.), ed. by Gardner Lindzey, and E. Aronson. New York: Random House.

Spence, J., and R. Helmreich. 1979. Comparison of masculine and feminine personality attributes and sex-role attitudes across age groups. *Developmental Psychology.* 15:583–84.

———. 1978. *Masculinity and Feminity: Their Psychological Dimensions, Correlates, and Antecedents.* Austin: University of Texas Press.

Spence, J. T., R. Helmreich, and J. Stapp. 1974. The personal attributes questionnaire: a measure of sex-role stereotypes and masculinity-femininity. *JSAS Catalog of Selective Documents In Psychology.* 4:43.

Spinley, B. 1953. *Deprived and the Privileged.* London: Routledge and Kegan Paul.

Staples, R. 1974. The black family revisited: a review and a preview. *Journal of Social and Behavioral Sciences.* 20:65–78.

Stensrud, J. R., and K. A. Feldman. 1982. The structural effects of life course change in patterns of friendship. *New York State Sociological Meetings.*

Stokes, J., A. Fuehrer, and L. Childs. 1980. Gender differences in self-disclosure to various target persons. *Journal of Counseling.* 27:192–98.

Stryker, S., and A. Statham. 1985. Symbolic interaction and role theory, in *The Handbook of Social Psychology: Volume I.* (3rd ed.), ed. by G. Lindzey and E. Aronson. New York: Random House.

Stryker, S., 1967. Symbolic interaction as an approach to family research, in J. Manis and B. Meltzer (eds.) *Symbolic Interaction.* Boston: Allyn and Bacon, Inc.

Thase, M., and R. A. Page. 1977. Modeling of self-disclosure in laboratory and non-laboratory interview settings. *Journal of Counseling Psychology.* 24:35–40.

Thomas, S., K. Albrecht, and P. White. 1984. Determinants of marital quality in dual-career couples. *Family Relations.* 33:513–21.

Tiger, L. 1969. *Men in Groups.* New York: Random House.

Tiger, L., and R. Fox. 1971. *The Imperial Animal.* New York: Holt, Rinehart and Winston.

Tignoli, J. 1969. Response matching in interpersonal information exchange. *British Journal of Social and Clinical Psychology.* 8:116–23.

Tognoli, J. 1980. Male friendship and intimacy across the life span. *Family Relations* 29:273–79.

Turner, R. 1962. Moral judgment: a study in roles. *American Sociological Review.* 17:70–77.

———. 1966. Role-taking, role standpoint, and reference-group behavior, in B. Biddle and E. Thomas (eds.) *Role Theory.* New York: John Wiley and Sons.

———. 1970. *Family Interaction.* New York: John Wiley and Sons, Inc.

Turner, J., E. Foa, and V. Foa. 1971. Interpersonal reinforcers: classification in a relationship and some differential properties. *Journal of Personality and Social Psychology.* 19:168–80.

Udry, J. 1974. *The Social Context of Marriage.* (3rd ed.). Philadelphia: Lippincott Co.

Walsh, W. 1967. Validity of self-report. *Journal of Counseling Psychology.* 14:18–23.

———. 1968. Validity of self report: another look. *Journal of Counseling Psychology.* 15:180–86.

Walster, E., E. Berscheid, and G. Walster. 1973. New directions in equity research. *Journal of Personality and Social Psychology.* 25:151–76.

Walster, E., S. Traupmann, and G. Walter. 1978. Equity and extramarital sex. *The Archives of Sexual Behavior.* 7:127–42.

Walster, E., G. Walster, and E. Berscheid. 1978. *Equity: Theory and Research.* Boston: Allyn and Bacon.

Walster, E., G. Walster, and S. Traupman. 1977. Equity and premarital sex. Unpublished manuscript. (Available from E. Walster, University of Wisconsin, Madison.)

Warren, N., and F. Gilner. 1978. Measurement of positive assertive behaviors: the behavioral test of tenderness expression. *Behavioral Therapy.* 9:178–184.

Wayne, J. 1979. As reported in *A Forum for Changing Men.* 56:2

Wiegel, R., V. Weigel, and P. Chadwick. 1969. Reported and projected self-disclosure. *Psychological Reports.* 24:283–87.

Weinberg, G. 1972. *Society and the Healthy Homosexual.* New York: St. Martin's Press.

Westman, J. 1972. Effect of divorce on a child's personality development. *Medical Aspects of Human Sexuality.* 6 (1): 38–55.

Wheeler, L., H. Reis, and J. Neylek, 1983. Loneliness, social interaction and sex roles. *Journal of Personality and Social Psycology.* 45(4): 943–53.

Whyte, W. 1943. *Street Corner Society.* Chicago: University of Chicago Press.

Williams, D. Gender. 1985. Masculinity-femininity, and emotional intimacy in same-sex friendships. *Sex Roles.* 12(5/6): 587–600.

Worthy, M., A. Gary, and G. Kahn. 1969. Self-disclosure as an exchange process. *Journal of Personality and Social Psychology.* 13: 59–63.

Zelditch, M. 1955. Role differentiation in the nuclear family: a comparative study, in T. Parsons and R. Bales (eds.) *Family, Socialization, and Interaction Process.* Glencoe, Ill.: Free Press.

# Index

# About the Author

Jack Balswick received his B.A. in Social Science from California State University at Chico and his M.A. and Ph.D. in Sociology from the University of Iowa. He has taught at Wisconsin State University, University of Georgia, and Fuller Theological Seminary.

Dr. Balswick has authored four books and published over 50 professional articles in the areas of marriage and the family and sociology of religion. He has twice been appointed a Senior Fulbright Scholar: to Cyprus in 1972 and to Korea in 1982.